New Technology and Education

A companion website to accompany this book is available online at:

http://education.edwards.continuumbooks.com

Please type in the URL above and receive your unique password for access to the book's online resources.

If you experience any problems accessing the resources, please contact Continuum at: info@continuumbooks.com

Other titles in the *Contemporary Issues in Education Studies Series* include:

Changing Urban Education, Simon Pratt-Adams, Meg Maguire and
Elizabeth Burn
Education and Constructions of Childhood, David Blundell
Multiculturalism and Education, Richard Race
Young People, Popular Culture and Education, Chris Richards

Also available from Continuum

Digital Games and Learning, Sara de Freitas and Paul Maharg
Foreign Language Learning with Digital Technology, edited by Michael Evans
Key Issues in e-Learning, Norbert Pachler and Caroline Daly
Mathematics Education with Digital Technology, edited by Adrian Oldknow
and Carol Knights

New Technology and Education

Contemporary Issues in Education Studies

Anthony Edwards

continuum

Continuum International Publishing Group

The Tower Building	80 Maiden Lane
11 York Road	Suite 704
London SE1 7NX	New York NY 10038

www.continuumbooks.com

British Library Cataloguing-in-Publication Data
A catalogue record for this book is available from the British Library.

ISBN: 978-1-4411-9774-0 (paperback)
        978-1-4411-8985-1 (hardcover)

Library of Congress Cataloguing-in-Publication Data
New technology and education / Anthony Edwards.
p. cm. – (Contemporary issues in education studies)
Summary: "An engaging look at the debates surrounding the benefits and dangers of the increasing use of technology in education"– Provided by publisher.

Includes bibliographical references and index.
ISBN 978-1-4411-8985-1 (hardback) – ISBN 978-1-4411-9774-0 (paperback) 1. Educational technology. I. Title.

LB1028.3.E4235 2012
371.33–dc23
                                                          2011022990

Typeset by Newgen Imaging Systems Pvt Ltd, Chennai, India
Printed and bound in India

To Matty and all other free thinkers

Contents

Acknowledgements

I would like to thank Dr Richard Race and Dr Simon Pratt Adams for their advice and encouragement, Dr Wendy Bignold for her support and, my family, for their endless patience.

Series Editors' Preface

The series *Contemporary Issues in Education Studies* is timely for its critical exploration of education in this period of accelerating change. Responding to this challenge, the books in the series have titles which correspond closely to the needs of students taking a wide range of courses and modules within Education Studies and related fields such as teacher education. Education Studies is an important subject area that should be at the heart of many faculties of education. There is a need for relevant, core texts within Education Studies, which explore and critique contemporary issues across the discipline and challenge prevailing discourses of what education is about. We also need to provide students with strong theoretical perspectives and frameworks, focusing on relevant literature in an accessible and readable format.

We set the authors of this series a number of challenges in terms of what to include in their text. Therefore, each book addresses a contemporary issue in education and has an international rather than only an English focus. The texts are structured to provide a clear grasp of the topic and to provide an overview of research, current debates and perspectives. Contextualized extracts from important primary texts ensure readers' exposure to dominant contemporary theories in the field of education, by demystifying essential vocabulary and educational discourse, enabling the education student to engage with these texts in a meaningful way. The extensive and appropriate literature review in each text gives a firm base for contextualizing the subject and promoting understanding at multiple levels.

This series is grounded in a strong conceptual, theoretical framework and is presented in an accessible way. Each book uses features such as case studies, reflective exercises and activities that encourage and support student learning. Key relevant and contemporary questions are inserted throughout each chapter to extend the readers' thinking and understanding. Furthermore, additional material is also provided in the companion website to each book.

Anthony Edwards is the author of *New Technology and Education*. Currently he is Director of Education Studies in the Faculty of Education at Liverpool Hope University. He writes from extensive experience as a school teacher and university lecturer, having worked in different educational settings both in the United Kingdom and other countries. His research interests include new technology and teaching and learning with a particular focus on creativity. His work is also underpinned by his interest in the history of education. He is carrying out different research projects in Finland and Australia involving E-Learning and New Technology.

Drawing on his own practice as an educator as well as his current research interests, Edwards's text analyses the contemporary, as well as historical relevance and importance of technology in education. The text is both a timely and welcome addition to the field because it contributes to the ongoing debate concerning pedagogy and new technologies. From a starting point of defining notions of pedagogy, Edwards proceeds to explore the link between pedagogy and culture. He offers an in-depth exploration of the key issues related to the changing relationship between the learner and the educator and how new technologies, using the interactive whiteboard as an example, can potentially be utilized in the classroom to support and extend learning and teaching.

Edwards emphasizes the importance of looking backwards to explore critically early technological developments such as books and printing and, more recently, the emergence of computers, in order to investigate the impact of innovative digital technologies on contemporary educational practice. He also explores the significance of digital poverty on education. It is vital that students of education understand and explore structural and material obstacles and Edwards provides the reader with a useful analysis of global issues that can exclude people from the Information society. Crucially, the reader is challenged to consider whether technology shapes society or whether, in fact, society shapes technology.

The text also explores the changing definitions of community resulting from the development of the Internet and the World Wide Web. The implications of such changes to learning and teaching are considered through discussion about forms of communication, blended and mobile learning, and virtual learning communities. The reader is challenged to consider critically how Web 2 technologies can transform our understanding and experience of education. The relationship between creativity, information and communication technology (ICT) and education is a fascinating element of this book. Edwards supports the view that ICTs can provide learners with the opportunity and facilitation to experiment in virtual environments and he encourages readers to reflect on key issues in the educational uses of virtual worlds and virtual schools. Edwards claims that computer modelling and simulations provide some of the most effective opportunities for creativity in educational contexts, especially when students are encouraged to take risks with their learning. However, he concludes that technology itself does not provide the opportunity for creativity; rather teachers need to know how to promote and use technology creatively and innovatively, working with learners who are digitally literate and can themselves be creatively expressive.

In the final section of the book, Edwards encourages the reader to look forward and consider the place of technology and education in the future and more broadly to think in new ways about the direction that lives might take. We believe that one of the key contributions that this book makes is in the way it encourages the reader to think critically and differently about new technology and education in rapidly changing times. Therefore, this text will become a major resource for all those interested in taking up this challenge.

Simon Pratt-Adams and Richard Race
June 2011
London

Introduction: Technology, Education and Change

Introduction

Today, there are few aspects of teaching and learning that are free from the influence of technology in some form or other (Luppicini, 2005). Indeed, Tinio (2003c) argues that in the developed world, technology is also at the heart of the process of educational reform. It is tempting, when thinking about the link between education and technology, to simply focus on devices such as computers or the digital camera and what they do. Indeed this reductionist tendency is characteristic of much early writing on the subject (Winner, 1993). But the premise on which this chapter and, indeed, the book are founded is that this approach, while having some value, is far too simplistic. A more sophisticated, even holistic, analysis is required. It is profoundly important to reflect on the link between technology and education. It is not just simply an issue of pedagogy. A deep examination of the ink between technology and education will help to reveal how we relate to each other, what values we currently hold and how they may evolve in the future. Therefore, any study should be founded on the application of a range of academic disciplines including history, philosophy, psychology and sociology. By adopting this approach, any judgements made about the taxing questions raised because of the link between education and technology are more likely to be founded on reason rather than rhetoric.

Partly because of the all pervasive nature of technology in contemporary society and the speed with which the nuts and bolts, the black boxes if you like, are changing, the link between education and technology now occupies centre stage in the minds of educators (Luppicini, 2005). This does not just apply to grandiose devices and systems. Nye et al. (2006) suggest that we should accept that the Neolithic axe has had as much (and possibly more) impact on our lives as the Space Shuttle. This notion is particularly apt in an educational context. It can be argued that writing slates, with the capacity to be wiped clean and reused, have as much right to an honoured place in the pantheon of technology that has generated significant educational change as things which have more spectacular properties.

It is also important at this stage to explore and subsequently place limitations on what is meant by education. It has both a normative and objective definition. The normative definition is one usually formulated by policy makers and educational experts, and usually relates to values and ideas and desired educational outcomes. The objective definition of education seeks to rise above specific contexts and offer a more generic explanation. Education in these terms could be deemed as simply the result of all the life experiences on an individual (Curoe, 2008). We need to be mindful in our exploration of this subject that the phrase 'educational technology' can represent a source of confusion. It has evolved into an intellectual discipline in its own right and is sometimes alternatively referred to as learning technology. At its broadest, educational technology is concerned with how best to shape the learning environment not only in terms of artefacts but methods of organization and systems of teaching which are employed in education. In practice, this could mean redesigning elements of the curriculum in order to best meet the needs of a particular group or altering the layout of a classroom to maximize learning opportunities. Educational technology as a doctrine can provide useful insights because it is underpinned by behaviourist, cognitivist and constructivist principles.

This chapter provides a starting point for an exploration of the key issues associated with this area by defining what we mean by technology in all its manifestations, and investigating whether it helps to shape society or whether society shapes it. These issues might include the following:

1. What can we usefully learn from the link between education and technology that has existed in the past?
2. Does technology make the traditional notion that schools or universities are definite physical entities fixed in one location an increasingly redundant feature of any education system?
3. Does technology inevitably change the relationship between the learner and the teacher?
4. Does the advent of more technology require us to abandon old pedagogies for new ones?
5. Will the increasing use of technology in an educational context exacerbate the divide between those who have and those who do not have?
6. Will our educational future be determined solely by technology?

There is one overriding issue that is woven either implicitly or explicitly into every section in the book – is technology in the classroom (wherever that may be) a force for good, acting to liberate and unite us, or does it enslave and divide us? One of the World Controllers in Aldous Huxley's dystopian novel *Brave New World* was amazed that a technology developed for educating people in their sleep was not universally welcomed. He remarked that it was prohibited because there was something called liberalism and Parliament which passed 'a law against it. The records survive. Speeches about liberty of the subject. Liberty to be inefficient and miserable. Freedom to be a round peg in a square hole' (Huxley, 1932).

Activity

The list of issues generated as a result of the growing link between education and technology is by no means definitive. What others would you add?

Towards a definition of technology

The entomological origin of 'technology' is from the Greek word *technologia*. The first part of the word, *techno*, relates to the arts and the second, *logia*, with writings on or accumulated knowledge of the arts. The meaning of technology that held sway in the seventeenth century closely resembles this Greek root. At that time, it was regarded as a discourse or a treatize on an art or the arts. To a certain extent, this definition has persisted, but with one significant difference. By the middle of the nineteenth century, the meaning of the word 'arts' had changed. Rather than simply embrace painting or sculpture, it now encompassed the growing application of science to manufacturing. The original meaning of technology, including this expanded notion of the arts, still has some currency today. Mullis (2009) is firmly of this persuasion. He suggests that technology is best characterized by the sort of science-based devices that began to emerge in the nineteenth century. He purposefully separates technology from the technical, suggesting that the latter term only relates to techniques of production. Mullis has adopted this almost reductionist viewpoint because he believes that technology is a 'slippery' term about which it is difficult to reach a consensus. While his approach might appear to provide clarity, it fails to grapple with some fundamental issues. For instance, there has been much debate about where science ends and technology begins. What is sometimes referred to as applied science, the sort you might find employed in an industrial context, appears to bear many of the characteristics of technology. This is a fraught subject that sometimes reveals more about the prejudices of those who comment upon it than the differences. Admiral Hyman Rickover, who developed the world's first nuclear powered submarine, likens technology to action, while associating science with pure thought (Kneszevich et al., 1970).

Activity

What do you think is the difference between science and technology?

Despite the difficulties, many thinkers in the past 50 years have sought to develop the meaning of 'technology'. They find the approach that Mullis has adopted wanting (Finn, 1960; Simon, 1969). Society has changed radically since the Victorian manufacturers first discovered that they could make things quicker and cheaper through mechanization. Simon (1969) proposed that technology is our way of interfacing between the inner (natural) and the outer (artificial) environments, a role that might equally be ascribed to science. Finn (1960) contends that technology represents a particular way of thinking about a problem through which a broad range of issues, including economic values, should be taken into consideration. He believes that technology should include all human and non-human processes, systems, and management and control mechanisms. Even international agencies have sought their own definition of technology because of the importance it has for the well being of many. The United Nations Education, Social and Cultural Organization (UNESCO) broadly regards it as the knowledge and skills and creative processes that may assist people to utilize tools, resources and systems to solve problems and to enhance control over the natural and made environment in an endeavour to improve the human condition (UNESCO, 1985). This definition implies that technology results from the purposeful application of knowledge and resources, that it is multifaceted, realized through the process of designing and making, and induces change in some form or other which meets the needs and wants of particular communities. However, whether this change is for the good or not is a vexed question. By making reference to improving 'the human condition', UNESCO raises the following dilemma – who decides what constitutes an improvement? Currently, economic growth in both China and India is manifest by increased industrial production (Goldstein et al., 2006). This has led to a vast demand for energy, which is largely generated by the combustion of fossil fuels. On the one hand, it can be argued that the resulting economic growth 'improves' the material well-being of some of the populace and, therefore, is to be welcomed. On the other hand, energy produced by highly polluting technologies contributes to atmospheric contamination and increasing CO_2e (carbon dioxide equivalent) levels that can lead to climatic change for both those in the immediate environment and all of us. Does anybody have the right to deny the people of China and India the benefits of these technologies, particularly since without them some may be condemned to a life of subsistence, on the basis of the greater good?

The current fashion for making more use of computers in a range of educational contexts is heralded by many as the dawn of a new age. The benefits are too numerous to mention here, apart from the potential this technology has for enabling access to learning material at any time and any place. This means that a range of individual study habits can be more readily catered for. The consequence is that the contact between the teacher and the taught is inevitably changed. To Cuban (1985) and others, teaching is as much about the relationships between individuals as it is about learning material, and he warns us of the dire social consequences if we dehumanize the learning experience through the use of computer. So who is right?

Luppicini (2005) points out that, as a result of the influence of social scientists, the meaning of technology has had to be extended. Simply considering the artefacts that Mullis is so fond of by themselves is not sufficient. The intellectual and social context in which they are used also needs to be taken into account. The social scientists also suggest that technology is an activity that is value laden and inextricably linked to cultural and environmental influences. This is perhaps best illustrated by an example from Mahatma Gandhi's India during the 1920s when mass-produced clothing made by machines in Europe caused severe unemployment. Gandhi urged his fellow countrymen to become self-reliant by spinning their own cloth on a hand-powered spinning wheel that would have been familiar to weavers 800 years before. While recognizing the need to address the economic situation, he also understood that by adopting the spinning wheel, he and his compatriots were making a bold statement about their desire for freedom from colonialism and dependency. It was also indicative of their desire for a simpler and more sustainable way of life. The device they used, called a Charakha, eventually came to represent the Indian independence movement and appears on their national flag. Interestingly, there are those who claim the 'techno' part of the word 'technology' originates from the Indo European word *teks*, which means to weave (Quiles, 2007).

Activity

Identify two things, one complex and expensive and one simple and cheap, that you think has had a significant impact on your education.

What are the advantages and disadvantages of using complex or high technology in education?

Do you think your viewpoint would be the same if you lived in a country that was significantly different from your own?

Aspects of technology

Technology is firmly associated in the minds of many, like Mullis, with objects, tangible products, that can do work of one sort or another under the right conditions. Such devices after all, surround us. They differ hugely in cost and complexity. Some, such as the immense electric earthmover found at Europe's Aitik copper mine in Sweden, are capable of dramatic acts, such as gathering 1,200 tons of material in one scoop (Earthmovers, 2010). Others are more prosaic but of equal value. Villagers in Mali trying to exploit the annual flood surge of the Nile in order to irrigate arid desert by digging channels use nothing more than the humble shovel (BBC, 2009). They rely as much (or perhaps even more) on this low-level technology for sustenance and income as the Swedish miners do on their massive machines. Both the shovel and the earthmover are similar in a number of ways. They are technological artefacts. They can also be regarded as elements in a technological process because they have been specifically designed to address a particular need or want, in which some sort of measurable change occurs. Layton (1974) argues that the concept of technology has to encompass knowledge in order for it to be elevated beyond artefact or a process. It is a many-faceted concept (Kline, 1985: 215–18). The creators of both the shovel and the earthmover require a fundamental understanding of soil and rocks, in particular how to deform and reform them, before an effective artefact can be created. Although the shovel and the earthmover differ significantly in their capacity to do work, there are similarities in how they are controlled. The shovel without its human operator is an inanimate object. It cannot function independently. The capacity it has to do work is governing not only by the strength of the individual, but also by his or her ability to sense load and position. Likewise, the earthmover cannot function independently and its capacity to do work is also dependent on a human being at the control, despite being driven by engine rather than muscle power. However, it is also capable of some form of self-regulation without human intervention. The earthmover by itself can halt the lifting process if it determines that the load in the bucket exceeds safety levels. This sensing ability results from input devices that assess weight, a processor that determines what to do with this information and outputs that control the physical manifestation of this 'thinking'. This is an example of technology as a system or a series of interconnected activities. You may regard this as a very recent innovation, but inventors and engineers have long been wrestling with the notion that you can develop machines with a brain. Charles Babbage, who built the first computer, was actively trying to create such a device in the first part of the nineteenth century with his Analytical Engine.

> **Activity**
>
> The shovel and the earthmover, although they do the same job, are at different ends of the technological spectrum. Try to identify devices that you may have seen used in teaching and learning that represent similar extremes.
>
> Provide an example of technology as a system or a series of interconnected activities from an educational context.

Technological determinism

To some, such as the Greek philosophers Leucippus and his student Democritus in the fifth century BCE (Before the Common Era), there is no such thing as chance or uncaused events. Their ideas were transformed into a school of thought, Determinism, which postulates that every decision and action is inevitable and is a necessary consequence of something that has happened beforehand. Technology, no matter how it is defined, is also sometimes regarded as an independent self-regulating phenomenon shaping the future despite rather than because of human aspirations and desires. This is called 'technological determinism'. Although the phrase was first accredited to Veblen (1921), the idea has been around since the industrial revolution that started in eighteenth-century England. Marx has often been associated with it because his writings appear to suggest that he conceived social processes in technological and not economic terms (Bimber, 1990). It is also found in other areas of study. Psychologists sometimes use the phrase 'biological or genetic determinism' which, at its most benign, refers to the innate capacity of some people to develop in a particular way. Language determines thought in linguistic determinism and not the other way round. All forms of this doctrine imply that human beings have little control or responsibility for what happens and that there is an inevitable and predictable path along which things (e.g. technology) will develop. For those who believe in the most extreme or hard notion of technological determinism, there is no choice about how technology and, hence, society evolves. This is preordained. Some such as Kanuka (2008) argue that our experiences of the world contradict this belief. We do have choice. This has led to a softer version of technological determinism, which acknowledges that there are many influences on events, including human beings. Technologies in this context act as causal agents that have a pivotal role in social change, but not an exclusive one. Common to the soft and hard versions of technological determinism is a linear mindset in which cause and effect feature heavily and in which a sequence of events can be traced from input to impact. Both are also associated with the notion that technological progress is inevitable and that social progress is linked unequivocally to it in a kind of benign technological embrace. The fact that it is difficult to reach consensus about what technology actually means undermines either viewpoint. Feenberg (1992) also argues that technological determinism is easily questioned. He contends that the development of technology, contrary to what the determinists believe, does not follow an unwavering path from low to high levels of complexity. Progress, if it can be called that when it emerges, is much more accidental. Feenberg (1992) also takes issue with one of the fundamental tenets of technological determinism, that society adapts to technology. He believes that social change is as much about politics as it is about artefacts. Technological determinism also raises interesting questions about free will and responsibility. Does the fact that, in deterministic terms, the development of weapons of mass destruction was inevitable mean that it is absolutely pointless in objecting to them?

Activity

1. Did suburbia create the car or did the car create suburbia?
2. Is there a link between the development of the Spinning Jenny (see URL link at the end of this chapter) and the necessity for a literate working class?
3. The technological determinists would argue what will be will be. Does this mean that if the development of weapons of mass destruction is preordained any form of moral education to halt their advance is pointless?

While technological determinism suggests that technology is autonomous and changes society, there are those that hold that technology emerges from and is shaped by society (Pool, 1999). In the latter model, artefacts result from the interaction between different social groups, who sometimes co-operate with each other and sometimes are in conflict. What emerges from this process are devices which encompass a wide range of needs and value systems. This is the constructivist view of technology. Constructivism is a philosophy of learning founded on the premise that, by reflecting on our experiences, we construct our own understanding of the world we live in (Fox, 2001; Cohen et al., 2007). It is both a theory of the way people learn, cognitive constructivism, and a philosophy, social constructivism. Cognitive constructivism owes its origin, in part, to the followers of Socrates, who in the fourth and fifth centuries BCE believed that learning was an internal process. Their contemporaries, the Sophists, on the other hand, believed that knowledge could only be acquired externally. Social constructivism is a more recent doctrine, which emerged from the work of Vygotsky (1962) and others, including Mead (1934) and Berger et al. (1966), who emphasized the importance of culture and social context in cognitive development.

Technology, education and change

The Social Construction of Technology (SCOT) emerged from constructivist thinking in part as a response to the increased pessimism about technology and its effects (e.g. in the generation of nuclear power) that has tainted technological determinism. It is a framework for coherently analysing the dynamics of technological change and the application of technology in order to examine carefully the inner workings of real technologies and their histories to see what is actually taking place (Winner, 1993). It resulted from the work of Pinch and Bijker (1984), both noted researchers into the relationship between technology and society. The model acknowledges that there is a link between social and technical processes and that both are human constructs. At its heart is the notion that the evolution of any technology, from many variants to one dominant strain (referred to as the process of stabilization) depends upon the influence of groups made up of what Bijker (1997) refers to as actors (individuals with specific traits or expertise), which form as a result of common cause. The important thing to stress about this framework is that it is built on the premise that technology develops through an organic or evolutionary process rather than as the result of a linear mindset. It has its critics. Jasanoff (2004) argues that the SCOT approach places too much emphasis on the social forces that shape technology rather than on the physical forces that surround us. Russell (1986) and Winner (1993) believe that the concept is too limited and cannot explain change fully. It may help to clarify how technologies arise but ignores the social consequences of the technology itself and too many of the wider forces that help to shape it. Winner (1993) is also adamant that it does not allow us to develop a view about technology and the human condition that matter most in modern history because it requires moral and political neutrality. Wajcman (1995) believes that the concept of relevant social groups is not straightforward. It can lead to oversights in which key players are easily omitted from the analysis. It is also important to ask who decides on the composition of these groups and, once identified, whether all members have equal influence.

Another similar approach to technological change is the theory of the diffusion of innovations (DoI) popularized by Rogers (1995) which resulted from the work of Gabriel Tarde in the early 1900s and Bryce Ryan and Neal Gross in the 1940s. It seeks to explain how innovation is adopted widely. Rogers (1995) describes it as an uncertainty reduction process. Innovation in this sense could be an idea, a behaviour, a practice or an artefact which is new to an individual. He contends that there are number of stages which lead to the widespread adoption of a new technology or innovation. They are manifest through a process in which an individual passes from the first knowledge 'of innovation, to the formation of an attitude towards innovation, to a decision to adopt or reject, to implementation and use of the new idea and finally to the confirmation of this decision' (Rogers, 2003: 20). The theory takes into account the fact that we don't all react in the same way or at the same time to things which are new to us, whatever form they take. There are five different types of adopter and the points at which they adopt an innovation:

1. innovators or risk takers, alternatively referred to as the opinion formers, who are the first;
2. early Adopters, alternatively referred to as the deliberators, are next;
3. early Majority, alternatively referred to as the sceptical, who adopt just before the average members of the system;
4. late Majority who adopt just after the average members of the system;
5. laggards who are described as traditionalists and are usually the last to adopt an innovation.

This is a useful framework. It allows different members of a group to be targeted accordingly to make it more likely that an innovation will be accepted It has very specific resonance in an educational context because it could help with the management of any change which might result from the introduction of a new technology in a classroom or lecture theatre, such as the interactive whiteboard.

Activity

1. Can you think of a device(s) used in schools or universities where many variants existed and now only one is available?
2. Can you suggest whom the actors and relevant social groups in the evolution of the device(s) identified above may be?
3. Using a recently developed technological device that you are very familiar with (it could be an iPod), identify which different social groups (old, young, etc.) could be ascribed to which adopter profiles.
4. From your own experience, identify a device that has been available but not widely adopted in school or university that would be useful in promoting teaching and learning. Suggest a reason why it has not been adopted.

In a recent paper, Timucin (2009) applied the DoI adopter profiles in order to analyse the introduction of new technology in a Turkish preparatory school connected to a state university. The research material on which he based his work resulted from a decision by the institution to introduce Computer-Assisted Language Learning (CALL) in English as a Foreign Language (EFL). The school had offered an intensive EFL course using the new technology to incoming students, but an evaluation revealed that it was not very successful. A significant number of those enrolled failed, due to low attendance. Teachers complained that this affected their ability to manage learning and students complained of dull classes and a singular approach to teaching. Timucin wanted to find out how well the technology had been accepted, particularly by the teachers. Qualitative data was collected through a process of recorded interviews which were then analysed using a modified form of Rogers's scheme developed by Hagner and Schneebeck (2001). Early and Late Majority adopters appeared to dominate his sample. The teachers' attitudes were shaped by a number of factors, including:

- A fear of being replaced by the computer.
- Failure as a result of a lack of technical expertise.
- Change fatigue. The system in Turkey had been subject to considerable recent changes as a result, in part, of the introduction of computer technology.
- Turkish EFL teaching had been characterized by an over-dependence on books and grammar-based syllabuses.

What emerged from this study was the importance of sensitivity towards Early and Late Majority adopters, particularly in relationship to how they were managed.

Timucin argues that administrators and boards of educational institutions must acknowledge the need for staff support to help them deal with change properly. He suggests that it is vital to create opportunities so that the teachers can take advantage of what they are familiar with, such as getting them to prepare support materials and evaluate feedback forms instead of simply asking them:

> to forget everything they have been doing for so long and adopt a completely novel way of teaching instantly. There is no doubt that change will occur in the course of time, but enabling the change to occur with the support of teachers is far more effective than just imposing an innovation on teachers. An innovation can only flourish if the teachers become vigorous, engaged participants, and if the teachers realize that there will be continuous attempts to make them integral parts of the 'novel' system. (Timucin, 2009: 267)

Conclusions

The preceding discussion serves to illustrate that understanding the link between technology and education requires us to think about this issue from a number of different perspectives. History, philosophy, psychology and sociology all have a part to play in developing understanding. What has emerged is that notions of technology have changed over time and that technology is a particularly difficult concept to grapple with. We need to be aware that technology used in education could equally include things, devices, as well as systems and processes. Neither can we dismiss the idea that educational change could be initiated by technology itself, while also acknowledging that societal forces may have a central role in shaping the technology and how we use it in education. Adopting one position or the other presents us with unique challenges. It forces us to contemplate whether technology is a morally neutral phenomenon or impossible to think about without considering values. If the former is the case, then how do we exercise control over what we develop and use in education. Santander-Gana et al. (2006) suggest that a consequence of this approach is that the technology is always:

> oriented towards improved efficiency and economic yield. Decisions result from a strict application of technical rationality. The understanding of the processes

is only accessible by experts that have the adequate specialized understanding necessary to make these decisions and therefore manage technology in a rational manner. (Santander-Gana et al., 2006: 437)

If the latter is the case, we need to ask ourselves whose values we use to guide any choices we make. Santander-Gana et al. (2006) also believe that this approach requires a consensus (regardless of how it originates) in which the expert is only one actor among many. Educational technology has emerged recently as an intellectual discipline in its own right, which has sought to establish general theories of how technology and education relate to each other. Modern thinkers associated with this movement have been particularly interested in establishing how change occurs in order to better manage it. The sheer multiplicity of technologies available today makes it essential for those involved in education to try and do so.

The UNESCO (1985) definition of technology will apply for the remainder of this book. Educational technology will generally mean the artefacts or devices employed in an educational context which aid learning unless otherwise stated.

Big question

Neil Postman in Olson et al. (2001: 9) muses that all technological change 'is a Faustian bargain – that every advantage is tied to a corresponding disadvantage'. We are fast approaching a point where the disadvantages of using technology in learning and teaching are outweighed by the advantages. Does it matter that we have reached this state?

Further reading

Bijker, W. (1997) *Of Bicycles, Bakelites, and Bulbs: Toward a Theory of Sociotechnical Change*, Cambridge, MA: MIT Press.

Layton, E. (1974) Technology as knowledge, *Technology and Culture*, Vol. 15, 31–41.

Luppicini, R. (2005) A systems definition of educational technology in society, *Educational Technology and Society*, Vol. 8, No 3, 103–9.

Pinch T. and Bijker, W. (1984) The social construction of facts and artefacts: or how the sociology of science and technology might benefit each other, *Social Studies of Science*, Vol. 14, 399–441.

Tinio, V. (2003a) *ICT in Education, E-Primers*, Available from www.eprimers.org/ict/index.asp, 69 – Last accessed 15/02/2011.

Useful websites

Babbage

www.computerhistory.org/babbage – Last accessed 15/02/2011.

Determinism

www.informationphilosopher.com/freedom/determinism.html – Last accessed 15/02/2011.

Indian National Flag

www.congress.org.in/national-flag.php – Last accessed 15/02/2011.

Mali Villagers fight against encroachment by the Sahara news.bbc.co.uk/1/hi/world/africa/8408568. stm Last accessed 15/02/2011.Social Construction of Technology

www.umsl.edu/~keelr/280/soconstr.html – Last accessed 15/02/2011.

Spinning Jenny

inventors.about.com/library/inventors/blspinningjenny.htm – Last accessed 15/02/2011.

Technology

http://atschool.eduweb.co.uk/trinity/watistec.html – Last accessed 15/02/2011.

Technological Determinism

/www.aber.ac.uk/media/Documents/tecdet/tdet01.html – Last accessed 15/02/2011.

What is technology?

www.nae.edu/nae/techlithome.nsf/weblinks/KGRG-55ZRMA?OpenDocument, – Last accessed 15/02/2011.

Part 1
SETTING THE SCENE

Early Technology and Education

1

Chapter Outline

Introduction

This is the first three chapters of the book that will examine the nature of the link between technology and education from an historical context in order to provide a rich framework for exploring contemporary issues.

Marcus Cicero (106 BCE to 43 CE), a Roman philosopher whose works greatly influenced European thought, stated that history is the witness of time, the lamp of truth, the embodied soul of memory, the instructress of life, and the messenger of antiquity (Holden, 1895). The Spanish American philosopher George Santayana, whose life spanned the transition from the nineteenth to the twentieth century, believed that those who cannot learn from history are doomed to repeat the mistakes of the past (Santayana, 1905). A considered approach to history can thus help to reveal the social imperatives, the economic forces, the alliances and the vested interests that produce new devices and new ways of thinking about teaching and learning. History also provides opportunities to explore how education and technological innovation are linked in ways that it is impossible to achieve through other means. It would be very difficult to set up a legitimate contemporary experiment that could reveal the impact of new technology in the same way that history can be used as a platform to reflect on similar events from the past. This chapter will, therefore, explore the key historical advances in technology that have had a bearing on the development of education. The canvass for this study will be recent rather than ancient history because the examination of distant events, before reliable records began to emerge, is problematic. In the main, it will feature those artefacts and devices from the fourteenth to the nineteenth centuries that have been employed in an educational context to aid learning. However, there are some advances, such as the advent of the spoken and written word, which emerged before this period that also demand some form of investigation.

What this chapter will seek to establish is whether it is possible, through the timeframe being studied to significantly address the constructivist or determinist conundrum referred to in the last chapter and later on in this one. In other words, using education as the principle measure, does technological change govern social change or vice versa? It will touch on elements of the other three disciplines – philosophy, psychology and sociology – mentioned previously when exploring this issue. Reference will be made to what is unique in the link between education and technology during the period that is covered.

The challenges of looking backwards

History is an imperfect social laboratory. We must remain vigilant in our interpretation of events from earlier periods. The French author François-Marie Arouet (1694–1778), more famously known as Voltaire, believed that history was nothing more than a tableau of crimes and misfortunes, a lie commonly agreed upon (Knowles, 1999). Despite the obvious enthusiasm for history exhibited by Cicero and Santayana, there is much sense in Voltaire's caution, because some of the sources on which we rely to form judgements about events in the past are usually compiled by conquerors rather than by the conquered. The vanquished, the oppressed and minorities rarely have a voice which is loud enough to be heard directly in the soundscape of history unless it is actively listened for. The mores and attitudes of the invaders usually prevail. In the first 400 years of the last millennium, the United Kingdom was subject to Roman rule. The wealthy indigenous population adopted the attitudes, dress and even the education of the invaders from the east to such an extent that they were difficult to tell apart from each other. To these new Britons, the customs from the past, which their far less wealthy compatriots might have still valued, were not worth preserving (de la Bédoyère, 2010).

It is also important when looking backwards that any judgements made about events in the past are not unduly swayed by present attitudes and experiences. For instance, it is tempting to regard education based solely on oral instruction, prevalent in India 2,500 years ago and in many subsequent cultures, as somehow less worthy or efficient than that supported by technology. Yet from this powerful tradition Vedic mathematical rules emerged which are still used today to make difficult computation simple to undertake (Scharfe, 2002). The debate about whether education should abandon the old for the new still has resonance today. In modern India and other countries, such as Australia, that are trying to embrace their indigenous past, this tension is particularly heightened (Nichol, 2010).

Activity

Think of a recent period of history you are familiar with and the technology that might have been used in education. It could be the 1950s or a time closer to our own. Write a few sentences on what you know about it and identify the sources on which you base your ideas. What else could you do to ensure the validity of what you write?

Just as Feenberg (1992) argues that technology does not follow an unwavering path from low to high levels of complexity, it is essential to recognize that technological change can occur differentially. For example, paper, which has a direct bearing on the development of education, first appeared in China as early as 100 BCE but it took 400 years to reach India and a further 1,000 years to reach Europe. In this sense, it would be better to regard the evolutionary journey of any technology in a historical context as a series of overlapping waves rather than as a straight line. Some waves have an uninterrupted journey, some disappear before they reach their final destination, while others coalesce and continue as new waves.

It is possible to misinterpret even basic terms in a historical context. What is meant by the word 'education' today had many different connotations in the past. 'Education' is derived from the Latin word *educatio* and in Ancient Rome (first century BCE onwards) referred to those things associated with child rearing and behaviour, rather than schooling and the development of the intellect. Thus, a child who was considered to be highly educated in this period of time was well brought up rather than erudite (Bonner, 1977).

Like the debate surrounding technology expounded in the previous chapter, history is also subject to dogma. There are those who adopt a deterministic view of history. They believe that history is shaped by forces which are beyond the control of human beings, be they serendipitous or as a result of some overriding law. Those of a Marxist persuasion argue that history is driven by the need to acquire basic material things like food and clothing (Olsen, 2004). They contend that individuals relate to each other solely as a result of the ownership of the means of production, which in turn is regulated by inexorable and immutable laws. This is sometimes referred to as historical materialism (Xiaoping, 2010). There is also a constructivist approach to history, which denies the possibility of a solitary explanation of events in the past and relies on a distinctive interpretative methodology based on case studies (Reus Smit, 2008).

There is a temptation to regard the story of technology and education as a continuum delineated by one invention or another. To a certain extent this is inevitable because the technology itself, or at least its antecedents, is the thing that stands out quite clearly in the fog of time, particularly the further back you go. Our knowledge of ancient cultures such as the Kerma in Sudan, one of black Africa's oldest civilizations, is based on artefacts. All that remains of their once mighty culture are the material things, the buildings and burial rites that were the precursor to some of the ancient Egyptian mummification practices. The Kerma had a profound impact on the region, but because they did not develop their own writing system, archaeologists can only guess at the social forces that helped shape their technologies or how they helped to shape society, particularly in relationship to education. It is important in the context of this book to look beyond the physical manifestation of their culture if any value from an examination of this period or any similar one is to result.

Activity

The caution about history issued by Voltaire suggests that it is prudent to suspect the veracity of witnesses or commentators on events or initiatives from the past. Read the following extract from the early part of the last century advocating the use of the blackboard in the classroom:

$\Rightarrow$

From other departments we have learned many things. Not the least of these is the value of blackboard work. Many English teachers, however, neglect this effective means of reaching the elusive minds of their pupils. It tends to noise and confusion, they assert. But if it helps to banish the sluggishness, the hands folded on desk attitude, the deadly inertness of the classroom; if it substitutes interest for forced attention, isn't it perhaps worth trying? It is time for the "perfect discipline" of the dry as dust teacher to go. Let us joyfully bid it farewell and greet in its stead a more thought producing, soul stirring spirit. I do not claim that blackboard work will of itself do all this, but it will help, and help greatly; chiefly, it seems to me, because it gives an opportunity of reaching a child's mind through his senses and through his nervous system, the only means of making knowledge useful and permanent. This is done by appealing to the eye and by providing an outlet for self-activity. Without these two – vivid sense perception and expression – mental images are sure to be faint hazy and ephemeral. (Monro, 1918)

What would you need to know about the source to determine the legitimacy of her comments? What additional information would help?

The first real technologies?

It could be argued that the first major technology used by human beings were not the crude tools that characterize prehistoric cultures but our ability to communicate, initially using the spoken, and much later the written, word. This may seem like an odd starting point for a historical exploration of the link between education and technology, but language in all its forms allows people to readily exchange and test knowledge, facilitate the transmission of culture and work more effectively for the common good, which some argue is at the heart of education (Bingham, 2005). Although the origins of human speech and language are unclear, the study of individual languages is a highly developed and precise science. Yet the theory of why speech and language evolved in the first place is highly contested. There are those who believe that speech and language are devices for fine-tuning social relationships and others that they are instruments for helping with day-to-day tasks such as keeping warm (Burling, 2007). Ambrose (2001) suggests that there is a direct connection between the development of grammatical speech and technology. He believes that the fine motor control required to produce speech and language and tools are similar in evolutionary origin, because the left hemisphere of the brain controls them both. In support of his thesis, he contends that the transition from simple handheld tools of the Early Stone Age (2.5 million years ago) to specialized composite technology found in the Later Stone Age (70,000 years ago) required a distinct change in the use of language. Simple artefacts can be produced from what is found in the local environment, while those of a more complicated nature require importation and exchange through extended networks and bartering. The language of diplomacy had to develop in order to facilitate this transition.

Activity

UNESCO suggests that technology is a combination of the knowledge and skills and creative processes that may assist people to utilize tools, resources and systems to solve problems and to enhance control over the natural and made environment in an endeavour to improve the human condition (UNESCO, 1985). Using this definition as a starting point for your thinking, identify reasons why speech and language should be regarded as a technology.

Because there is some doubt about whether speech is an entirely innate process rather than a developed capacity, perhaps writing rather than speech could be more readily described as a technological tool (Brown, 1991; Chomsky, 1996). Writing can be defined as a system of visible or tactile signs used to represent units of language in a systematic way. The origins of writing are unclear but it appears to have emerged independently in different cultures and places across the world. The earliest known forms, in which pictures were used to resemble real objects, became evident in the Middle East more than 5,000 years ago. China and Central America also developed their own writing systems independently, and some elements of them are still in existence today. McLuhan (1962) claims that the advent of the phonetic alphabet necessary for effective writing, which no longer depended solely on pictures to represent sounds, was deeply significant in that it allowed abstract concepts to be more readily codified. Because learning to write was usually the preserve of the priesthood or commercial classes, it remained an activity from which the majority of the population were excluded. The fact that for a long time it had mystical overtones also helped to limit those who were allowed to acquire this skill. What the emergence of writing did was to begin the process of converting knowledge into a commodity that could potentially be more widely exchanged. It also gave ideas more permanence. Transmission through the oral tradition was subject to many vagaries and inconsistencies. Writing required the development of additional technologies before the knowledge it contained could be given this permanence and transferability. This was initially achieved by carving on wood or stone, and later by writing on beeswax or clay tablets. The Egyptians developed papyrus and the Greeks their own version of parchment. With the corresponding development of the stylus and inks made from soot and water, the tools necessary to record information in all its guises more permanently were in place. Greeks from the classical period (fifth to fourth centuries BCE) embraced this opportunity with gusto. They were fanatical about noting down everything from finance to philosophy. The letters and hand-copied books which they created have enabled us to derive a great deal of information about them which otherwise would have been impossible to glean. In relationship to education, we learn that Plato's famous Academy (387 BCE), which flourished for 900 years and produced a number of eminent thinkers, was no more than a house and a large garden with probably fewer than a dozen students at any one time (Power, 1964).

Activity

Although Plato and his followers had much to say about the theory of education, they provide very little insight into what education in general was like at the time. However, it is clear from the literature that there was a gradual shift during this period towards providing education for its intrinsic value and enjoyment rather than solely to meet the needs of the state or in support of some higher being (Cubberley, 2007). Do you think that the advent of the recorded word made this more possible? Justify your conclusion(s).

Books and Printing

Another technological shift, the ability to mass-produced books, was required to give knowledge greater permanence and transferability. Since they had first emerged, books and tracts had been unique, handmade treasured works of art that served mainly as a repository for sacred knowledge. The earliest known printed book still in existence, the Diamond Sutra, which was produced in China in 868 CE, is likely to have been made by the transfer of an image from a carved wooden block to paper. The technology was not robust, however. Woodcuts were easily damaged and the time-consuming and costly process of creating a new book had to be undertaken if the information changed. Johann Gutenberg, a goldsmith and stonemason from Mainz in southern Germany, invented a way of printing in 1436 that was far more durable than woodcuts. By using metal type made up of an alloy of lead, tin and antimony, which could be infinitely arranged and rearranged, his printing press could mass produce any text. Thus, costs could be reduced and mistakes more easily rectified. Knowledge could be standardized, preserved and disseminated with much greater ease. New ideas could be developed and challenged by a wider range of people. Using borrowed money, Gutenberg's first and only large-scale activity was to produce 200 copies of the Bible in Latin, a small number of which were printed on vellum (calf-skin). The *Gutenberg Bible* as it became known was hugely popular and sold out almost immediately. This is hardly surprising, given that education during this period, particularly in Europe, was strongly tied to religious organizations, which established schools to promulgate their teachings rather than advance other forms of scholarship (Willmann, 2009). Despite his best efforts to maintain secrecy, the techniques Gutenberg had developed quickly spread to Italy and along the principal trade routes of Western Europe. The books and other materials printed between the middle and the end of the fifteenth century are commonly known as *incunabula* (Latin for cradles). It is quite important to note that although many were religious, others such as Maphaeus Vegius's *De Educatione Liberorum* (*On Education*, 1500 CE), Marsilio Ficino's *Consiglio Contro la Pestilenza* (*On the Plague*, 1481 CE) and Poggius Florentinus's *India Recognita* that contained the report of Niccolò Conti's travels in the Far East (1492 CE) also began to emerge. Gutenberg is credited with modernizing the production of books. Mechanized printing also enabled books to be produced that were used to promote education for its own sake rather than solely for religious training (Füssel, 2005: 108). By the late nineteenth century, the extent to which the book and printed material had become an integral part of the education process is illustrated by the following report on an International Exhibition held in London in 1871, in which education featured prominently. A commentator noted that there were atlases, bibles, copybooks, diagrams, dictionaries, drawing books, examination papers, exercise books, grammar books, lists of vocabularies, maps, posters, multiplication tables, spelling books, text books, wall sheets and school registers on display and remarked, 'who shall say where educational publications end' (*Chambers Journal*, 1871). Tracts, which were essentially religious in nature and had once populated what passed for a classroom in the Middle Ages were now superseded by a multiplicity of books and resources to aid learning and teaching across a wide spectrum of subjects. The variety of printed resources available reflects a growing acknowledgement that education was not simply a matter of incantation and rote learning. Thomas Field, the first Warden of Radley College (an English independent school) between 1897 and 1913, suggested that all the senses needed to be stimulated in order to imprint ideas on the young mind more readily. He believed that it was not enough simply to drill pupils, but that the teacher 'must present to the eyes that through them instruction may reach the imagination' (Field, 1897: 105). He contended that the judicious use of pictures and models, as well as books, would facilitate this process. However, old ideas persisted. Many still held to the notion that the schoolroom was for work and the playground for play and that 'children should never be allowed to convert the school into the playground' (*The Leeds Mercury*, 1880).

Print Culture

Print culture brought about a number of significant changes, apart from serving to commodify knowledge, which had a direct bearing on how education was perceived and delivered. McLuhan (1962) referred to printing as the technology of individualism. Reading, in general, is a solitary activity that takes place in silence. This promotes a sense of personal space and redefines the relationship between the teacher and the taught. Incantation and collective activity, which were the hallmarks of learning prior to the age of what Evans (1998) refers to as Typographical Man, no longer predominated.

McLuhan (1962) suggests that with the advent of the printed book a standardized form of punctuation was required. This meant that speeches were increasing replaced by texts and pamphlets because the written word could portray all the complexities and nuances of the spoken word. A much wider audience could also be reached. Oral or manuscript culture, which was heavily reliant on the spoken word, was therefore in decline. Thus, the dominant means of transmitting ideas and knowledge became vision rather than through a combination of the senses. This interesting notion, if followed to its logical conclusion, has significant implications for the way learning changed during this period. Eisenstein (1990) takes issue with this proposition, claiming that in the 300 years after Gutenberg, the spoken word was not superseded by the printed word, because literacy was still not extensive. She contends that public oration of some form or other was necessary in order for ideas to spread. However, speakers also had to read and write and be more circumspect, because their words could be recorded and published more readily. Postman (1986) believes that the need to be able to read and write, generated in part by Gutenberg's invention, added a new rite of passage separating the child from the adult – that of acquiring literacy. This has great significance for the nature of education and who provided it. The transmission of skills and knowledge through father to son, mother to daughter, or the initiated to the uninitiated that characterized much learning in oral culture was no longer sufficient to meet contemporary needs. As a result, across Europe and America in the late nineteenth century, the provision of education by the state became an increasing necessity. McLuhan (1962) suggests that printing had a profound effect on how easily analytical thought could be undertaken. He argues that because certain types of writing require coherence and an orderly arrangement of ideas, those who are literate can more readily separate the emotional from the rational. In addition, he speculates that the capacity to remember things becomes less important because books, rather than the brain of an individual, now function as the repository for information. Postman (1986) claims that this new rationality resulting from the widespread adoption of print culture signalled the beginning of what the Anglo American radical Thomas Paine (1737–1809) referred to as the 'age of reason', in which orthodox views about religion and the natural order of things was challenged. Logical thought and freethinking above all were cherished rather than an unquestioning acceptance of the sacred word (Paine, 1819). Mass-produced books also enabled the minutiae of any canon to be forensically examined and reexamined by many minds, which aided the development of new ideas and exposed those that were flawed. Charles Darwin's theory of evolution, which raised the spectre that man was descended from apes, generated much controversy when it first appeared in print in 1859. His book, *Origin of the Species*, was an immediate bestseller. It was written for non-specialist readers and attracted the widespread attention of the open-minded, who generally supported him, and an equally vociferous group of scientists and theologians who were violently opposed to his ideas. Although Darwin was reluctant to engage in public debate, both his supporters and detractors invested considerable effort in compiling and publishing pamphlets and essays on aspects of his theory (Campbell, 1989). Those who were literate read these publications voraciously. Those who were not literate flocked to the public lectures on the subject eager to engage in the complexities of the debate.

Activity

The advent of print enabled those including governments who controlled access to the presses to promote their own views. What affect do you think this had on the curriculum material used in the burgeoning education systems that appeared in Europe an America at the end of the nineteenth century?

Conclusions

There is no doubt that the previous pages establish that the transition from educating the few to the many can be linked to the development technology. First the spoken, and then the written and the printed word, were instrumental in promoting change. In Ancient Greece, boys, or at the least those who came from families that were free of bondage, attended schools and learned to read, write and undertake simple arithmetic. Education of the poor was confined to the transmission of the skills and knowledge associated with tasks they were required to perform. In the Roman Empire, high-status Greek slaves introduced the children of the wealthy to the mysteries of geometry, history, literature and public speaking. There was no significant change in the educational provision for the poor. There was a shift, albeit a small one, in the Middle Ages. A few children of the poor were taught to read and write by sympathetic priests in chantry schools, supported by an endowment from a rich benefactor who wished his soul to be prayed for. Education was, nevertheless, still the preserve of a select few. It was in the nineteenth century, particularly in Europe and America, that significant change occurred. Education for all provided by the state began to emerge. In the United Kingdom, the 1870 Education Act, sometimes known as the Forster Act, was passed which signalled the beginning of a state-funded system of education in the United Kingdom that eventually became free of charge, compulsory and catered for children of all ages. The act concentrated on establishing a network of nondenominational elementary schools to complement existing schools already run by churches and individuals and guilds. Religious instruction, although still part of the curriculum, was not compulsory. This seminal event appears to be linked to the rise of the book that could not have evolved without Gutenberg. Indeed, Eisenstein (1980) suggests that his presses acted as a catalyst for every department of human activity at some point or other, claiming that the invention and development of printing with movable type brought about the most 'radical transformation in the condition of intellectual life and history of Western civilization'. She contends that it opened new horizons in education (Eisenstein, 1980). However it took more than 300 years for the Foster Act to emerge after Gutenberg, and it is important to ask why. Other forces, both economic and social, could have been at play. Perhaps a realignment of the relationship between religious agencies and the state was equally important, since much early education was provided by religious rather than secular agencies. The social imperatives, alliances and vested interests that could have been additional influences are, however, difficult to identify. It is equally possible that this timeframe is suitable and that the causal link is real. We live in a time of rapid technological change and it is more problematic for us to regard 300 years as acceptable. This period is of only limited value in trying to shed new light the constructivist or determinist debate. However, what it does do is to establish a number of key points. Writing, and then printing, did commodify knowledge and make it less vulnerable to frailties of human memory. This enabled great social change and the development of new ideas, especially in education. The mass produced book was one of the first technologies to radically affect all aspects of learning and teaching. However, the full psychological and sociological impact alluded to by McLuhan (1962) and Postman (1986) could only be achieved through widespread literacy. It is important to note that, even today, we still do not have universal literacy.

Big Question

Are there contemporary examples of technology that have made such a radical difference to education as the printing press and the mass-produced book and what lessons can we learn from history?

Further reading

Burling, R. (2007) *The Talking Ape: How Language Evolved*, USA: Oxford University Press.

Cubberley, E. (2007) *The History of Education*, Vol. 1, Charleston: BiblioBazaar.

Eisenstein, E. (1980) *The Printing Press as an Agent of Change*, Vol. 1, Cambridge: Cambridge University Press.

Füssel. S. (2005) (Translated by Martin D.) *Gutenberg and the Impact of Printing*, Aldershot: Ashgate.

Postman, N. (1986) *Amusing Ourselves to Death*, London: Methuen.

Scharfe, H. (2002) *Education in Ancient India*, Leiden: Brill.

Useful websites

Diamond Sutra

See the section on the Oldest Printed Book www.bl.uk/onlinegallery/ttp/ttpbooks.html – Last accessed 14/02/2011.

Gutenberg Press

www.gutenberg.de/english/erfindun.htm – Last accessed 14/02/2011.

History of Education

www.localhistories.org/education.html – Last accessed 14/02/2011.

Historical Materialism

www.marxist.com/historical-materialism-study-guide.htm – Last accessed 14/02/2011.

History of Paper

www.historyforkids.org/learn/literature/paper.htm – Last accessed 14/02/2011.

Range of *Incunabula*

www.bl.uk/catalogues/istc/ – Last accessed 14/02/2011.

The Miracle of Language

www.duke.edu/~pk10/language/psych.htm – Last accessed 14/02/2011.

The 1870 Education Act

www.parliament.uk/about/living-heritage/transformingsociety/livinglearning/school/
overview/1870educationact/ – Last accessed 14/02/2011.

Writing in Ancient Greece

www.fjkluth.com/writing.html – Last accessed 14/02/2011.

2 The Automation of Education

Introduction

This chapter will explore the link between education and technology from about the end of the nineteenth century until the last quarter of the twentieth century, before computers were widely in use. Studying this period has particular relevance for the present-day reader because many of the issues that the supporters and their opponents raised about the use of technology in education at the time still have resonance today. The timeframe concerned is close enough to our own to be recognizable even by those least informed about it. This proximity also means that archive material about the challenges and the accompanying debate is readily accessible. We can, therefore, avoid one of the major limiting factors of any historical study, the availability of primary sources. At the same time, the period is distant enough from our own to offer proper points of comparison. A study of the shift from the use of mechanical contrivances to those which are digitally based to do our bidding in learning and teaching that took place during this era offers rich opportunities to study the complex relationship between technology and education.

What this chapter will seek to establish are the key technological and social developments that had a significant bearing on teaching and learning during the period being explored. It will examine the rise of the teaching machine in both its passive and active forms. Attention will be paid to the growing interest by psychologist in the scientific basis of learning and how a few of them sought to convert theory to practice. The new media of radio and television will be investigated in order to shed light on how technology was beginning to redefine the scope of learning and what cultural issues any changes that ensued might have been generated. Above all, it will encourage the reader to apply what has been discovered about the link between education and technology during this time frame to a contemporary context, specifically through the activities provided.

Activity

It could be argued that, in the past, the advent of popular newspapers made major events such as war and pestilence much more immediate to those in the community, at least to those who were literate. Schools of that time needed to reflect this change in the curriculum they delivered. Identify contemporary equivalent technologies that have forced changes in the curriculum.

In the beginning

To the fertile minds of those innovators who helped shape the world at the beginning of the twentieth century, the idea that technologies other than the book could be usefully employed in the classroom was not anathema. After all, it was the period in which we made our first hesitant attempts at assisted flight and the mechanized vehicle emerged as the desired form of transport for, in the first instance, a few, and then many. At the same time, various devices that made use of some of the new technologies were being developed in support of learning and teaching in both Europe and America. An American industrialist and master mechanic Halcyon Skinner has been credited with inventing the first patented teaching machine in 1866 (Lawson, 1973). His machine was designed to teach children to spell. Using a series of keys, pupils were required to type out a word in a lower window located on the front of the device that represented a picture, which was exhibited in an upper window. The pictures could be changed as required (Benjamin, 1988: 704). How far this machine reflected a significant breakthrough in the utilization of technology in education is debatable. Many devices, such as charts and maps and models, had been around in one form or another since the first tentative steps at formal education were made. They had a number of things in common with Skinner's machine. They required the active participation of the teacher in order to be effective and had no innate capacity for feedback. It was quite possible for a user of the Skinner device to type in nonsense without correction unless the teacher intervened. It could, therefore, only be described at best as an appliance for assisting learning and not a machine that teaches. The shift to developing a technology that did the latter required a change in mindset and the application of many new areas of knowledge that only emerged in the next century.

A glimpse of the future

The first patented device that 'taught' was attributed to Herbert Austin Atkins, an American psychologist and academic, who in 1911 created an appliance that could be used in a range of different curriculum areas. His machine consisted of a wooden case into which blocks of a particular shape could be inserted if they represented the correct response to a specific question. This denotes something new, because psychological research into how we respond to external simulation had been employed as the basis for its development. It was one stage closer to what Benjamin (1988) regarded as a real teaching machine, in that it contained discreet units of information, provided some means for the learner to respond to this information and used feedback to improve performance. However, Atkins's device was not automatic or self-regulating. Sidney Pressey (1888–1979) is regarded as the true father of the teaching machine. Pressey, a Harvard psychology graduate and recognized innovator, published widely on educational matters. He held that education during his time was grossly inefficient, limited by its addiction to procedural issues and conservatism, and stymied by intellectual inertia. He suggested that the catalyst for change or modernizing agent would arise from a combination of educational science and inventive educational technology. Pressey believed that no less than 'an industrial revolution' in education was required, which he would help to start by creating his own teaching machine (Petrina, 2004: 305). He had been inspired by Edward Thorndike (1874–1949), an experimental psychologist, who as early as 1912 wished that the means existed to create what he described as a book that would only allow a reader to advance from one page the next when the content had been properly absorbed and understood. Thorndike believed that if such a device was available, 'much that now requires personal instruction could be managed by print (Thorndike, 1912: 165). Besides being fascinated with miracles of mechanical ingenuity, he was also committed to developing a theory of learning. His experiments with animals, particularly cats, led him to believe that behaviour could be modified by positive reinforcement. From this work, he developed what he referred to as the 'law of effect', which stated that the strength of that connection between stimulus and response depends on whether rewards or sanctions follow the stimulus (Catania, 1999). He believed that rewards were more important than punishment. Later, Thorndike added the laws of exercise and of readiness.

Activity

In his experiments on learning, Thorndike confined a hungry cat in what was referred to as a puzzle box. In order to get at food, which had been placed outside the box and in a position where it was clearly visible, the cat had to depress a lever which opened an access gate. Random actions were replaced eventually once the cat learned the correct response. If you were presented with the results from a similar study today that advocated a particular approach to teaching and learning based on the modification of behaviour through reward, would you be willing to adopt them and why? What do you think the difference between attitudes then and now would be?

Thorndike's laws were important because they helped to shape how Pressey approached the task of designing his machine. His first device which tested intelligence was patented in 1928. It was mainly composed of typewriter parts that could be easily and cheaply replicated. It could be operated in two different ways. In its testing mode, subjects chose answers to the list of 30 multiple-choice questions, graduated from easy to difficult, by depressing one of four keys. The machine then moved on to the next question automatically. When all of the questions had been answered, it 'counted' how many were correct, thus providing an indication of intelligence or, in some cases, test score results. In its teaching mode, achieved by raising a small lever on the back of the device, a user could only advance from one question to another by entering the correct answer. Multiple responses were allowed until the correct key was pressed. Pressey, unlike some other teaching machine designers, believed that learners had to be allowed to make mistakes in order for them to clarify their learning (Pressey, 1962). He continued to develop his devices so that they could accommodate a wide range of subjects for testing, eventually referring to them as 'Automatic Teachers'. He argued that his machines could give instant feedback to students about their performance. He claimed that they allowed for the development of self-regulation and self-instruction in accordance with the laws that Thorndike had evolved. At the same time, he wanted to free teachers from repetitive tasks that did not require specialist skill.

Activity

Pressey explored the link between technology and education for some considerable time and mused that schoolwork, in what to him was the future, would be:

> marvellously though simply organized, so as to adjust almost automatically to individual differences and the characteristics of the learning process. There will be many labour saving schemes and devices, and even machines – not at all for the mechanizing of education, but for the freeing of teacher and pupil from educational drudgery and incompetence both. (Petrina, 2004, 328)

Do you think that Pressey's vision of the future has become a reality and what evidence do you base your conclusion on?

Skinner's machine

Another beneficiary of Thorndike's work was B. F. Skinner (1904–1990), an American psychologist with strong views on both childrearing and human behaviour. Skinner's journey into the world of teaching machines began in 1953 with a visit to his daughter's school, where he noticed that during a maths test, all pupils were required to work at the same pace and then had to wait 24 hours for their results (Skinner, 1983). He wanted to address these issues by developing his own primitive machine to teach mathematics. He wrote a seminal paper, 'The Science of Learning and the Art of Teaching', which explained both his device and the reasoning behind it (Skinner, 1954). He believed firmly that if teachers were to benefit from recent advances in the study of learning they must have the help of mechanical devices. In his view, these devices had to be capable of timely reinforcement and have the capacity to provide for differentiated and sequential learning (Skinner, 1954: 95). His own device consisted of a box with a window on its top surface in which questions or problems printed on paper could be viewed. Sliders allowed the user to construct answers to these questions. Correct answers resulted in a bell ringing to provide a form of conditioned reinforcement and transition to the next question. Incorrect answers resulted in the user not being allowed to progress until the error was corrected. Although Skinner acknowledged Pressey's contribution to the development of his own teaching machines their approaches were fundamentally different. In Pressey's device, students had to study some material prior to using the machine. In contrast, Skinner's machines were based on the premise that new material was only to be introduced to the student in manageable packages. This was a critical difference. He argued that learning proceeded most easily:

> in small steps; thus, student success could be maximized, and errors could be kept to a near zero level. To ensure this kind of learning, the material had to be organized in a coherent fashion, building a response repertoire, step by tiny step. (Benjamin, 1988: 708)

He also believed that the most valuable teaching machine would be one that allowed students to compose or construct their responses rather than select one from a set of predetermined alternatives. James Holland, one of Skinner's colleagues, commented that learned behaviour is only possible when it is:

> emitted and reinforced, gradual progression . . . is necessary to establish complex repertoires, gradual withdrawal (fading or vanishing) of stimulus support is effective, it is necessary to control the student's observing and echoic behaviour and to train for discrimination, the student should write his response. (Morill, 1961: 365)

Skinner based his ideas partly on work done with hungry pigeons in the laboratory that were taught certain behaviours for rewards of food. Drawing parallels between animal and human behaviour would be hard for some to accept. He countered any criticism of this ilk by pointing out that he had established universal truths about learning which could be applied to any species. His animal studies had led him to conclude that there was a link between certain behaviours and the mental states necessary for learning to take place. Therefore, any tool that allowed modification of these behaviours was an essential component in the armoury of the teacher (Skinner, 1954). He anticipated that there would be other objections to the use of such devices in the classroom. He regarded the spectre of the teacher being replaced by a machine as unfounded. He believed that 'mechanical devices will eliminate the more tiresome labours of the teacher but they will not necessarily shorten the time she remains in contact with the pupil' (Skinner, 1954: 97). In his view, the opposite was far more likely. Nor did he regard cost as an issue, arguing that the economies of scale, particularly in a country surrounded by labour-saving devices, would help reduce prices. Perhaps the most significant obstacle he anticipated was that of cultural inertia. Skinner argued that Pressey's machines had not been successful simply because the world of education at the time of their development was not ready for them. The 1930s in America was a period of the Great Depression when there was mass unemployment. Devices which appeared to increase efficiency in education, making it possible to use fewer teachers, were bound not to find favour with the educational establishment of that time (Benjamin, 1988, 708). Skinner was convinced that conditions had changed and 'a sweeping revision of educational practices is possible and inevitable' (Skinner, 1954: 97).

Activity

Despite the fact that his own efforts to market a machine were not very successful, Skinner's ideas generated a revolution in teaching. However, the 1960s saw a vast increase in the number and type of teaching machines used in a range of educational settings in America. By 1962, the Grolier Company had sold a 100,000 teaching machines based on his principles at $20 each (Benjamin, 1988: 709). Can you suggest reasons why a slow uptake was followed by wide adoption of these devices and what bearing this has for today?

Other devices

Rather surprisingly, Skinner, who was now being described by some as a behavioural technologist rather than a psychologist (Kitchener, 1972), contended that when a student or a pupil engaged in machine-supported learning something was happening all the time, but while, in contrast, watching television, they 'may just sit and stare' (Skinner, 1960: 189). Unlike Skinner, other educators recognized the value of both radio and TV broadcasting in learning and teaching.

In the same decade that Pressey was developing his prototype machines, in America the School of the Air (SOA) movement, linking radio and education, was beginning to emerge. Bianchi (2008) speculates that some in the early 1920s believed that radio offered a quick technical solution to the deficiencies in the American education system, persuaded by the notion that a single dazzling teacher using this form of communication could inspire thousands of bored students to greater learning. The movement started in Chicago in 1924 as a result of funding obtained from the Sears Roebuck and Company that enabled lessons on topics as diverse as farming, transportation and science developed by teachers and pupils to be broadcast on local radio in a programme called 'The Little Red Schoolhouse'. It was well received and within a year had reached nearly 28,000 students in classrooms spread across three states. Benjamin Darrow, who was responsible for the Chicago experiment, believed that the central purpose of education by radio was to create a global village to 'bring the world to the classroom, to make universally available the services of the finest teachers, the inspiration of the greatest leaders . . . and unfolding world events' (Hackbarth, 1996). Although Darrow and his supporters were unsuccessful in getting federal support for their initiative, many Schools of the Air (SOA) emerged in subsequent years which were either sponsored by commercial network broadcasters such as the Columbia Broadcasting System (CBS) or were endorsed by states, such as Wisconsin. The Wisconsin School of the Air was commissioned in 1930 to provide for the educational needs of school children, particularly those in rural communities, who, because of their isolation, faced special difficulties in accessing appropriate learning and teaching resources. At the same time, it was also designed to compensate for the dearth of experiential learning in most American schools. However, great care was taken to make it clear that this initiative was not a means of marginalizing or even making the teacher redundant. The School of the Air, like the machines by Plessey and Skinner, were underpinned by scholarly values. The programmes were created by professors from the University of Wisconsin with the support of local public school teachers. As a result of its success, a sister agency, the Wisconsin College of the Air, was developed in 1936 to address some of the learning needs of adolescents in high school and adults who could not attend university. There were no tuition fees or restrictions on the number of programmes an individual could enrol in, and no need to attend a campus (Bianchi, 2002). The courses included historical, musical and scientific subjects and were more concerned with informal rather than formal education. While not definitive, these two schools are indicative of the many experiments (including the Portland

School of the Air, which lasted well into the mid-1990s) in utilizing this technology in an educational context that were being undertaken at the time. The Portland initiative was distinctive because it continually broadcast a full day of in-school and after-school programs and involved students and teachers in writing, producing, performing, announcing and engineering. Lester Ward Parker, the director of a schools broadcasting research project hosted by the University of Wisconsin, noted that it was significant that in 'almost every civilized country, the radio has been recognized as a powerful instrument for the wide dissemination of whatever kind of education and culture suits its national need' (Parker, 1939: 296). He had attended the World Conference of Education Associations held in Oxford in 1935 and was impressed with the work of the *British Broadcasting Company* (*BBC*) in developing radio for schools in the United Kingdom. While Darrow was piloting 'The Little Red Schoolhouse', the *BBC* was making its first broadcast to a single school in Glasgow in 1924. By the time it had become the official state broadcaster in 1927, this experiment had been transformed into a national service. However, despite appointing Mary Somerville as the *BBC's* first Director of Schools Broadcasting (1929–1947), output was less than enthusiastically received by some who 'doubted the power of the disembodied voice to hold children's attention, while others were concerned that listening to the radio might create a race of listeners rather than of thinkers and men of action and introduce robot teachers into schools' (Crook, 2007: 219). Interestingly, another objection to an expansion of the service was the potential broadcasting had to make provision in schools too standardized. Nevertheless, there were many passionate advocates of schools radio in the United Kingdom who recognized its potential to bring new voices into the classroom, which could supplement teaching or provide materials way beyond the resources of the ordinary school. This meant that subjects such as biology, in which there was a shortage of trained teachers, could still be delivered through broadcasting. The important thing to stress here is that the *BBC* was an official broadcaster and, as such, had all the apparatus of the state behind it and could rely on a guaranteed income.

In both America and the United Kingdom, radio has mainly been employed as a curriculum supplement but attempts were made to broaden how it was used. In the early days of American educational radio, contact with individual listeners was fostered by allowing them to mail questions on subjects related to broadcasts for experts to answer. There were even efforts to take registers in the form of questionnaires, which were designed as a means of quality assurance. In the United Kingdom, Parker observed how in a rural school, radio was not only used to bring history alive but the broadcasting process itself was modelled by the children to improve their spoken language. He described how each child went out to a little improvised studio and actually broadcasts to the class. He noted that

> their papers are original and exactly timed to two minutes and their childish voices come through very clearly to the listening class. Each does his best to interest his audience and hold their attention and some succeed surprisingly . . . and one did not need to use the word motivation to express the enthusiasm and interest these youngsters showed both in their composition and in their speech. (Parker, 1939: 291)

However, real contact between broadcasters and listeners only occurred as the result of special circumstances, such as those that led to the introduction of the Australian Schools of the Air movement. Children in the more isolated parts of Australia had little or no access to traditional schools. Their education was generally done through correspondence courses, which relied on an infrequent and sometimes unreliable postal service. In 1944, Adelaide Miethke, a former inspector of schools and a member of the Council of the Flying Doctor service, suggested using shortwave radio to give educational talks to children in the Outback. This led to the first School of the Air being established in 1951 in Alice Springs, which linked its remote 'pupils' to both a teacher in a town and to each other. Initially, lessons were delivered in a similar way to that found in American and British radio, but very quickly, question and answer sessions were added to the end of each broadcast and the whole experience became more interactive. By 1968, there were 13 such schools in various locations in Australia.

Television was to extend and change the reach of broadcaster's involvement in education. Although TV had been around since the 1930s, the Second World War delayed the point at which broadcasters were in a position to begin to seriously think about education. Provision for schools evolved in many different countries at about the same time. What they had in common was a suitable technical infrastructure and a community with access to affordable mass-produced sets. However, they differed in that broadcasting began in the United Kingdom, Canada and Europe 'as public, government established programming, with private commercial television coming much later; while in the United States, government and foundation efforts served to squeeze out a space for classroom instruction and public access educational television in an otherwise commercial environment' (Levin et al., 2003: 264). In 1952, the *BBC* undertook an experiment that involved transmitting 20

TV programmes on a range of subjects, including art and science, through a closed circuit television link to six secondary schools in Middlesex. A BBC spokesperson stated that '. . . no one yet knows the value of television to the work of schools, and the only way to find out is to try it' (Thomas, 1952). By 1957, both the *BBC* and its commercial rivals were preparing to broadcast a range of TV programmes made specifically for schools. However, these initial efforts were not universally acclaimed. Problems lay not only with technical issues but with how broadcasting was used. A commentator writing in 1958 asked why those involved in schools television appeared not to make use of the basic rules learned from using radio and films in learning and teaching when creating TV programmes (Field, 1958). This criticism emerged from the practice known as direct teaching or instructional television, in which an expert undertook the role of the teacher (albeit at a distance) whose task was to guide the viewer through a lesson. The important issue here was integrating this provision into the school curriculum. A much looser use (although not universally recognized) was referred to as enrichment television, in which any serious drama, documentary or news programme was regarded as educational as long as it enhanced the learning experience (Lawler, 1965: 327). The same threat identified in all the new twentieth-century technologies used in the classroom, that they hastened the point at which the teacher becomes redundant, was also evident with television. It had the potential to offer:

> the studio teacher and the master schedule as a replacement for the classroom teacher. In the interest of reaching mass audiences of students, school administrators [in the United States] at first seized upon TV as an all-or-nothing medium which could deliver packaged courses that seemed to result in as much pupil learning as did traditional instruction. (Freeman, 1967: 198)

Perhaps the emergence of the Open University in the United Kingdom represents the point at which all the technologies that appeared to impact on education came together. As early as 1926, J. C. Stobart (historian and educator), who was the *BBC*'s first Director of Education, suggested establishing a wireless university. In 1962, Michael Young, British sociologist and author, proposed that a university be established to:

> prepare people for external degrees at London University, with three key functions; to organise new and better correspondence courses for the degree; to promote lectures and residential schools; and to teach by means of television.

Convinced of the need to free education from the limitations of school, class and even location. . . . (Stanistreet, 2009, 8)

It was Young who stated that if the student can't come to the lab, then 'the lab must come to the student' (Stanistreet, 2009). This notion was embodied in a government White Paper on the University of the Air, presented to Parliament in 1966, which advocated setting up a new university to provide undergraduate and postgraduate opportunities to those (over the age of 21) who, for whatever reason, were excluded from attending full-time higher education but deemed capable of it. The first courses of the Open University (OU) as it became known (it was also sometimes referred to as the University of the Second Chance) were available in 1971 and the first degrees were awarded in 1973. It was technology that made this possible. Students received study material by mail from a central campus, completed set readings, listened to weekly radio broadcasts, watched weekly or biweekly television programmes (usually transmitted at what some regarded as antisocial hours of the day or night), then completed and mailed back assignments. Either individual or group telephone calls involving other students and their tutor were used to enrich the learning experience, and summer schools provided additional opportunities to meet. Despite high ideals of social justice the majority of the initial 25,000 students selected for study (from 43,000 applicants) were distinctly middle class. This situation was to continue into the next decade (Craig, 1980).

Activity

In relationship to the use of television in the classroom, Freeman (1967) commented that for generations the

> . . . quality of instruction in the schools has depended, fundamentally, upon the teacher working alone in his self-contained classroom. Subject to a minimum of supervision, the schoolmaster determined the learning objectives and the learning experiences to which pupils were exposed. Textbooks, curriculum guides, and instructional aids increasingly influenced the nature and quality of instruction, yet the teacher continued to be the master of his own domain, choosing his texts, deviating from curriculum guides, adopting only those aids. (Freeman, 1967: 199)

Do you think that nature of the contemporary teacher's role has changed because of the increasing use of technology? Does this matter?

Conclusions

The rise of machines employed in education had a slow beginning at the start of the last century. They were initially no more than devices to enhance learning and teaching, in the same way that the book or a globe might do. The technology used to create them was borrowed from other devices, such as the typewriter, and the number of things that these machines were capable of doing was fairly limited. However, increasingly, designers aspired to produce teaching machines that could automate the process of learning and teaching. It is interesting to speculate what this objective sprang from. Was it simply the result of intellectual curiosity or a means of making education more efficient? The latter would certainly be in keeping with an age that saw the advent of time and motion studies. The use of some form of technology certainly was regarded as a cure for shortages of specialist teachers. However, automated teaching machines could not evolve until a better understanding of how people learn had been developed. Psychologists, who were in the vanguard of constructing learning theories, became interested in machines. Learning and teaching was suddenly no longer the sole preserve of educators. Theses innovators appeared to be motivated by the best of intentions.

The introduction of radio and then television in the classroom that occurred during this period also had a significant effect on education. The needs of pupils in remote communities could now, in theory, be readily met without some form of relocation. Both brought education within the reach of other groups, such as those who could not undertake higher learning by traditional means. To those facing less pressing resource issues, the world outside the classroom was now also only the touch of a button away. Radio and television, like the book, are examples of technologies not designed specifically for educational use that have employed in teaching and learning. Similarly, the computer is widely employed in education today, despite its origins as a both a military and business tool. The teaching machine and radio and television inexorably began to change the way the teacher and the taught related to each other. They also signal the growing importance of technology in the classroom. However, a suitable technical infrastructure needed to be in place and unit costs needed to be low enough before they could be adopted widely.

Big Question

Skinner and his colleagues were convinced that the process of teaching and learning could be made much more effective by the use of technology, developed using sound scientific principles. Teachers were deeply sceptical about this notion, concerned that the real agenda was to find ways of replacing them by the machine. It took many years for the profession to accept some technologies in the classroom, although this was not just because of the spectre of job losses. Is the modern teaching workforce equally as reluctant to accept innovation and how best can this tardiness, if it still exists, be overcome?

Further reading

Crook, D. (2007) School broadcasting in the United Kingdom: An exploratory history, *Journal of Educational Administration and History*, Vol. 39, No. 3, 217–6.

Hoth, W. (1961) From Skinner to Crowder to Chance: A Primer on Teaching Machines, *The English Journal*, Vol. 50, No 6, 398–401.

Kitchener, R. (1972) B. F. Skinner: The Butcher, the Baker, the Behaviour-Shaper, *The Philosophy of Science Association*, Vol. 1972, 87–98.

Levin, R. and Hines, L. (2003) Educational Television, Fred Rogers, and the History of Education, *History of Education Quarterly*, Vol. 43, No. 2, 262–75.

Petrina, S. (2004) Sidney Pressey and the Automation of Education, 1924–1934, *Technology and Culture*, Vol. 45, 305–30.

Skinner. (1954) The Science of Learning and the Art of Teaching, *Harvard Educational Review* Vol. XXIV, No 2, 86–97.

Useful websites

BBC Education
www.bbc.co.uk/schools/ – Last accessed 14/02/2011.
Edward Thorndike
http://psychology.about.com/od/profilesmz/p/edward-thorndike.htm – Last accessed 14/02/2011.
History of the Open University
www8.open.ac.uk/about/main/the-ou-explained/history-the-ou – Last accessed 14/02/2011.
Instructional Design http://internettime.com/itimegroup/Is%20it%20Time%20to%20Exchange%20Skinner's%20Teaching%20Machine%20for%20Dewey's.htm – Last accessed 14/02/2011.
Learning Theories

www.brookes.ac.uk/services/ocsld/resources/theories.html – Last accessed 14/02/2011.

Pressey's Teaching Machines

www.nwlink.com/~donclark/hrd/history/machine.htm – Last accessed 14/02/2011.

Schools of the Air (Australia)

www.abc.net.au/arts/adlib/stories/s857521.htm – Last accessed 14/02/2011.

Skinner Machines

www.thecrimson.com/article/1956/4/18/skinner-machines-make-classroom-like-kitchen/ – Last accessed 14/02/2011.

Wisconsin School of the Air

www.wcftr.commarts.wisc.edu/collections/featured/madisonradio/schoolofair/ – Last accessed 14/02/2011.

The Computer and Education

Introduction

This chapter will explore the impact of the programmed learning movement and the computer on education. Programmed learning, which was developed in the 1950s, is worthy of examination because it helps to raise issues about the relative value of software (programme) versus hardware (machine) in a learning and teaching context. Investigating programmed learning also provides unique opportunities to determine the impact of theories of learning on the use of technology in education. While traces of the programmed learning movement are fading today, it nevertheless still has significance in relationship to the rise of the computer. An examination of the genesis of the computer in education, before the advent of the Internet, has much to offer in establishing why this technology has become so ubiquitous today and the challenges faced by the first adopters. It has become so rooted in educational practice, in developed countries, at least, that to a certain extent we forget how limited it appeared to be as an educational tool in the early days. The late 1960s and early 1970s saw the first tentative experimentation with computers. The 1980s was the decade in which many large-scale projects involving computers were initiated. All raised similar questions about how best to use them in an educational context, and what the economic and technological challenges were in their widespread adoption.

What this chapter will seek to establish is the impact of key players, including educational administrators, on the uptake of technology in learning and teaching. It will also establish how technologies used extensively in the wider community do not readily transfer to the classroom without suitable forethought. In addition, it will posit that some technologies, like the computer, require every aspect of educational activity, from curriculum content to the timetable, to be adjusted in order for them to be effective. Even financial and technological infrastructures must be modified. The interdependence syndrome, which posits that useful technologies do not exist in isolation from each other, is also a relevant consideration in this context. This chapter will assert that while technologies in the past have been used to bolster existing educational practice, newer ones have the potential to reform and deform it quite radically. At the same time, it will make the case that, because the sum of all knowledge is ever increasing, educators could not afford to ignore any technology that gave them the ability to access information more readily. Finally, it will emphasize that the spectre of teachers being supplanted by technology was brought into even sharper relief by the rise of the computer. Inevitably relationships between users of these machines, regardless of whether they were learners or teachers, were also changed.

Programmed learning

Skinner's efforts to devise teaching machines referred to in the previous chapter (Skinner, 1953) were founded on the notion that any subject, be it astronomy or zoology, could be broken down into a series of component parts and taught in small steps or frames. The parts built upon each other like the bricks in a house. Each ended in a series of questions that participants needed to answer correctly in order to advance to the next part in the sequence. This was known as programmed learning or programme-led learning, and it remained popular with educators throughout the 1960s and 1970s. It was widely adopted in America and was also employed elsewhere. While teaching machines and programmed learning are sometimes regarded as interchangeable terms,

there is an important difference. Teaching machines required learning programmes to function properly, but programmed learning could be undertaken without a machine. A book or paper would suffice. Some regarded this
lack of dependence on more complicated technology as the most attractive
feature of programmed learning (Stewart, 1963). It was free from the need for
specialist support and was not subject to excessive costs or concerns about
reliability. However, it did require very careful design. Programmed learning
allowed users to work at their own pace, but within a clear and highly regulated framework (Field, 2007). Educational administrators and those responsible for budgets quickly recognized that this was an apparently effective way
of delivering the curriculum which could be readily costed and measured.
This is not surprising, since the founders of programmed learning, including
Skinner, had been attracted by the notion of efficiency in education. They
were convinced that in order to succeed, it was necessary to devise ways to
teach more in less time (Dale, 1967; Skinner, 1968). Programmed learning had
other potential benefits. It could be used to address the shortage of specialist teachers. As a concept, it was also highly transferable across cultural and
geographical divides because the principle of breaking a subject down into
frames was universal. Consequently, there was much interest from Africa in
the 1960s (Stewart, 1963). However, there were a number of problems associated with programmed learning. Kay and others contended that it was based
on a gross over-exaggeration of the link between behaviour and learning to
which Skinner and Crowder were so attached (Langeveld, 1967). It did not,
as had been promised, bring about a revolution in education. Programmed
learning failed to improve performance in examinations or make students
'feel more positively about the subject matter they were studying or about the
quality of the teaching at their schools' (Kulik et al., 1982: 133). It could not
compensate for differences in natural aptitude between pupils. There were
issues with how programmes were devised and used. If programmers wanted
to develop material for a topic that did not reduce easily, they moulded it into
something that did (Gagné, 1965, in McDonald et al., 2005). This often led
to oversimplification, changed meanings and constrained learning. When
programmes that had been created by specialists in commercial agencies
were adhered to rigidly without any contextualization, they generally failed
to meet student need (McDonald et al., 2005). Furthermore, it was difficult to modify a typical programme, which might contain between 500 and
3,500 frames, without compromising the integrity of the package as a whole.
Programmed learning often failed to promote genuine exploration (Garner,

1966, in McDonald et al., 2005). Learners were given little responsibility for directing their own learning. The need to provide positive feedback in order to promote desired behaviours also meant that the steps in programmes were very often determined by the lowest common denominator. The necessity for small steps in any sequence meant that the transition points were not challenging enough. Users could only establish that subsequent items were 'connected with preceding ones, but is unable to experience this link sufficiently clearly' (Langeveld, 1967: 21). There was also some criticism generated by the necessity for logical sequencing in the development of frames. McKeachie suggested, somewhat irreverently, that randomness 'may not make sense conceptually, but it may be more fun' (McKeachie, 1974, in Vredeveld, 1982: 15). It was also possible in programmed learning to give a succession of correct answers without having gained any insight into what was being studied.

The best that could be claimed for programmed learning was that it was no less effective than traditional methods of teaching. However, without any apparent gain, it raised the spectre of teacher marginalization again. Unsurprisingly, programmed learning was abandoned almost as swiftly as it was taken up.

> ### Activity
>
> Early adherents claimed that programmed learning was as old as education itself and followed in the tradition of great thinkers such as Socrates, whom they thought of as the first programmer (Fonseca, 1965). Why do you think they made this assertion?

Computers

By the time computers were readily available, educators had already been exposed to a number of new technologies that either failed to deliver what had been promised or appeared to pose too much of a threat to the status quo to be easily absorbed. Recording devices in early language laboratories were supposed to improve foreign language teaching. Poor learning materials and lack of understanding of the technology on the part of teachers meant that they were largely ineffective. Television may have added richness to the learning experience but it distanced teachers from their pupils. Teaching machines and programmed learning turned out to be tedious to use and blighted by uninspiring materials (Sharpes, 1968). The dogma associated with behaviourist learning theories did not help. It's hardly surprising, therefore, that the majority of teachers greeted the first computers with a singular lack of enthusiasm. Trials in computer-based instruction began as early as 1959. Donald Bitzer, while at the University of Illinois, was the first to experiment with a large-scale project focussing on computers in learning and teaching. He built a system known as PLATO (Programmed Logic of Automated Teaching Operations) to be used with a range of pupils from neighbouring elementary schools and student at the university or local colleges. It is a tribute to the longevity of the system he developed that it endured for more than four decades in one form or another. The initial funding for PLATO came from military grants designed to address concerns about the education of veterans. During 1963, Patrick Suppes and Richard Atkinson at Stanford University were experimenting with computer-assisted instruction in mathematics and reading. They worked with children from local elementary schools. Their objective was to individualize learning, but despite the innovative nature of what they were trying to achieve, the traditional tools of drill and practice still underpinned the resulting programmes (Molnar, 1997). These trials relied on either direct or indirect funding from external sources. Both projects were also restricted to one locality and dependant on centralized systems and equipment. Outside the university sector, educators were forced to enter into time-share agreements for the use of computers because they were so expensive. This meant that access was restricted to key personnel (Molnar, 1997). Even then, computers were mainly used as administrative tools. Nevertheless, Sharpes was warning that the:

> felicitous wedlock of industrial and electronic corporations with the educational enterprise is an indication that the world of electronic instruction, willy-nilly, is rapidly approaching. Imaginative parents and educators had best be prepared. (Sharpes, 1968: 13)

The opening of the world's first retail computer store in Los Angeles in 1975 by Dick Heiser was an indication that the future had indeed arrived. He sold kits and accessories to service the needs of local computer enthusiasts. By 1977, fully assembled computers (from Radio Shack and Commodore) were on sale to the general public in his shop. Molnar (1997) commented that the computer could no longer be regarded as a luxury but a necessity for many schools and universities. Isaacson (1978) noted that low-cost, abundant computers brought the dawn of a new era in which information processing power will not only be:

> the exclusive tool of government and large business. Rather we will have computers for people to use in a near limitless variety of ways in our work, our play, and all aspects of our daily lives. (Isaacson, 1978: 359)

There were a number of key factors that hastened the introduction of computers in education. The knowledge base on which many subjects were founded had increased exponentially. Molnar (1997) estimated that it would take 22 centuries to read all the medical research papers generated in one year, and a mere seven centuries to do likewise in chemistry. The Nobel Laureate Herbert Simon (one of the most noted social scientists of the twentieth century) believed that as a result of this vast increase in information, the verb 'to know' could no longer be simply associated with memory, but had to encompass the notion of how to access knowledge, as well. Hilberry (1957) hinted at how the computer might also be able to help to address the issue of a much expanded knowledge base when he stated that computers permitted the study of the behaviour of entire complex systems and:

> since the information is presented to us with fantastic speed, our actual knowledge of complex systems has greatly increased. Equally important, our capacity for control and prediction and our capacity for insight into these complex systems has also been greatly extended. (Hilberry, 1957: 149)

At the same time, there was a growing disquiet about the provision of compulsory education. There were demands to make it more relevant, particularly in America (Hansen, 1970). Taylor suggested that the reason for this unrest lay with the very art of traditional teaching itself. Despite the best efforts of reformers and teachers alike, the basic technology of teaching remained that of the direct, face-to-face presentation of what is to be learned 'by the teacher and its recitation by the learner. Talking the learner into knowing the lesson is still very much how the business of education gets done' (Taylor, 1975: 163).

To some, this process stifled creativity and was inefficient. Yet it had endured, largely because it was highly adapted to the context in which most learning and teaching took place – the conventional classroom. Gerard (1965) believed that computers were as significant, in evolutionary terms, as was the development of language and considerably more significant than the development of printing. It is clear that during this era, most education-alists recognised their capacity to change things, but few were ambivalent about them.

Perceived benefits of computers

First and foremost, those who regarded computers in a benign light were quick to recognize that computers had the potential to provide completely individualized 'instruction in which the pace and sequence of materials are independently controlled for each student, based on his or her responses to the materials' (Coulson, 1966: 340). It was envisioned that computers would allow students to proceed through learning material at their own pace, while being guided by an unseen electronic hand which monitored their responses and adjusted the programme of study accordingly. Skinner and the other proponents of teaching machines could have only dreamed of this degree of adaptability from their electro-mechanical contrivances. Teachers would benefit because computers thus used had the potential to take away the drudgery of record-keeping, allowing more time for what many considered to be real teaching. Access to the latest and most relevant resources, created in some cases by master teachers, was also possible. Responding to or initiating changes in learning and teaching would, therefore, be much easier. The opportunity to use computers to coordinate schools more effectively was perceived to be an additional benefit. Records of attendance and performance, stored electronically rather than on paper, could be accessed by any authorized person much more readily. This would allow teachers to plan the delivery of their teaching more effectively and administrators to make best use of the resources at their disposal. Scheduling, in theory at least, could be liberalized. The hidden potential of the curriculum would then be released. Simulation and modelling could be used to make predictions about future events, such as the effect of fluctuating student numbers, making planning more accurate. This was already being done extensively in the commercial sector. Gerard identified another possible benefit as early as 1965. With great insight, he envisaged that in the not too distant future, there would be opportunities for individuals to interact 'through a console with the great array of knowledge and even with other humans, so there may not be geographic entities like a campus' (Gerard, 1965: 15).

Early issues with computers

The use of computers in education, like many technologies, was not universally welcomed. There were those who worried that their use would irretrievably change the relationship between the teacher and the taught. They feared the onset of a depersonalization or dehumanization in schooling would result in a loss of identity and individuality (Gerard, 1965). They contended that many skills and sensitivities which are needed for communal living could not possibly be learned on a screen (Loop, 2006). Cuban (1986) believed that the bond between the teacher and the pupil is compromised when computers mediate this relationship. He suggested that it is impossible to disconnect the emotional component from learning and teaching and in the:

> fervent quest for precise rationality and technical efficiency, introducing to each classroom enough computers to tutor and drill children can dry up emotional life, resulting in withered and uncertain relationships. (Cuban, 1986: 89)

Gerard, who acknowledged the validity of some of these concerns stated rather mischievously that books, as a form of technology, had also similarly interposed between people without leading to dehumanization and neither had the 'mechanization of the kitchen ruined the home' (Gerard, 1965: 14). New technology had enthralled many in the 1960s, no matter what their political persuasion. Harold Wilson, who was the leader of the Labour Party and soon to be prime minister in the United Kingdom, confidently declared in 1963 that Britain would be forged anew in the white heat of the scientific and technological revolution. President John F. Kennedy in America was encouraging his scientists and technologists to place a man on the moon at the same time. Such was the belief in the fundamental importance of technology. However, there was a suspicion at the time, fostered by philosophers like Martin Heidegger, that it was far too easy to assume all problems could be solved through technology (Krause, 2000). Hansen (1970) suggests that, in relationship to education, it was dangerous to embrace computers unquestioningly, because their effects would rapidly outpace the ability of teachers to assimilate them. McCluskey (1994) believed that if more and more advanced technology was introduced into education without a concomitant emphasis on knowledge acquisition, it would allow some learners to operate at increasingly lower levels of thought. Those who 'possess knowledge will use technology as a tool; those who do not possess knowledge will use it as a crutch (McCluskey, 1994: 552). It is a mark of the general acceptance of computers in education that critics thought far more about the consequences of their uptake than trying to resist the change.

Activity

Computers were either regarded as a universal panacea for all educational ills or as a force that would compromise the relationships between people, particularly in education (Coulson, 1966). Do you think any element of this statement holds true today? Justify your conclusion.

Uptake of computers

An extensive study into the use of computers in education was undertaken by the International Association for the Evaluation of Educational Achievement (IEA) between 1987 and 1993 in America, Austria, Belgium, Bulgaria, Canada (British Columbia), China, France, Germany (FRG), Greece, Hungary, India, Israel, Italy, Japan, Latvia, Luxembourg, Netherlands, New Zealand, Poland, Portugal, Slovenia, Switzerland and Thailand (IEA, 2011). The study indicated that there was a growing international desire to involve computers in education, particularly in the post-primary sector. However, many participants in the study were concerned that the aspirations of early proponents of the computer remained largely unmet (Plomp et al., 1996). Rather than being employed as a means of achieving more pupil-centred learning and for enriching the existing curricula, they were mainly used in support of either general or specialist computers studies and very occasionally in other subjects (Plomp et al., 1996). The explanations offered for this lack of progress varied. The Belgian, Bulgarian and American participants highlighted the paucity of hardware within the classroom as a key factor. More prosaically, the Irish observed that locating computers in specialist rooms militated against their integration across the curriculum. The Thais attributed the lack of progress to a dearth of specialist teachers. However, there were also deeper problems hinted at in the study. The Japanese noted that an adherence to the written examination made the structural changes necessary for widespread use of computers in school difficult to achieve (Plomp et al., 1996). Teaching was driven by the need to perform well in question papers. This orthodoxy was characteristic of many other systems which appeared to be unduly wedded to both the written and spoken word. Taylor (1975) neatly describes the paradox that this led to in the age of the computer when he stated that educational systems deliver:

> lettered people to societies saturated with visual images and dense with instant communication; people whose capacities for processing information are limited by the minds of their teachers . . . as well as by a curriculum based on an arithmetic of subjects – two periods of Mathematics, one of History, two of English and one of Music. (Taylor, 1975: 159)

This mindset, conceived in the nineteenth century, seemed hardly fitting for a world full of scientific and technological innovation in which persistent and continual changes in the knowledge gathering process and systems of communication was taking place beyond the school gate (Taylor, 1975).

Activity

The IEA study appears to indicate that the rate at which computers were being adopted for educational use in the early days varied considerably between countries. Can you suggest what factors affected uptake? What principles can you derive from your reflection that can be applied to the introduction of any new technology into the classroom?

The Chinese and Germans and others who had participated in the IEA survey pointed out that the absence of suitable software, particularly that employing languages other than English, was one of the factors that restricted the widespread uptake of computers. It was clear from this finding that the hardware alone was of limited value in an educational context. However, some were experimenting with radically new approaches to the development of educational software. Seymour Papert instigated what perhaps should be regarded as one of the most influential and enduring projects. While working with others at the Massachusetts Institute of Technology (MIT) in 1967, he created a computer programming language called Logo. The resulting programme was able to promote mathematical understanding in a wide range of pupils through experimentation in virtual environments because it did not rely solely on numerical input. It went through many stages of evolution but was underpinned by a strong Piagetian conviction, held by Papert, that children build their own intellectual structures. He wanted to make the computer an expressive medium in which the child was a producer rather than simply a consumer. Despite great initial enthusiasm, Logo was criticized because studies undertaken by James Hassett and others seemed to indicate that it promised more than it delivered (Papert, 1987). However, Logo did represent quite a radical departure from more-accepted notions of how the computer should be employed and was embraced widely in both America and the United Kingdom. Molnar (1997) justifiably claimed that Papert had tried to shift education from what he referred to as an appreciation of computing to computer fluency in which the computer was applied to solving real problems.

The Luxemburg contributors to the IEA survey believed that the slow pace with which teaching methods could be adapted was responsible for the limited uptake in computers. This was quite a common notion. It is hardly surprising, therefore, that there was confusion about how best to employ the computers in the classroom (Plomp et al., 1996). They had been used either as just another source of information and data processing, or as a devices for directing learning. It appeared that the underlying educational philosophy in whatever country computers were employed helped to determine which predominated. There was also a strong belief that, regardless how they were used, it would become increasing necessary to teach all pupils about computers because of their growing application in business. Staff development was one of the factors most strongly associated with the successful implementation of computers in schools. However, many countries were aware that there was a general lack of interest and motivation among teachers to fully embrace the computer into their practice (Plomp et al., 1996) To this end, a large number of teachers in the 1970s were taught how to write programmes in a language called BASIC (Beginners All-purpose Symbolic Instruction Code) in the hope that it would increase their understanding and that they would develop their own teaching material. A majority returned to their schools to find that 'they had no use for their training and, as is almost always the case, no time for reflecting on or developing new directions for using technology' (Morton, 1996: 417). They quickly became disillusioned. Indeed, as a result of the IEA survey, Plomp et al. (1996) concluded that the high hopes at the beginning of the 1980s for the computers potential:

> to bring improvements and fundamental changes in education, actual changes in the daily practices of schools develop very slowly or not at all. Although the capacities for communication and information technologies have developed

considerably, the questions with regard to solving educational needs, increasing perceived relevance, and assuring the practicality of computer use for educational practice at large remain substantially the same and insufficiently resolved. (Plomp et al., 1996: 26)

Activity

Morton (1996), when referring to the introduction of computers, suggests that educators were far too eager to look 'studiously backward' and that, as a result, their thinking was destined to be flawed, rather like the Laputans in *Gulliver's Travels* who always rejected new ways of doing things, regardless of the consequences. Do you think teachers today still have this Laputian mindset? What do you base your conclusions on?

Conclusions

Programmed learning made teachers more aware of the 'importance of system and design in instruction, and it taught them to value more such pedagogical basics as behavioural objectives, active pupil response, and positive reinforcement' (Kulik et al., 1982: 133). It also rekindled interest in the notion of individualizing learning. Perhaps the most important thing that programmed learning (and teaching machines) did was to help the teaching profession recognize the potential for changes in learning and teaching that computers could offer. At the same time, it helped reinforce the notion that technology is of limited value unless appropriate support material, either in the form of software or guidance material, is developed. Change in an educational context did not occur as quickly as some had anticipated as result of these technologies. Feurzeig (2006), who collaborated with Papert on Logo, claimed that the new learning technologies made possible by computers should have been well established throughout education but 'their powerful potential as expressive tools for knowledge construction and design, and for extended inquiry and investigation, has yet to be realized' (Feurzeig, 2006: 30). There are many reasons why this faltering progress should have occurred, but perhaps the most significant was a general reluctance or even misunderstanding of how best to use computers in an educational context. This reluctance originated from a number of sources, but it was a manifestation that some of the key actors, teachers in particular, held deeply conservative views. Waller refers to schools as 'museums of virtue' which were dedicated to upholding values and mores belonging to a bygone age that most had long since abandoned (Tyack et al., 1982). At the same time, educators generally chose to regard the computer simply as an extra resource rather than make full use of its true capacity to transform practice in learning and teaching. After all, they had managed to successfully absorb previous technological advances into the classroom without significantly disturbing accepted pedagogical practices, so why should the computer be any different (Krause, 2000: 12)? Regarding the computer as simply a tool meant that traditional curriculum structures could be less readily dismantled in favour of the integrated, cross-disciplinary learning approach that some argued was necessary in order for education to better reflect the real world (Morton, 1996: 417). This was a serious matter, because Coulson (1966) recognized that the real contribution computers could make to education would only materialize if the structures of schools were altered to take advantage of them.

There was still a lingering suspicion that the computer would supplant the teacher or, as Gerard (1965) puts it, 'artificial intelligence will replace natural stupidity' (Gerard, 1965: 11). While some could see benefits in this, others regarded computer-mediated learning as an ersatz form of education that was bound to be second best. Loop (2006) suggested that playing in a simulated orchestra can never be the same as performing with 100 other musicians and that acts of caring for human beings, animals or plant life require nuances of touch and perception that cannot be transmitted remotely. Perhaps Loop misses the real point. What educators are faced with is not the real versus the simulated, but a 'symbiosis of both, combining the attributes of great speed and vast memory of the idiots that we call computer systems with the imaginative, creative, idiosyncratic, pattern-forming capacities of the human brain and mind' (Gerard, 1965: 11–12).

There is another significant point raised by studying the origins of the computer in the classroom. The extent to which any technology is used effectively in any educational context depends in good part 'on the ability of technologically minded reformers to understand the realities of the classroom and to enlist teachers as collaborators rather than regarding them as obstacles to progress' (Krause, 2000: 15). The IEA survey adds that collaborative effort will be needed among the:

> main actors in the domain of education, namely the policy makers, on the one hand, and the teachers on the other hand. In this context, at least two factors will be important: achieving a good balance between 'top down' [national, state or

local imperatives] and 'bottom up' [prompted by teachers or the school] strategies for bringing about change and teacher training. (Plomp et al., 1996: 22)

Activity

It is clear from examining this period that even until quite recently, and despite great potential for change, the computer has been used falteringly. However, while it has been possible to choose the extent to which the technology is involved in the process of learning and teaching, that option is no longer available. What has altered between than and now?

Big Question

Are there any current technologies that appear to have as little potential to be used in education as the computer did in the early days that should be employed in learning and teaching?

Further reading

Cuban, L. (1986) Teachers *and Machines: The Classroom Use of Technology Since 1920*, New York: Teachers College Press.

IEA (2011) *The Computers in Education Study*, www.iea.nl/computers_edu_study.html?&type=98&no_cache=1&sword_list[0]=computers – Last accessed 14/02/2011.

Loop, Liza. (2006) Why look back? Arguments for a history of computing in education. In ICALT 2006 – *Proceedings of the 6th IEEE International Conference on Advanced Learning Technologies* 5–7 July 2006, Kerkrade, The Netherlands, 1087–8.

Papert, S. (1987), Computer criticism versus technocentric thinking, *Educational Researcher*, Vol. 16, No. 1, 2, 22–30.

Plomp, T., Anderson R. E. and Kontogiannopoulou-Polydorides, G. (eds) (1996) *Cross National Policies and Practices on Computers in Education*, Dordecht: Kluwer Academic Publishers.

Useful websites

Early Computers

http://oldcomputers.net/ – Last accessed 14/02/2011.

History of Computers in Education

www.csulb.edu/~murdock/histofcs.html – Last accessed 14/02/2011.

International Association for the Evaluation of Educational Achievement

www.iea.nl/ – Last accessed 14/02/2011.

John F. Kennedy's Call for a Man on the Moon

www.youtube.com/watch?v=Kza-iTe2100 – Last accessed 14/02/2011.

Laputa in Gulliver's Travels

www.gradesaver.com/gullivers-travels/study-guide/section5/ – Last accessed 14/02/2011.

LOGO

www.softronix.com/logo.html – Last accessed 14/02/2011.

Seymour Papert

www.papert.org/ – Last accessed 14/02/2011.

Martin Heidegger

www.iep.utm.edu/heidegge/ – Last accessed 14/02/2011.

Programmed Instruction

http://viking.coe.uh.edu/~ichen/ebook/et-it/program.htm – Last accessed 14/02/2011.

Part 2
ISSUES

Digital Poverty and Education

Introduction

This chapter will explore the link between education and what is sometimes referred to as the digital divide or digital poverty. Nowhere has the rate of change been more evident in the last 30 years than in what are referred to as digital technologies, such as computers and the Internet. Indeed, they now play a central role in how people purchase goods and services, and, in some cases, determine how they engage in 'civic or political affairs as well as the consumption of leisure and entertainment services' (Selwyn et al., 2007: 9). However, not everyone is in a position to benefit from this form of technological embrace. Currently in Africa, only 10 per cent of the population uses the Internet, in comparison with 80 per cent who do so in America (Internet World Stats, 2011a). Of the 1 billion PCs available today, 60 per cent are located in developed countries such as Japan and Germany, which collectively only represent 15 per cent of the entire population of the world

(Gartner, 2010). A new phenomenon, digital poverty, has arisen. What this chapter will seek to establish is the nature of digital poverty and whether it is simply another manifestation of exiting social divisions, or if there is a new dynamic associated with it. Selwyn et al. (2007) contend that those suffering from digital poverty appear to be excluded from the very best of what is on offer in society, including an education fit for the rapidly changing world in which we live. UNESCO is convinced that unless something is done about digital poverty, developing countries face 'digital and knowledge gaps that threaten to leave them far behind' (UNESCO, 2005: 17). This chapter will also establish that in order to fully understand digital poverty, something more than a simple point of comparison, such as access to hardware, must be used in order to capture the full complexity of the issue. This chapter will assert that in the apparent headlong rush to address digital poverty through schemes to improve digital literacy, one solution cannot fit all social and educational contexts. It will also directly address the constructivist or determinist conundrum by exploring the notion that a future based on the increasing application of digital technology is not inevitable. Clegg et al. (2003) contend that the debate about education has been unduly hijacked by technophiles guided by a belief that the link between globalization, information and ICT competencies is beyond question. The term 'globalization' in this context refers to a phenomenon in which a new cultural and economic order has emerged, one governed by increasing integration and interdependence between nation-states. Political and geographical boundaries are fast becoming blurred, partly as a result of the emergence of information technology. Although the world appears to be more homogeneous, this phenomenon has also meant that those who do not have access to the technology are potentially disadvantaged (Ochoa Morales, 2004).

All these points have serious implications for thinking about how technology in general can be applied to education.

Activity

The gap between the information rich and poor is the most pressing civil rights issue of the millennium and education in both traditional and new settings is the key to creating equitable knowledge societies. Why do you think such significance is placed on access to information?

Digital poverty

There was much debate at the end of the last century about what has been called the 'digital divide', which in its broadest sense referred to the gap between those individuals and communities who had access to, and made use of digital technology, and those who did not (BECTA, 2001). When the price of hardware began to fall and the Internet became more common, this led some to maintain that the differences between the *haves* and *have nots* was no longer as stark as it had been in the past (Compaine, 2001). The digital divide seems to have been poorly understood, because it had been reduced to a question of whether or not computers or the Internet were available. The impact of the cultural, economic, educational and social forces that have a bearing on this phenomenon could not be readily taken into account because of this mindset (BECTA, 2001). By thinking less about a digital divide and more about this as a form of poverty, it is possible to consider these forces more fully in the search for understanding (Galperin et al., 2007). Digital poverty is defined, at its most basic, as a lack a multidimensional range of goods and services with three basic attributes:

- Connectivity – this encompasses all fixed and wireless networks that will allow devices such as radios, static or mobile phones and computers to function.
- Communication – this relates to the nature of any exchange (one or two way) and the reasons why it is undertaken. TV, for instance, can provide information but cannot easily facilitate any other form of exchange.
- Information – this is categorized by how information is created, stored, broadcast, exchanged and consumed (Galperin et al., 2007: 32).

These goods and services are collectively referred to as information and communication technologies (ICTs). UNESCO has developing a methodological framework that allows digital poverty to be measured and permits accurate international comparisons to be made. The relative digital poverty or wealth of a nation, referred to in the framework as its Infostate, is expressed as a numerical score. This score is based on an evaluation of two aspects of ICTs, Infodensity and Infouse, which are also expressed as numbers once all the information on both has been aggregated. Infodensity is determined by the spread of networks and the ICT skills of the population under examination. Networks in this sense are measured by the number of telephone lines and the number of cell phones per 100 inhabitants, cable TV subscriptions per 100 households, the number of Internet hosts per 1,000 households and the international band width. Rather surprisingly, skills in this context are not those associated directly with the use of the technology but refer to levels of adult literacy and participation rates in primary, secondary and tertiary education. Infouse is determined by the uptake (consumption) of various ICTs by households, businesses and governments, and the intensity with which they are applied. It is measured by the number of TVs per 100 households, PCs per 100 inhabitants, Internet users per 100 inhabitants, the quantity of international outgoing telephone calls and the quantity of incoming telephone calls. The difference in Infostate ratings between countries is an indication of relative digital poverty or wealth. Those with very high Infostate ratings include Western Europe (all of Scandinavia, the Netherlands, Switzerland, Belgium, Luxembourg, the United Kingdom and Germany), America, Canada, Hong Kong, Singapore, South Korea, Japan, Australia and New Zealand, while African counties including Chad, Ethiopia, the Central African Republic, Eritrea, Malawi, Myanmar and Bangladesh have the lowest Infostate rating (Sciadas, 2003). In order to provide a benchmark with which to make comparison more meaningful, the framework includes an imaginary country, aptly named Hypothetica. It is given a rating of 100. The highest rating in the most recent survey was 200 and lowest was 5. Clearly, there is a major gap between the countries at the top of the Infostate league and those at the bottom that will take many decades to address (Sciadas, 2003: x). Besides revealing the differences between countries, the UNESCO framework also helps to expose the differences within countries, thus helping to emphasize the notion that digital poverty is not simply confined to those with the lowest score.

Activity

According to the World Hunger Education Service (WHES) more than 1.3 billion people worldwide live in extreme financial poverty (WHES, 2011). Their daily income is less than one dollar a day. Becket and others argue that, rather than emancipate, digital technologies aggravate such inequities (Beckett, 2010; Guillén et al., 2005: 682). Why do you think Becket has reached this conclusion?

Demography and digital poverty

It is likely that those social groups within a country who are marginalized or undergo deprivation through lack of employment or low income will be excluded from the benefits of digital engagement (Selwyn et al., 2001). There are other aspects of demography, including age, disability, gender, language and geographical location, that either on their own or in conjunction with each other exacerbate digital poverty.

Selwyn et al. (2001) argue that ICTs remain culturally focussed on the young. This is clearly reflected in data from the United Kingdom, which, despite a very high Infostate rating, indicates that the majority of those approaching retirement age fail to engage with digital technology. Individuals over the age of 55 are significantly less likely to own a computer than are their younger counterparts, or even have the prerequisite skills to use one. Despite the apparent emergence of what has been referred to as the 'silver surfer', some in this age bracket express no interest in addressing either of these deficits (BECTA, 2001). While 67 per cent of adults of all ages have Internet access at home, only 37 per cent of those aged over 65 do so, even though they represent more than one-fifth of the population in the United Kingdom (HMG, 2008: 25). This figure drops significantly to 22 per cent for those aged 75 or over.

Disability and digital poverty are related. Among those with special needs, the use of ICTs is markedly lower than among those in other groups. While 70 per cent of the general adult population in the United Kingdom either use the Internet currently (or have done so in the past), only 40 per cent of the disabled do so (Office for National Statistics, 2007 and Jones, 2010). This may be because that part of the population officially classified as disabled contains a greater number of older individuals than does the general population. However, although approximately only 10 per cent of the general population between 16 and 54 are likely never to have used the Internet, this figure doubles for the equivalent disabled population (Williams et al., 2008: 72). The disabled are clearly more liable to digital poverty.

Gender also has a bearing on the propensity towards digital poverty. Women in the United Kingdom are 14 per cent less likely than men to have used a computer. While 52 per cent of men have access to the Internet, only 39 per cent of women do so. These differences are apparent even among what has been referred to as the digital generation. Boys appear to own and use more ICTs in the home and display more confidence in how they engage with them (BECTA, 2008). There is a robust body of evidence that suggests, despite a narrowing gap between the sexes, the use of the Internet in everyday settings including the home, workplace and classroom is still subject to inequality. There are a host of firmly established ways 'in which gender continues to fundamentally mediate engagement with new technologies, regardless of an individual's age or technological background (Cranmer, 2006, and Lally, 2003, in Selwyn et al., 2007: 20).

The language that dominates the Internet at the moment is English but is closely followed by Chinese and Spanish (Internet World Stats, 2011b). Translating existing sites and software into a range of other tongues to accommodate those who do not speak any of these languages cannot be done at the same rate as new material is being produced in them. It is a situation of perpetual deficit, and one without an easy remedy. It can leave those for whom English is not a first or even second language at a disadvantage, especially in communities whose mother tongue is only spoken by a relatively few people (Gorski et al., 2002). The issue of language in this context is also often closely aligned to ethnicity or race.

Geographical location is also an important factor in digital poverty both within and between countries. It has already been established that digital wealth is more likely to be closely associated with countries that are in the developed rather than the developing world. Within countries, ICTs are generally used less in rural and inner-city areas. Surprisingly, once other socio-economic variables are taken into account, the effect of location is less pronounced.

There is one further determinant of digital poverty that is of possibly the greatest significance – whether an individual has the minimum ability required to use ICTs effectively or not. The notion of what constitutes minimum ability can vary according to context. However, it is usually typified by the capacity to create and modify content and engage with commercial and other agencies using the technology (Galperin et al., 2007).

The principle characteristics of at least three major groups who suffer from digital poverty can be identified in the following ways.

It is clear from the table (Figure 4.1) that if one or more of these three elements applies, then a group or an individual can be regarded as digitally poor.

There is an additional minor group composed of individuals who are economically poor and/or marginalized, who choose not to engage with ICTs because of cultural or social imperatives, even though they have access to the necessary infrastructure and the prerequisite technical competences (Galperin et al., 2007).

Group	Are economically poor and/or marginalized because of one or more demographic factors	Have access to the relevant ICT services and facilities	Have minimum ability required to use ICTs effectively
1	Yes	No	No
2	Yes	Yes	No
3	Yes	No	Yes

Figure 4.1 Characteristics of digitally poor groups or individuals

---

Activity

Neill suggests that the savage inequalities of the past extend into 'the wired savagery of the future. There is neither empirical nor theoretical reason to believe this scenario will change for the better' (Neill, 1995: 184). Do you think he is right, and what would you do about it?

Digital literacy

It is clear that digital poverty is closely aligned with those communities in society who are already disenfranchised or marginalized, and part of the solution involves addressing a range of social issues. However, UNESCO, recognizes that education has a pivotal role in the human capital element of Infodensity. Barrantes (2007), who suggests that digital poverty or wealth can be classified by a four point connectivity scale based on different ICT attributes, also identifies general education as a defining component. Those with a rating of 3, the highest level of connectivity, use digital interaction for both commercial and civic reasons, have access to broadband, and are well educated and young. The next group, with a connectivity level of 2, engage in electronic messaging, have access the Internet and mobile telephony, are reasonably well educated and young and not so young. Those with a rating level of 1 receive and communicate information electronically through telephone services, are poorly educated but not illiterate and are generally elderly. The group with the lowest (0) rating receive information only through radio and television, and are illiterate and elderly. It is interesting to note the association between age and education made apparent by the table. It is clear that both formal and informal general education and ICT training are important in addressing digital imbalance. In some countries, it is a declared policy aim to enable all citizens to become digitally literate by training them to use ICTs confidently in both their personal and working lives (Sciadas, 2003). Digital literacy in this context is closely aligned to the acquisition of skills. Commentators such as Hague et al. (2009) believe that digital literacy should be less about keyboards and their like, and more about ideas. They define digital literacy as the ability to comprehend, discriminate between and utilize effectively the many different forms of information generated by a computer. Whilst acknowledging the importance of skills, they suggest that the digitally literate must also understand wider issues, such as how and why we use computers and the effect this has on our interpretation of what we generate and receive (Hague et al., 2009: 23). Thoman et al. (2005: 4) concur, suggesting that everybody from young children to adults must be able to 'critically interpret the powerful images of a multimedia culture and express themselves in multiple media forms'. Digital literacy in this sense is characterized by social awareness, a propensity for critical reflection and enough knowledge of digital tools to be able to select the right technology for the job. These notions of digital literacy are encapsulated in a Digital Taxonomy created by Church (2011). He uses the key skills identified in Blooms Taxonomy and suggests that: Creating with programming, filming, animating, blogging, video blogging, mixing, remixing, using wikis, publishing, video casting, podcasting, directing, broadcasting; Evaluating with blog commenting, reviewing, posting, moderating, collaborating, networking, refactoring, testing; Analysing with linking, validating, reverse engineering, cracking, media clipping; Applying with executing, operating, uploading, sharing, editing; Understanding with advanced searches, Boolean searches, blog journaling, Twittering, categorizsing and tagging, commenting, annotating, subscribing; Remembering with finding, bullet pointing, highlighting, bookmarking, social networking, social bookmarking, favourite or local bookmarking, searching and using Google. This digital taxonomy is interesting from a number of points of view. The fact that it was deemed necessary to create this version of such an iconic tool indicates that the digital word and education are deeply interconnected. Although the digital component may be subject to some disagreement, it does serve to illustrate digital literacy in a way that practitioners can relate to. This can help with the planning of teaching and assessment. It is also clear from the taxonomy that many of the skills that are seen as part of digital literacy are generic, particularly those relating to analysis and effective study techniques. However, in its current form, the digital taxonomy is tied to technology as it exists today and will need constant revision in order for it to be truly useful.

> ## Activity
>
> Which do you think is the most important feature of digital literacy – skills or understanding and how would you teach it?

Defining what digital literacy means is a necessary task in order for educators to be able to plan how to deliver it. There are additional educational challenges that must also be addressed. The problem for countries with a low Infostate rating, such as Mozambique, is how to effectively prepare its populace to become what is sometimes referred to as cybercitizens when basic literacy levels are as low as 57 per cent for men and 33 per cent for women (UNESCO, 2007). The scale of the digital challenge that faces this country and others in a similar situation would not be revealed by simply counting computers per head of population or even measuring Internet usage. For children in countries with a high Infostate rating, basic literacy is generally not a major concern. It appears that digital literacy is similarly less of an issue because young people tend to make extensive recreational use of new technologies. There is a temptation to regard this group as a digital generation who think and process information differently from preceding generations (Prensky, 2001). They are purported to be native speakers of the digital language of computers, video games and the Internet. This commonly held belief is largely unsubstantiated by research (Bennett et al., 2008). It often leads to an overestimation of the level of digital literacy that this group possesses and requires educators to think carefully about how to manage any deficit (Deed et al., 2010). Similarly, there is no longer a sharp division between technologies used in education, as there was in the age of Skinnerian teaching machines, and those used in the wider community. Indeed, they are often employed to bridge the gap between the two. However, whilst the uses of ICTs in school tend to be planned and linked to a particular curriculum focus, the use of ICTs in the home is characterized by unstructured and exploratory individual rather than collaborative activity (Grant, 2010). Thus, digital participation cannot be assumed to develop automatically from exposure to ICTs in the home even where the 'engagement is of a very high level and involves extremely sophisticated types of activities, associations and affiliations' (Hague et al., 2009: 25). Indeed there can be tension created by this misalignment, which can make it more difficult for digital literacy in its widest sense to ensue unless properly managed by educators (Walker et al., 2009).

Activity

The educational establishment in Europe and America has been reluctant in the past to abandon its traditions and structures, particularly as a result of the advent of new technologies. Competing demands and limitations on spending and staff time mean that educationalists find it difficult to fulfil their current mandate yet alone embrace a visionary new one. What implications do you think this has for digital poverty?

Educational projects

Different countries and communities start their digital journey at different points. Kenya has one of the highest Internet penetration rates in Africa but only 10 per cent of the population are regarded as ICT literate (Gathanju, 2010: 18). A public/private initiative has been established to tackle this issue. The government is in the process of setting up a digital resource in every one of the 210 (soon to be expanded to 290) parliamentary constituencies, to serve the commercial, developmental and educational needs of local communities. In each of these digital villages, the Internet is broadcast from special masts. Solar and wind power are used to address the issue of intermittent electricity supplies. The resources are housed in a variety of locations ranging from cargo containers to office blocks. Mundeku in the Butere District of western Kenya has been designated as a digital village. In most senses, it is an archetypal rural village with thatched huts, mud paths and tracts of farmland. What sets it apart from others is a small modestly furnished cubicle in the Martha Guesthouse, which contains seven computers linked to the Internet and various peripheral devices, such as digital cameras. Villagers can learn how to use ICTs and stay in contact with those in other locations who face the same issues as they do. More importantly, teachers, who are regarded as central to improving digital literacy, can receive ICT training readily. In the past, they have had to travel and pay for this themselves (Butuny, 2008). Although these digital villages are in rural areas, the project will eventually incorporate the slums that are usually found on the periphery of major centres of population. There are plans to create digital libraries containing information on local culture and history, as well as having national and international content. The Kenyan Ministry of Education has also recognized that by digitizing learning resources, it can reduce costs because there will be less need to buy expensive textbooks. Another advantage of digitizing learning resources is that they do not require any form of Internet connection in order to be utilized. However, a growth in the number of computers available to schools is necessary. Gathanju suggests that for most African governments, the digital villages and libraries offer endless opportunities 'to adopt technologies that empowers its people . . . and . . . are the first steps to a new era' (Gathanju, 2010: 22).

An early effort to link education and ICTs occurred in American Samoa. H. Rex Lee, one of the first governors, regarded the local education system as unfit for this purpose and decided to bring in American educators and experts to improve the situation. After consultation with the Unites States National Association of Educational Broadcasters in 1961, he proposed that a completely new system of education should be created which would be underpinned by the extensive use of television. The resulting system was highly structured and centralized, with a team-teaching approach to learning which sought to 'shape and reinforce both student and teacher behaviours through the medium of educational television' (Baldauf, 1981: 235). American expert teachers were at the heart of this initiative. American money funded the TV production facilities, the transmission system and the TV sets required to view output. Every effort was made to give the curriculum a South Pacific orientation by using local contexts. However, the system remained fundamentally American and, despite broadcasting material in the indigenous language, it was still regarded as essential that Samoan children learned to speak English. Structural problems meant that many of the 6,000 TV programmes required each year had to be remade the following year and, consequently, quality was poor (Baldauf, 1981: 237). By 1973, television was being phased out as a medium of educational instruction because *fa'a Samoa*, the Samoan way, was remarkably resistant to cultural change. The Samoan tradition of *matai* or family headship based on talent rather than heredity did not sit well with leadership roles defined and occupied by foreigners. The school programmes were underpinned by Western notions of individualism, competition and evaluation and remained alien to *fa'a Samoa*. Equally important was the fact that, even after ten years, few local teachers had gained positions of sufficient power to be able to affect appropriate change.

Activity

What lesson can be learned from both the Kenyan and American Samoan approaches to addressing the issue of digital poverty in countries with very low Infostate ratings?

Determinism or social constructivism

There is a basic assumption in both the Kenyan and American Samoan projects that a future dominated by digital technology is inescapable. Citizens and workers who do not become proficient in the use of ICTs will be increasingly isolated and marginalized (Hague et al., 2009: 27; HMG, 2008). Furthermore, Selwyn et al. (2007) believe that the notion of finishing ones education at the age of 16 or 18 or even 21 is now firmly a thing of the past because of this technology. In numerous government and corporate documents, there are constant references to the risk of being left behind and the need for speedy action to address this issue (Clegg et al., 2003). Yet there is a vocal anti-technology lobby which includes Cuban, Colon, Oppenheimer, Simpson and Reynolds, which refuses to accept either the inevitability of the digital future or that the educational use of ICTs is desirable or straightforward (Underwood et al., 2010). They condemn the apparent passive acceptance by the educational establishment that ICTs will shape how we will live. They contend that technology is not an unconstrained phenomenon with its own inevitable trajectory. Furthermore, they argue that it is a social imperatives resulting from the needs of the military and scientists which have spurred the development of ICTs in the past and that, by implication, social and not technological imperatives will do likewise in the future (Clegg et al., 2003). Block (2004), another sceptic, is even more strident. Although he acknowledges that digital technology brings many benefits, he suggests that vigilance is required to see through the:

> economic and moral fallacies that underlay programs to shove computer literacy down the throats of innocent people. We must reject the conclusion that there is any meaningful digital divide; that even could this somehow be proven, that it would constitute a problem; and even if, somehow, it was considered such, that the solution would not involve the initiation of violence against those who were innocent of such uninvited border crossings. (Block, 402)

Some research appears to support the counterview held by Cuban and his colleagues, indicating that:

- The current rate of expansion of digital technologies may not continue.
- Digital technologies tend to supplement rather than supplant existing ways of organizing and doing things.

- The impact of digital technologies depends on the social context in which they are applied (Clegg et al., 2003: 45).

Even if it is difficult to resolve the arguments about whether social or technological determinism is driving change, Selwyn believes that digital technologies are not a universal panacea for all types of learning. He suggests they appear to be more suitable for knowledge transfer rather than as genuine agents of transformative educational experiences (Selwyn et al., 2007). Additionally, the rate at which technologies become redundant or are superseded makes the rush for digital literacy somewhat futile.

Activity

Clegg et al. (2003) contend there is a presumption that 'in order for citizens and workers to meet the challenges of the information age, they must become ICT proficient. In terms of debates about education the use of ICTs is over-determined by assumptions that link globalization and information to particular ICT competencies. As Michael Apple (1998) and others have pointed out manufacturers have been quick to capitalise on this assumption using parental anxiety as a way of targeting sales' (Clegg et al., 2003: 46). Do you think that sales and not need drives our desire to become digitally literate?

Conclusions

Sciadas suggests that the core of human progress, endeavour and well-being, are inextricably linked to education and the use of ICTs. He believes that the rapid progress of digital technologies opens up 'completely new opportunities to attain higher levels of development . . . and . . . for the first time in history makes it possible to use the potential of these technologies for the benefit of millions of people in all corners of the world' (Sciadas, 2003, Point 8, 10). Yet, the heady prediction that ICTs (particularly the World Wide Web) would liberate the individual and shrink the world, with all the benefits that might entail, remains largely unfulfilled because of a number of issues, including digital poverty (Guillén et al., 2005). Concerted action is required by the international community to address this issue to avoid leaving 'substantial population masses behind, with all the negative consequences that this entails' (Sciadas, 2003: x). The challenge has been to recognize that it is digital poverty rather than a digital divide that separates communities and that empowering the deprived to use ICTs meaningfully is dependant upon a complex mixture of social, psychological and economic factors (Selwyn in Livingston et al., 2007: 673). Defining digital poverty and identifying the groups who are most likely to suffer from it means that educational policy can be more readily created. Developing an empirical means of measuring it using the Infostate framework has allowed a clear idea of relative poverty, or wealth, to materialise. Education is central to this new world order. The notion of digital literacy, a key tool in shaping educational provision, has emerged from the process of having to reconcile the teaching ICT skills with the need to promote understanding at the same time. There is no universal panacea to address digital poverty through education. Kenya has adopted an incremental approach to solving the issue of digital poverty, which is mindful of local sensitivities and realistically matches the resources available. The American Samoan experience, despite belonging to period of time that was on the cusp of the digital age, highlights the importance of getting the link between technology, education and acculturation right. Finally, even the vociferous minority who challenge the legitimacy of allocating significant resources for developing digital literacy also recognize that technological determinism has had 'a profound effect on educational policy as the "forces of globalization" and its artefacts are perceived as overwhelming and unchallengeable' (Clegg et al., 2003: 42–3).

Big Question

Will giving the populace Pentiums (or the equivalent) prove any more useful in addressing social ills such as digital poverty than Marie Antoinette's apparent *cri de coeur* to the poor of Paris in the late eighteenth century that they should overcome hunger by eating cake? (Attewell, 2001)

Further reading

Church, A. (2011) *Bloom's and ICT Tools*, Available from http://edorigami.wikispaces.com/Bloom%27s+and+ICT+tools – Last accessed 07/03/2011.

Light, A. and Luckin, R. (2008) *Designing for Social Justice: People, Technology and Learning*, Bristol: FutureLab.

Postman, N. (1992) *Technopoly: The Surrender of Culture to Technology*, New York: Vintage.

Selwyn, N. and Facer, K. (2007) *Beyond the Digital Divide: Rethinking Digital Inclusion For the 21st Century*, Bristol: Futurelab.

Useful websites

Africa and ICTs

http://cto.int/Default.aspx?tabid=446 – Last accessed 14/02/11.

American Samoa

www.ipacific.com/samoa/ – Last accessed 14/02/2011.

Digital Divide

www.digitaldivide.net/ – Last accessed 14/02/2011.

Digital Literacy

www.ictliteracy.info/ – Last accessed 14/02/2011

Digital Literacy Projects

http://ec.europa.eu/information_society/tl/edutra/skills/projects/index_en.htm – Last accessed 14/02/2011.

Digital and Other Poverties

www.chronicpoverty.org/ – Last accessed 14/02/2011.

Digital Poverty

www.economist.com/blogs/babbage/2010/10/digital_technology_and_poverty – Last accessed 14/02/2011.

UNESCO

www.unesco.org/new/en/unesco/ – Last accessed 14/02/2011.

5 Technology and Pedagogy

Chapter Outline

Introduction

Roth (2009: 125) suggests that traditional approaches to learning and teaching are 'quickly losing their ability to challenge, motivate, and engage students in ways that are compatible with their digital lives in a techno-centric society'. It follows then that in order to successfully work with current and future generations of learners, educators need to be mindful of their attitudes towards these new technologies and how they exploit them in their teaching (Cox et al., 2003). They can be utilized as either a core component or an associate feature of learning and teaching. Core technologies are those around which all other elements of the learning experience are built. Associate technologies are optional and can be dropped without unduly compromising the validity of what the teacher is trying to achieve. Both core and associate technologies necessitate changes in how teachers teach but it is the former, most familiar to the majority of Roth's cyber kids, which requires the greatest adjustment. An examination of the amount of investment by governments across the world on ICTs in an educational context reinforces how seriously this issue is being regarded (Kennewell, 2006). Yet, despite the undoubted importance of these technologies, they remain poorly understood by teachers (Phipps et al., 1999; Lipponen, 2002 quoted in Jefferies et al., 2007).

This chapter will explore the link between technology and pedagogy, examining the widely held belief that the use of technology inevitably leads to changes in pedagogy. It will seek to establish that the pedagogical approach adopted by the majority of teachers is heavily influenced by their own experiences of school as children. Practical issues rather than theoretical concerns also tend to dominate their thinking. This strictly utilitarian and orthodox approach to pedagogy has had a direct bearing on how technologies have been used in the classroom. In some parts of the world, there is little attempt to use technology to change practice. It is deliberately employed to reinforce traditional approaches to learning and teaching. This chapter will suggest that by developing a comprehensive understanding of the affordances of ICTs a shift in these rather prosaic attitudes can occur. In informing the debate about technology and pedagogy, it will make reference to the negative aspects of the culture of immediacy that appears to result from the capacity of digital technologies to provide instant information. The notion of the existence of a universal pedagogy will also be challenged. This chapter will contend that it is an evolving rather than a fixed concept and that it is important to consider technology in this changing tableau.

Activity

The computer and Internet might be used as core technologies in series of lessons on the daily lives of people in different parts of the world. They could be employed to allow pupils to gather information and even engage in direct communication with those in other locations. How would the roles of the learner and the teacher be changed, given the same educational context, if these technologies were unavailable?

What is pedagogy?

Pedagogy, at its most basic, is concerned with teaching methods and the organization of learners (Alexander, 1992). It is sometimes referred to as the science of teaching although it is claimed to be an art. It is a subject about which a great deal has been written and as our knowledge of it deepens new degrees of complexity emerge (Webb et al., 2004). It is not a fixed concept. It has evolved over time, particularly as our understanding of cognition and metacognition have developed. Current notions of pedagogy seek to establish the interconnection between the teacher, the context in which learning takes place and the nature of the learning itself. Pedagogy is inexorably linked to theories about how we learn and the nature of knowledge, which is sometimes referred to as epistemology. Broadly speaking, these theories can be grouped into two categories, positivist and constructivist. Positivists believe that the world exists independently 'of any observer, and that nothing can be treated as real unless it can be measured and described objectively' (Jefferies et al., 2007: 113). They for Positivists which can be taught without discourse, emerge from rational thought. To them, knowledge is a commodity that can be readily packaged and transmitted. Positivist thinking about education is grounded in behaviourist theories and is underpinned by the principle that learning is a conditioned response. Skinner used this notion as the foundation for the development of his teaching machines. In positivist pedagogy, teaching is characterized by the transmission of known objective truths to individual learners. It is associated with more traditional notions of education (Balakrishnan et al., 2007). Constructivists, on the other hand, maintain that reality 'is a construct that cannot be determined independently of the observer' (Jefferies et al., 2007: 113). They believe that truth can only emerge (or be constructed) from agreement between individuals or social groups. To them, knowledge changes according to context and is socially and culturally mediated. Constructivism represents eclectic group of theories, some of which are widely divergent, and caution must be exercised when trying to categorize it. However, constructivist thinking about education has two overriding principles in which learning is characterized as an active means of constructing rather than acquiring knowledge, and teaching is regarded as an activity that supports the process of acquisition (Duffy et al., 1996). In constructivist pedagogy, the teacher uses negotiation and cooperation to foster learning and is not simply a transmitter of truth. Learners are not passive recipients of knowledge but active interpreters and constructors of meaning appropriate to the context in which they are working. They undertake a cognitive apprenticeship in which they acquire the crucial negotiation skills to develop multiple perspectives on reality. This process is very closely associated with problem solving, in which challenges from real life with multiple possible solutions are used to promote learning.

Summary

Positivism is inclined towards:

1. Teacher-centred and didactic classroom activity
2. Teachers mainly acting as fact-givers and subject experts
3. Pupils and/or students who are listeners and recipients
4. An instructional emphasis on facts and memory

Constructivism is inclined towards:

1. Learner-centred and inductive classroom activity
2. Teachers who adopt a variety of roles, including collaborator and facilitator
3. Pupils and/or students who have a variety of roles, including subject expert and provider
4. An instructional emphasis on relationships, inquiry and invention (Cohen et al., 2007: Suter, 2005: UNESCO, 2004)

Activity

Read the extract below from the *High School Journal* and try to determine when it was written.

> In order to teach successfully, one must be extremely careful in the selection and use of texts. It is always inadvisable to make the pupils believe a thing because a book says it is so. He will, in this way, acquire the pernicious habit of believing all that is printed and this will gradually but surely put an end to his own independent thinking and reasoning. Textbooks, like everything else, may be useful or harmful, depending entirely upon the way they are used. . . . The texts, however, in all subjects should merely be a guide to the pupil's own thinking and the successful teacher will see to it that too much dependence is not laid upon the text. (See Marshall, I. V. in the Reference section for the date when the extract was written.)

Does this represent a positivists or a constructivists approach to pedagogy?

It is clear that constructivist pedagogy relies on 'higher forms of literacy and skills, self reliance and cooperation', while positivism assigns more traditional roles to the teacher and the taught (Balakrishnan et al., 2007: 47). New technologies can support either approach. Virtual learning environments (VLE), which allow pupils or students access to learning materials remotely through computers, have this capacity. Teachers can use them to select and control learning experience, in line with positivist thinking, or to facilitate the discussion and construction of knowledge that the social constructivists are so fond of (McRobb et al., 2007). However, Tinio (2003) believes that because of the emergence of what she refers to as the information society, traditional pedagogies must be replaced by those more firmly based on constructivism. In her view tradition pedagogy, which she equates with the industrial society, is characterized by activities prescribed by teacher, whole class instruction, little variation in activities, pace determined by the teacher, individualism, homogenous groups, everyone for him/herself, reproductive learning, a fixation with known solutions to problems, no link between theory and practice, separate subjects, disciplines, summative and highly directed learning and teaching. New pedagogy, which she equates with the information society, is characterized by activities determined by learners, small groups, many different activities, pace determined by learners, working in teams, heterogeneous groups, support, productive learning, finding new solutions to problems, integrating theory and practice, interrelated subjects, thematic, teams of teachers, student led and diagnostic. Educational agencies in many different countries are seeking to achieve the transition from the old to the new that Tinio (2003) has implied is necessary and inevitable through the use of technology in the classroom (Insight, 2011).

Activity

Discuss whether the transition from traditional to new pedagogies is solely dependent on the introduction of ICTs into the classroom? List any other factors that might influence this change.

The link between pedagogy and culture

There is a risk of adopting what Goethe et al. (2006) refer to as false universalism, in which a singular approach to pedagogy fails to take into account the unique social and historical contexts that affect it in different countries. Those who live in Confucian Heritage Cultures (CHC), such as China, Korea, Japan and Vietnam, are far less likely to subscribe to constructivist principles based on a propensity to individualize the curriculum and encourage dialogue. The value of an individual in such societies is measured only in the context of his or her role in a network of kinships, although things are changing. Conflict and challenge are not encouraged in traditional CHC classrooms. There is little interactivity between group members. In seeking to illustrate typical CHC attitudes, Goethe et al. (2006) refer to a Vietnamese proverb that cautions the individual to think seven times before speaking out. Goethe et al. (2006) do not prohibit the use of constructivist and cooperative approaches to learning with CHC students, but warn that this could result in the erosion of cultural identity. There are a number of other factors which influence the pedagogical approach adopted by teachers. Their own value system, as well as beliefs which could have been forged by their own childhood experiences at school, has a powerful affect on the choice they make. The curriculum area in which they work is also a contributing factor. Some subjects, such as those from the sciences, lend themselves more readily to positivist approaches, while the arts are more akin to constructivism. Paradoxically, new technologies lend themselves readily to being used in any curriculum area and can blur the division between them. Outside forces, such as the ethos of the school or education system in which they work, may dictate that one pedagogical approach is favoured above another. However, teachers are sometimes driven by more mundane concerns. The evidence suggests that practitioners often base how they use the technology in the classroom on common sense rather than pedagogical theory, which they find alien and overwhelming (Conole et al., 2004). Research undertaken by Watkins et al. (1999) confirms this tension between the theoretical and the practical. They reveal that there is a difference between what researchers suggest is the right approach and what is actually happening in the classroom. Laurillard (2007: 11) similarly believes that while academics develop hypothetical models that focus on the nature of learning, 'teachers may adopt a simplified model of practice in the face of contextual constraints'.

Activity

Goethe et al. (2006: 6) contend that CHC males have more influence in group discussions than females do. What implications do you think this has for the educational use of social networking technology in these countries?

Affordances and ICTs

Teachers appear to go through a number of developmental stages when employing technology in the classroom. They begin by regarding the computer in particular as either a substitute for pencil and paper, or as a machine tutor. Some move towards viewing it as a support for cognitive activity, which learners could not undertake without it (Somekh, 1994). The rate at which they move through these stages is not only dependant on pedagogy, the local context and the subject discipline in which they are working, but also on their own ICT competence. Research indicates that once they have acquired an appropriate level of proficiency, they adopt an integrated, enhanced or complimentary approach to utilizing technology (Laurillard, 2007). An integrated approach involves carefully reviewing the curriculum and only employing ICTs when they can contribute to specific aims and objectives. An enhanced approach is one in which the technology is used to enrich the learning experience in the classroom. A complimentary approach is one in which the technology is used to support aspects of pupils' work, such as helping to bridge the gap between school and home. Competence by itself is not sufficient to guarantee that teachers, regardless of pedagogy, use ICTs effectively in the classroom. They must also understand the potential the technology has to affect teaching and learning. This is referred to as affordances. The theory of affordances was first developed by the American psychologist James Gibson (1904–1979) as a result of work he did with pilots during the Second World War on the depth of perception. He argued that there are features of the environment:

> that afford (i.e. enable) perception and action in that environment. They are not constructed by the person. They exist independently in the environment, and are discovered rather that constructed by the human (or animal) actor. Thus, a rigid surface stretching to the horizon under our feet affords locomotion; an object of a certain size affords grasping and so on. (Boyle et al., 2004: 296)

Affordances, therefore, are the perceived 'and actual properties of a thing, primarily those functional properties that determine just how a thing could possibly be used' (Salmon, 1993: 51). Wertsch (1998) applied Gibson's theory to digital technologies. He regarded the computer as a tool that amplified opportunities to combine physical with symbolic forms of action. This interchange often reflects complex thought processes that are dependent on both the learning environment and the capability for action of the learner.

Taxonomy of affordances

Conole et al. (2004) have developed a taxonomy of ICT affordances that helps to extend understanding. The taxonomy seeks to establish the possibilities for action that ICTs offer not only to the teacher but to the learner, as well. They are categorized as accessibility, change, collaboration, diversity, multimodality, nonlinearity and reflection, and are explained below.

Accessibility

A vast amount of information is now readily available to teachers and learners from many sources, including shared networks and websites. For the teacher, the challenge is helping learners to know how to use what is available. For the learner, the challenge is not searching but selecting.

Change

Rapid change to the information available can be made as a result of new technologies. News about political unrest or freak weather can be transmitted around the world in an instant, regardless of the proximity of the recipient to the event. While this provides unprecedented opportunities to remain *au courant*, the information can be subject to inaccuracies, lacking in authority and posted with little reflection. For the educator, the challenge is to help learners to make informed decisions despite this immediacy.

Collaboration

Digital technologies have the potential to link people together through new forms of online communication, including chat rooms, forums and mailing lists. This can foster discourse but also lead users to engage with each other on a superficial level, and for them to lack a clear identity. For the educator, the challenge is to ensure that learners have the appropriate communication and literacy skills (Deed et al., 2010).

Diversity

ICTs can expose learners to things beyond their immediate environment and can draw on the experiences of others, including subject experts who are necessarily close by or teachers. Computer simulations also offer the user the opportunity to model complex behaviours and systems that would not be available otherwise. For the teacher, it raises questions about how well those in their care are taught to distinguish what 'is real and what is rendered real via the technology' (Conole et al., 2004: 117).

Multimodality

A combination of touch, vision and voice can be used to access some technologies. By employing voice-activated software, users can issue commands at the same time as writing, reading or sending a message. This not only enables multitasking, but it makes it more possible for learning to take different forms. Learners can easily hear, figuratively feel (through simulation), read and see material in whatever combination is appropriate to their needs.

Nonlinearity

Some technologies such as the World Wide Web (www, or web) allow those using search engines to approach their task in any number of different ways. Web pages, unlike the rooms in a house, can be entered or exited from any point, not just by the equivalent of the front or back door. This equates to a system in which output is not directly related to input and from an educational perspective is an important facility. It allows learning to be based on experimentation and trial and error rather than as a series of graded steps with none of the shortcuts that the behaviourists are so fond of. ICT affordances may not only reside in a computer but also in software packages, websites and multimedia, or connected peripheral devices.

Reflection

Technologies which allow for discourse to occur over an extended period time (asynchronous) and can make use of archived material (such as forums) without the need for immediate responses have the potential to nurture reflection and present 'new opportunities for knowledge claims to be considered and subject to the critical gaze of much wider and more diverse communities of practice' (Conole et al., 2004: 118). For the educator, the challenge is how to make sure the learners take the time to reflect properly.

> ## Activity
>
> Conole et al. (2004) wanted to develop a checklist which practitioners could use to help them make informed decisions about how to map specific pedagogical approaches to learning design. What is missing from it if anything? Upon what do you base your conclusions?

Constraints of ICTs

This taxonomy also makes reference to some negative consequences of the use of ICTs rather than the more positive features generally associated with the concept of affordances. These are sometimes referred to as constraints. Technologies can and have been used in unintended ways. For example, the emergence of new forms of plagiarism has been made possible as a result of the development of the web. Conole et al. (2004) contend that digital networks are subject to the malign effects of viruses and technical failure. Over-reliance on systems unduly blighted by these fallibilities can have a profound effect on learning and teaching. They note that while there are clear educational benefits from increased accessibility, there is a concomitant demand for quick response times and effortless information retrieval. The culture of immediacy is beginning to shape attitudes (not always positively) towards learning and teaching. The disproportionate influence on the development of hardware and software by a limited number of companies raises the spectre of a market place with little competition. This can lead to a form of over-reliance that limits innovation and widens the gap between those who can and cannot afford to use the technology. A proliferation of tools that can monitor performance, behaviour and location may well mean that assessment can be undertaken more readily but also raise the spectre of the surveillance society in which individual liberty is under threat. Interestingly, Conole et al. (2004) note a surprising constraint that has arisen from the risks associated with the development and utilization of new technologies. They have arisen from recent human activity rather than from natural disaster and are typified by concerns about global warming and climate change. Consequently, technology is no longer regarded as the panacea for all ills. It now has negative undertones, which, in an educational context, can inhibit the rate at which it is embraced.

Challenge to the concept of affordances

The concept of affordance has been widely adopted by those who comment on how ICTs can support learning and teaching. However, Boyle et al. (2004) believe that many fail to recognize the difference between the real and perceived affordances of an object. They suggest that it might be more productive to develop a framework that matches the communicative context in which learning is to take place with the appropriate ICT tools, that is, enhanced interaction or aids to writing through software. Oliver (2005) also believes that, even though useful, the concept of affordances is problematic and has limited value unless we are prepared to modify how it is applied to digital technologies. He suggests that the premise is undermined because of a basic paradox that either allows us:

> to talk about technology as part of the environment . . . but not about minds; or is rendered analytically ineffectual by recognition of the cultural, constructive nature of learning. (Oliver, 2005: 412)

In order to reconcile this contradiction, he advises that we keep the label but abandon the concept.

New technology, new pedagogy?

Tinio (2003) suggests that when used appropriately, ICTs can 'enable new ways of teaching and learning rather than simply allow teachers and students do what they have done before in a better way' (10). She contends that these tools permit a teacher to do a number of things including:

- Promote greater engagement by the learner in the process of learning. He or she can also choose what and when and how much to learn. This is sometimes referred to as just-in-time learning.
- Expand the scope of learning by including a range of mentors and experts drawn from a number of different fields.
- Encourage learners to more readily create rather than simply repeat existing information.
- Eliminate the artificial separation between different subjects and between theory and practice.
- Allow for different learning pathways.
- Support exploration and discovery, based on an overview of pedagogy in the industrial versus the information society (Tinio, 2003).

Interactive whiteboards (IWB) are typical of the sort of technology to which Tinio refers. They were specifically designed for whole class or group activity, rather than as devices for supporting individual learning and, therefore, serve as a useful tool with which to examine her contention that the introduction of a new technology in the classroom results in changes in pedagogy.

Interactive whiteboards and pedagogy

SMART Technologies pioneered the development of an electronic whiteboard consisting of an input device and projection system that could be operated either through the touch-sensitive screen or a by computer connected to the IWB. Whatever was running on the computer was displayed on the screen. It could replicate, through appropriate software, non-digital technologies often used in learning and teaching such as flip charts, dry wipe boards, overhead and slide projectors. Thus, students and their teachers could interact with the images displayed, write notes and highlight items. First introduced in 1991, it subsequently became possible to utilize many associated technologies, such as digital cameras, data capture devices, electronic microscopes, scanners and various voting systems through the IWB. These combined features meant that a multimedia approach to learning and teaching, through the spoken word, music, and still and moving images, could be readily employed in the classroom. The scale of what the teacher or the pupil could attempt and accomplish also increased considerably by connecting the IWB to the Internet. Bearing in mind how reactionary the educational establishment is normally (Cuban 2001), the spread of IWBs has been quite remarkable. Nearly 750,000 IWBs were sold worldwide in 2009 and it is predicted that 1 million will be sold in 2010. One in six classrooms with the appropriate infrastructure will have an IWB by 2012 (Futuresource Consulting, 2010). They are expensive, but such is the desire to incorporate them into learning and teaching that Professor Thinh, from the South East Asian Ministry of Education Organizational Regional Training Centre in Vietnam, demonstrating great ingenuity, has identified a way of building a low-cost system using a traditional whiteboard and $79 worth of electronic equipment, including an infrared pen and a Wiimote camera (Thinh et al., 2009). Those who administer education systems across the world also appear to be keen to make IWBs a key feature of their education policy. As part of a ten-year plan, the government of the Bahamas has made the spread of modern technology, including IWBs, a key objective. The Greek Ministry of Education has plans to equip every classroom in their lower secondary schools with an IWB (European Schoolnet, 2010). Kennewell (2006: 3) suggests that because the IWB is 'so suited to supporting whole-class teaching that it has been adopted so rapidly in comparison with more personal technologies which integrate less readily into traditional teaching methods'.

Activity

Can you remember the first time you saw an Interactive Whiteboard being used in an educational context? What were you studying at the time and was it a tool dominated by the teacher or by those being taught?

Interactive whiteboards in action

There are three specific ways that IWBs can influence classroom practice. They can affect the pace of delivery, increase the use of multimodal resources and offer more opportunities for interactive whole-class teaching (Moss et al., 2007). The experience of an English Primary teacher is typical of many who work with this technology for the first time. Although confident using ICTs, the teacher was very sceptical of the IWB at first. She had to train herself how to operate the IWB in her classroom before term started, but claims it changed the way she taught in a very short period of time. It made her lessons more visual, lively and interactive and encouraged independent learning in all areas of the curriculum (Prior, 2005). A history lesson on Ancient Egypt was enlivened because a website which she could access through the IWB involved the children in making decisions about the correct procedures and tools to use in the mummification process. In a lesson on how to grow plants, she found a resource that could illustrate what happened if too much (or not enough) heat, light or water was applied. This would have been far more difficult to demonstrate to the whole class without the IWB and would have taken many weeks to replicate in real life, with the distinct possibility that the learning objectives would not have been achieved (Prior, 2005). The introduction of nine IWBs into classrooms rearranged to promote discussion and foster group collaboration in a public primary school in Hong Kong resulted in similar changes to both learning and teaching. Teachers became better managers of their time and used more visual clues to support the teaching of abstract concepts. Pupils became more discursive and creative thinkers. Consequently motivation and levels of concentration improved. Before IWBs were introduced, there was little interaction between the teacher and the taught. Subsequently the relationship has changed. A general studies teacher at the school suggests that such tools not only allow teachers to 'put more content more flexibly but also give the students opportunity to contribute through a writing pad on their desks. Students are also allowed to cast their vote on questions and issues through voting devices connected to the interactive whiteboard' (Li, 2009). Perhaps more significantly, teachers have been able to develop peer support networks through which they can share can their experiences, swap ideas and provide advice on new ways of using IWBs. These networks assist teachers to widen their horizons by 'giving them access to resources that simply weren't available before which, in turn, helps them with better lesson design and teaching strategies' (Anderson, 2010: 106). Forming support groups seems to be an internationally universal feature associated with the introduction of IWBs. Thinh et al. (2009) report that by using their ersatz IWB device, teachers of English language classes in Vietnam showed greater spontaneity and flexibility and changed their pedagogy.

Although the IWBs represent a convergence of a wide variety of digital technologies, there is much debate about whether they promote pupil- or teacher-centred pedagogies. Rudd (2007) notes that because a technology theoretically has the potential to promote greater interactivity and collaboration embedded within it, there is a misguided assumption that this will automatically translate into more interactive classroom practice. IWBs are typical of this misconception. There is no doubt that they can radically change how educators approach their work, but they can also reinforce traditional approaches to learning and teaching. This is why they can be useful when employed in both school systems with a propensity for constructivism (England) and those of a more traditional nature (Hong Kong). IWBs can promote high levels of pupil collaboration, communication and interaction, but equally pupil activity can be highly regulated and constrained by the teacher. Thus, although IWBs have the potential to induce the changes in pedagogy described by Tinio, the reality is that 'the design, the positioning, the school ethos, teacher experience and understanding, and so forth, can all mediate the extent to which it is used as a truly interactive pedagogical tool' (Rudd, 2007: 7).

Conclusions

An assumption has been made that a compelling rationale for using ICT in schools is its potential to act as a catalyst in transforming the teaching and learning process. However, technology by itself cannot promote significant pedagogical change, no matter how desirable, without a willingness on the part of teachers to embrace this change. Their predisposition to accept change is not always based on ideology, but results partly from the cultural and personal history of the individual concerned and the context in which they work. John et al. (2004: 102) believes that the way in which the technology is incorporated into teacher pedagogy is 'dependent upon the impact it has on the epistemologies and personal theories of the teachers deploying the technology in their classrooms'. It is clear that they need to be receptive to the social and philosophical mores that accompany a particular theoretical stance in order to incorporate it into their practice. However, it has been suggested that the knowledge, beliefs and values of teachers will alter in line with affordances provided by new technologies (Cox et al., 2003). Way et al. (2009: 14) highlight an additional incentive for teachers to change. They conclude that there appears to be correlation between using the features of an IWB that 'closely replicate other standard tools such as chalkboards or flip charts, and lower levels of student involvement and autonomy'. On the other hand, 'lessons that make greater use of the more advanced affordances of the IWB appear to stimulate higher levels of student involvement'. Kennewell (2006) concurs, suggesting that the former approach does not encourage deep learning. He neatly summarizes how pedagogy has changed and is changing. He believes the teacher's role is now to manage affordances and constraints of a new technology in order to maintain:

> a gap between existing abilities and those needed to achieve the task outcome, a learning gap which is appropriate to the development of intended abilities. If students find the task easy, little learning will result and the affordances and constraints need to be reduced. Similarly, if they find the task too hard, other features can be added or the current ones adapted in order to provide more appropriate support. This orchestration involves adding, removing and changing features of the setting as the students become attuned to the features and then focusing their attention on the features during subsequent reflective activity in order to develop conceptual schemes and improve the students' subsequent performance. (Kennewell, 2003: 2)

More prosaically, Cox et al. (2003) conclude that teachers need to develop a series of specific pedagogical reference points in order to shift their practice appropriately to accommodate new technologies. This framework includes the need to:

- Recognize subject specific nuances of using ICTs
- Use this subject-specific knowledge to select the most appropriate ICT resources
- Be aware of the capacity of ICT resources to extend pupil learning
- Understand that knowledge can be presented differently by ICTs
- Plan appropriately for the use of ICTs
- Use the most suitable organizational models in conjunction with ICTs
- Develop their own ICT expertize

Big Question

Resta (2002) contends that the most important aspect of infusing technology in the curriculum is pedagogy. Is this true and upon what do you base your answer?

Further reading

Boyle, T. and Cook, J. (2004) Understanding and using technological affordances: a commentary on Conole and Dyke, *ALT-J, Research in Learning Technology* Vol. 12, No. 3, 295–9.

Cox M., Webb M., Abbott C., Blakeley B., Beauchamp T. and Rhodes V. (2003) *ICT and Pedagogy: A Review of the Research Literature*, Annesley: DfES Publications.

Goethe, J. W. and Karabab, G. (2006) Culturally appropriates pedagogy: The case of group learning in a Confucian Heritage Culture (CHC), *Intercultural Education*, Vol.17, No. 1, pp. 1–9.

Law, N., Pelgrum, W. J. and Plomp T. (eds) (2008) Pedagogical Practices and ICT use around the World: Findings from an International Comparative Study, *CERC Studies in Comparative Education*, Hong Kong: CERC.

UNESCO (2004) ICT in Education, Available from www.unescobkk.org/education/ict/online-resources/features/ict-pedagogy/ – Last accessed 11/03/ 2011.

Webb, M. and Cox, M. (2004) A review of pedagogy related to information and communications technology, *Technology, Pedagogy and Education*, Vol. 13, No. 3, 235–86.

Useful websites

Affordances

www.interaction-design.org/encyclopedia/affordances.html – Last accessed 14/02/11.

Constructivism

www.uis.edu/colrs/learning/pedagogy/constructivism.html – Last accessed 14/02/11.

Interactive Whiteboards

www.jisc.ac.uk/uploaded_documents/Interactivewhiteboards.pdf – Last accessed 14/02/11.

Metacognition

www.teachingthinking.net/thinking/web%20resources/robert_fisher_thinkingaboutthinking.htm –
Last accessed 14/02/11.

Multimodality

www.ai.rug.nl/~lambert/projects/miami/taxonomy/node6.html – Last accessed 14/02/11.

Pedagogy

www.teachingexpertise.com/articles/pedagogy-what-does-it-mean-2370 – Last accessed 14/02/11.

Pedagogy, Language, Arts and Culture in Education

www.educ.cam.ac.uk/research/academicgroups/pedagogy/ – Last accessed 14/02/11.

Positivism

http://changingminds.org/explanations/research/philosophies/positivism.htm – Last accessed
14/02/11.

Community, Technology and Education   6

Introduction

The Internet and the World Wide Web (web or www) enable people to create a range of new social spaces in which to meet and interact with one another (Smith et al., 2002: 7). Education professionals are beginning to recognize that the highly personalized and multi-dimensional experiences that the Internet and the web provide have significant implications for learning and teaching. They also recognize that much activity in the virtual world is communal in nature. Texting, voice chat, wikis, blogs and, in particular, virtual worlds with avatars have the potential to provide a rich and immersive experience for all. They can transform ideas about how education can be delivered in both formal and informal settings. This has led to rekindled interest in notions of what constitutes a community despite much work having been already done on this subject during the second half of the last century. The term 'community' has been used in the past to describe the bond between people who were connected by location or activity. More recently, it has been used to describe the relationship between people who exhibit a unique set of behaviours that have meaning to the members of that group. These behaviours are based on shared expectation, values and beliefs (Sackville et al., 2010). As a result of technology, the strength and nature of the relationship between members of a group are more likely to become key determinants of community rather than familial ties, common work or physical proximity. Online learning, a significant change agent in transforming notions of community, has been one of the fastest growing educational trends in America. The National Centre for Education Statistics estimated that the number of 17 year olds in public schools engaged in a distance education driven by of technology grew by 65 per cent between 2002 and 2005 (Zandberg et al., 2008). By 2007, more than 1 million pupils in the same age bracket were undertaking online courses (Picciano et al., 2007). In 2009, nearly 12 million students, in some form of post-compulsory education, undertook part or all of their classes online. By 2014, this number is expected to increase to 22 million. At the same time, it is predicted that the number of those in higher education being taught in a physical classroom will decrease substantially (Nagal, 2009). This trend, most prominent in America, is likely to become universal.

What this chapter will seek to establish is the nature of communities formed with fulfil some form of formal educative function. It will identify the key relationships within them, particularly how the roles of the teacher and the taught are defined. It will also establish that, because of new technologies, having a presence in or making a contribution to these learning communities is no longer entirely dependent on physical location. The growth of mobile, virtual and social networking technologies is bringing immediacy where there previously was none and heightened levels of connection between group members that would be impossible to achieve without them. This provides many rich opportunities but also generates challenges that good educators strive to address, not least of which is that functioning virtual communities of learners do not occur by accident. It is necessary to understand that the mores of how they operate is as significant in them as it is in traditional communities. It will also contend that an awareness of how technology has altered the way group members communicate with each other is also important in an educational context. Above all, this chapter will make the case that although new technologies support the creation of communities of learners in new and innovate ways, a mixture of the real and the virtual, rather than one or other, is the most effective way of learning.

Communities of learners

Traditionally, a community in which learning was supposed to take place was very easily identified by both its location and purpose. It could be found in a centre for teaching apprentices, a seminary for novice priests or in a school for secondary-aged children overseeing the last stages of their compulsory education before they go on to work or higher learning. This notion of where learning could legitimately occur was predicated on many assumptions, not least of which was the belief that the teacher and the taught had to be in close proximity to each other. The emergence of radio and then television and other new forms of communication forced a re-evaluation of this assumption. Computer technology, in particular, has made it possible for more expansive notions of community to evolve, which are not just simple clones of those already used. The concept of a community of learners is one derivative. This form of community is founded on constructivist principles, which advocate that education should be suitably contextualized, and encompasses the perspective of the learner (Brooks et al., 1993). An equal partnership between the teacher and the taught is essential if the community is to function appropriately. Consensus and negotiation are paramount. The process of learning that occurs within communities of learners is based on the transformation of the individual rather than the transmission of knowledge (Pringle, 2002). As the number of people who need to engage in what Kruger (2000) refers to as perpetual learning increases, virtual solutions become more and more appealing, especially to administrators and those who control the finances. Building ever more schools, colleges and universities to meet the demand is just not feasible. Understanding how virtual communities of learners should be established and maintained, therefore, is important.

Activity

Kruger (2000) suggests that communities of learners based on new technology will not look or feel like those found in a traditional classroom. Make a list of the best features of a community of learners located in the physical rather than the virtual world. What could you do, if anything, to make sure these features are available to a virtual community of learners?

Communities of practice and inquiry

Communities of learners come in many forms but in the context of this work, communities of practice and inquiry are of the most interest. The concept of a community of practice was first introduced by Lave and Wenger in 1991 as a result of work they did when studying apprenticeship as a learning model. It is used to describe groups that share a common concern or passion. Participating members help each other to improve their understanding and/or practice in the field that unites them through regular interaction in the real or virtual world. Molphy et al. (2007) believe that this educative function is at the heart of what they do. Learning occurs as the membership exchange ideas and develop solutions to problems associated with their shared passion. Some communities of practice are highly regulated and formal, while others are only loosely structured. However, they all have three basic characteristics, a domain, a community and a practice. 'Domain' refers to the area of interest that the group shares. 'Community' refers to the corporate nature of their engagement with each other and 'practice' refers to the fact that members are practitioners of some art or skill for pleasure or profit or even basic survival. Daele et al. (2007) also believe the community could be made up of professionals seeking to improve understanding among peers and fellow practitioners (Jackson, 2010 and HIF-net, 2011). The community in Lave and Wenger's (1991) original construct is populated by members who have different roles. There are 'experts' at the centre who are tasked with helping to move newcomers from the margins to the core of the community by inducting them into the conventions and common goals of the group. Thus, a fresh recruit undertakes a journey in which he or she becomes 'ever more legitimate, less peripheral and theoretically more engaged' (Belgrove et al., 2008: 92).

As the community evolves and shifts focus, roles can change as illustrated in Figure 6.1. Newcomers can become experts, and vice versa. A successful community of practice is more than just a forum for information exchange. Membership involves an 'emotional as well as an intellectual component and the process is transformative rather than transmitted' (Molphy et al., 2007: 711). Communities of practice have been around in many different forms for as long as human beings have learned together. However, they have been widely applied in an educational context as a means of professional development for teachers. Changing the focus of a school, perhaps in relationship to new developments in learning theory, requires quite significant change that

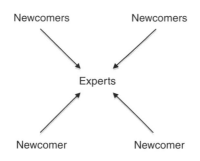

Figure 6.1 Roles in a community of practice

is not readily achieved without external help. Communities of practice offer like-minded educationalists the opportunity to engage in professional discourse that can lead to a change in practice (Wenger, 2007). This might mean teachers and administrators forming a group exploring how best to apply a technological advance such as the interactive whiteboard in the classroom. Indeed, many such groups already do so.

Activity

A community of practice is not just people who meet because of shared interests such as films or antiques. Identify what a group of teachers meeting regularly for lunch should do if they wish to convert their recreational activity into a community of practice.

An alternative perspective on the nature of community was developed by a group of academics, including Garrison, Anderson and Archer, at the start of the new millennium (Sackville et al., 2010). The resulting conceptual framework – communities of inquiry – had its genesis in the work of John Dewey and was prompted by the emergence of online learning. From an educational perspective, Garrison et al. (2003) suggest that a typical community of learners would be composed of teachers and the taught, interacting with the specific purpose of constructing and validating understanding and:

> developing capabilities that will lead to further learning. Such a community encourages cognitive independence and social interdependence simultaneously.
> (Garrison et al., 2003: 23)

Purposeful critical discourse and reflection to assemble personal meaning and confirm mutual understanding underpin the activities of any community. The model was designed to be consistent with constructivist theories of learning and teaching (Brooks et al., 1993). Within a community of inquiry, there are three interdependent elements: a social presence, a cognitive presence and a teaching presence. A social presence refers to the ability of members of the community to participate fully, both socially and emotionally, as a result of the medium of communication being used. The willingness of participants to project their identities as real people through open communication, self-disclosure and humour are indicators of a social presence. A cognitive presence refers to the capacity of the group members to construct understanding through collaboration. Thus, any conflict that sometimes results from being exposed to the unknown should be transformed by insight gained as a result of participation in the community. A teaching presence refers to the structure and leadership associated with the process of learning. It includes the 'design, facilitation, and direction of cognitive and social processes for the purpose of realizing personally meaningful and educationally worthwhile learning outcomes' (Anderson et al., 2001: 1). It is characterized by what Garrison et al. (2000) call 'instructional management', involving curriculum setting and assessment, and what Shea et al. (2010) identify as directed intervention. Of the three presences, Garrison et al. (2000) suggest that teaching is essential in balancing social and cognitive issues.

The diagram in Figure 6.2 illustrates the interconnection between the social, cognitive and teaching presences (Garrison et al., 2000).

The way members of the community respond to each other, teachers affirming success, learners respecting each other, is the pivotal connection between

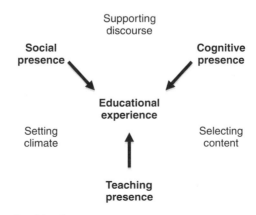

Figure 6.2 A community of inquiry

the social and teaching presence. The content that guides the learning journey is at the interface between the teaching and cognitive presences. The supporting discourse is dependent upon both the social and cognitive presences. Lim (2007) investigated a typical community of inquiry that was formed at Murdock University, Australia, studying Organizational Informatics. The community was composed of third year undergraduates and their tutors who were engaged in weekly virtual tutorials formed to discuss computer mediated work processes. Every participating student was required to manage at least one of the tutorials while their tutors acted as both facilitators and assessor throughout. Lim (2007) suggests that because those students with a leading role were expected to encourage less confident members to engage in debate, to support the right of others to express their views and to keep discussions relevant with guidance, both they and their tutors were involved in establishing:

> teaching presence in the online environment. Furthermore, as all parties share individual knowledge, negotiate new understandings during dialogic interaction, build relational ties that bind virtual communities, they would essentially be engaged in providing cognitive and social support to each other. (Lim, 2007: 159)

She concluded that this model was useful in helping to shape the way virtual communities operate (Lim, 2007).

Activity

Both communities of practice and communities of inquiry provide models of how a community of learners might be organized. Summarize what the key differences are between the two. Identify which type of community you might use to encourage students to lead rather than just participate in learning and say whether this could be readily done virtually. State the reasons why you made these choices.

Synchronous and asynchronous communication

Learning communities are sometimes affected by the way in which participants communicate with each other. They have always been able to employ synchronous and/or asynchronous tools to facilitate dialogue. However, the increasing use of technology has brought the argument about the value of one as opposed to the other into sharp relief. Synchronous communication occurs in real time and depends on all those involved in a virtual discussion or an exchange of ideas to be simultaneously engaged, but without the need for them to be in the same place. Video conferencing and chat rooms are typical of this type of technology. Video conferencing offers all the benefits of face-to-face (FtF) interaction to members of a virtual community. Chat rooms offer instant messaging facilities and an interactivity that mimics elements of FtF conversation. However, using text alone cannot easily provide all the nuances of meaning afforded by being able to see others (Deed et al., 2010). Nevertheless, Blanchard (2004) argues, virtual communities founded on synchronous communication still have a strong identity because the rituals and conversations between members serve to reinforce their sense of belonging. Although freed from the need to be in close proximity to each other, the necessity for participants to 'meet' in their virtual synchronous environment at the same time can be restrictive. Interaction can become difficult to manage and chaotic when the number of contributors increases (Olaniran, 2006). Moderation of what is said or posted is difficult to achieve.

Asynchronous communication is also free from the constraints of place but, additionally, does not require those involved to participate at the same time. Discussion or an exchange of ideas is not dependant on simultaneous engagement. Email facilitates this form communication. Meaningful conversation can occur without the sender or the receiver being at the keyboard at the same time. Indeed, there is much to be said for the reflection that this allows for, particularly when a hasty response may be inappropriate. Rather than stultify, virtual learning communities that use asynchronous tools offer a rich menu of opportunities to their members. They reduce the competition for airtime and all voices can be more readily heard because they are freed from the limitations of time and place. By enabling those participating to determine their own working patterns, the development of rational discourse is encouraged (Pringle, 2002). This is partly achieved because more time for reading and reflection is possible (Donaldson et al., 2002). Multi participant discussion is also more manageable.

Activity

The characteristics of face-to-face (FtF) communication are that it is time dependent, has many opportunities for interactivity, low expediency, few opportunities for feedback, a low technological component, possible opportunities for peer to peer communication, anonymity is not possible, it possible for the leaner to control learning and

⇨

takes insignificant time to establish. The characteristics of synchronous communication are that it is time dependent, has many opportunities for interactivity, medium expediency, many opportunities for feedback, a high technological component, many opportunities for peer to peer communication, anonymity is possible, it is probable that the leaner can control learning and takes significant time to establish. The characteristics of asynchronous communication are that it is not time dependent, has limited opportunities for interactivity, high expediency, many opportunities for feedback, a medium technological component, opportunities for peer to peer communication, anonymity is possible, it is highly probable that the leaner can control learning and takes t time to establish (Olaniran, 2006). Using these characteristics as a guide, can you suggest reasons why asynchronous learning, rather than synchronous learning, has been at the heart of developments in distance learning and has been widely used in education?

Blended learning and community

The question of whether to use asynchronous and/or synchronous communication ideally should be determined by learning need rather than other factors, such as expense. Both should be employed in conjunction with each other as the context demands. The multiplicity of technologies now available to learners and teachers makes this blended approach more feasible. They allow for communities to form and transform readily and can set learning in range of contexts. Blended learning is said to occur when traditional (synchronous) and online learning environments (asynchronous) are integrated to create a learning system that fosters meaningful exchange between the teacher and the taught (Graham, 2006). Over time, the concept has variously embraced different contexts for learning, different learning theories and a multiplicity of learning outcomes as it has evolved. It has also been used to label any learning milieu, including those involving digital technologies, in which a multiplicity of tools and media are employed. This has led some commentators such as Clark (2006) to claim that, although the term has only emerged recently as part of the educational lexicon, the ideas that underpin it have a long history. Teachers in the 1940s were as much concerned about using more than one approach to learning as are contemporary educators, particularly in the light of technological changes that they faced. The difference between them is that the earlier educators did not have an appropriate label to describe what they were doing. Blended learning is sometimes confused with distance education or distributed learning. Both are characterized by a physical separation between the teacher and learner. Perhaps this is why some, such as Oliver et al. (2005), suggest that blended learning is ill defined and at its best it a compromise term encouraging the avoidance of either a purely online or a purely FtF system. They contend, rather cynically, that the concept was introduced to justify the millions of pounds invested unwisely in purely online tuition when the training industry discovered e-learning. Despite their concerns, the term is now widely employed when technology-mediated learning (TML) involving the web is combined with FtF teaching.

Advocates of blended learning suggest that there are a number of benefits from adopting this approach, including:

1. Getting the best of all educational worlds with none of the pitfalls
2. Improved learning effectiveness
3. Increased access and convenience
4. Cost effectiveness (Graham, 2006)

A report commissioned by the US Department of Education that examined the results from 46 studies comparing online learning with FtF techniques seems to confirm these claims. It concluded that blended approaches are more effective than either online learning or FtF on their own (Means et al., 2010). The evidence from examining many studies (a meta-analysis) undertaken by the report authors indicated that learners who carry out all or part of their instruction online performed better than those undertaking the same activity through FtF instruction. Blended learning appeared to generate by far the best results of all. However, the level of teacher engagement was a strong mediating factor in the success or relative failure of this approach. Both limited and over-participation on the part of the teacher nullified any benefit (Means et al., 2010).

Stacey et al. (2008) believe that in order for blended learning to be effective it should be regarded as a scholarly construct that can transform teaching and learning and not simply as a means of incorporating technology. However, they strongly recommend that, rather than a strict adherence to any dogma, local community and organizational needs should be paramount. The Tel Aviv University Virtual TAU (VT) project is typical of this approach. In 2001, the university, which is the largest research-orientated institution in Israel, initiated the project to encourage faculty members to employ the Internet and the web in their teaching. A bespoke course management system that made it possible to store information, create didactic teaching material, and use either synchronous or asynchronous communication tools was used as the primary vehicle to facilitate this change. No predesigned template was imposed on the tutors taking part. Each was given an opportunity to develop his or her own pedagogy in relationship to how this system should be employed. After eight years, 75 per cent were utilizing some aspect of VT in their work. Soffer et al. (2010) regard this transition as a great success but Nachmias et al. (2006) point out that although this initiative prompted the adoption of some aspect of blended learning, in the majority of courses the degree to which this was done varied. At its most basic, tutors used VT simply as an administrative tool and repository for information. This is not unusual. Very few tutors gave up FtF meetings or utilized all the virtual facilities available to them. Nachmias et al. (2006) suggest that for greater transformation of teaching and learning to occur in the context of blended learning, most tutors needed 'appropriate support to make the conceptual shift toward the generation of more sound technology based learning activities' (Nachmias et al., 2006: 384).

M learning and community

Mobile technologies such as cell and smart phones, palmtops, handheld computers tablet PCs, laptops, and personal media players are increasingly being used in support of blended learning. They bring an increased portability that can have a significant number of educational benefits. A growing number of educators are beginning to recognize that such handheld devices can facilitate the personalization of learning and enhance learner responsibility (Faux et al., 2006). More importantly in the context of this chapter, they can also help to forge coherent links between the sometimes-disparate groups learners belong to, in the school, home and wider community. Park (2011) suggests that these handheld devices have unique technological attributes, which can lead to a number of useful pedagogical affordances. These are identified as portability, small screen size, relative computing power, use of diverse communication networks, application rich environments, ability to synchronize data with other devices and a range of methods of input. Mobile devices are also generally much cheaper than other digital equipment, and more ubiquitous. The Dudley Handhelds Initiative, the first large-scale investment in mobile technology for students in the United Kingdom, provided approximately 300 handheld palmtop devices to students across Years 5 to 10, in eight schools (6 primary schools, 1 secondary special school and 1 mainstream secondary school), for use at both school and home. At the time of the initiative (2005), Dudley had low levels of access to technology and poor family involvement with learning. The devices were used differently in each setting. For example, in the mainstream secondary school, they were given to high-ability students who took them to all their lessons, while in the special school they were given to those who had limited access to ICT at home. In all cases, the objective was to raise student standards of literacy and numeracy and to address adult literacy and numeracy by engaging families with their own learning. Faux et al. (2006: 11) concluded that using handheld devices had extended community access to ICT by helping to 'forge stronger links with parents. Indeed, the impact of the devices on parents was generally perceived positively. There was also some evidence of positive impact on engagement with learning in the community'. However, they warn that in order to develop collaborative self-supporting communities of practice using mobile devices adequate and appropriate training for both the teacher and the taught is a fundamental requirement (Faux et al., 2006). This caution is important because, as mobile technology advances and greater functionality is built into handheld devices, their owners will 'use this functionality, along with a range of other technologies, to support both intentional and unintentional mobile informal learning' (Clough et al., 2007: 370).

Virtual worlds and community

Another interesting if incidental development made possible through the Internet and the web has added to the range of things that can be included in blended learning. Advances in computer technology have meant that it has become possible to develop more powerful gaming software. This has led to the creation of a number of computer-based simulations that offer the opportunity for a unique form of social interaction. These simulations also have the potential to support the creation of virtual learning communities, in some cases populated by avatars that represent the real community members. Although education in a virtual context is dealt with more thoroughly in a later chapter, it is worth examining the implications for communities of learners here. Second Life (SL) is a package typical of this genre that has found wide use in education. The Department of Biosurgery and Surgical Technology at Imperial College, London, is involved in a project called SciLands, which is a specialized area of SL dedicated to science and technology. SciLands consists of more than 65 'islands' that are populated by virtual representatives of more than 20 agencies, such as the National Physical Laboratory (NPL), the National Oceanic and Atmospheric Administration (NOAA) and various universities. The islands are docked together to create interdisciplinary communities in which engineers, designers, researchers, educators, students, operational staff and even members of the public attend virtual meetings. The objective is not only to foster dialogue between like-minded professionals remote from each other in virtual communities of practice, but also to encourage communication between residents, forming communities of inquiry. Thus, in their avatar form, participants can 'interact and learn from one another without the social, organizational and age barriers that serve to separate their communities from one another in the real world' (Taylor, 2009). These 3-D virtual worlds, as Boulos et al. (2007: 243) suggests, offer educators and learners the opportunity to be 'more creative and to develop new effective ways of teaching and learning, rather than to purely replicate real life and classrooms in Second Life!' Warburton (2009) asserts that virtual worlds offer rich opportunities for social interaction between individuals and communities, and promote a sense of belonging and purpose that coheres around groups, subcultures and geography. Dreher et al. (2009) contend that by immersing themselves in a virtual community, participants not only benefit from the connection with others at a distance, but also that simply engaging with the technology inevitably leads to the development of valuable knowledge and skills. Baxter (2008) claims that being able to step into a 3D world as an avatar is a much more real experience, and by implication, more effective in helping to form a learning community, than having a Skype video conference, or being part of a mailing list. Dudeney (2009) concurs, suggesting that SL activity affords opportunities for participants to

> Prosume (that is, 'produce' and 'consume') rather than simply be passive participants in their learning, and a freedom to experiment in a safe and controllable environment. Providing a space where groups can get to know each other and work together with an increased feeling of presence over chat rooms or forums in virtual learning environments such as Moodle, and without the scheduled urgency of a video conference. (Dudeney, 2009; 69)

Viable social communities leading to socially constructed learning can thus emerge.

Pesce (2008) believes that the continued development of virtual worlds will likely force educational institutions to either fully embrace the technology or fall far behind as social institutions and risk becoming a less significant in community life. However, Warburton (2009) has identified a number of challenges that users of SL face in relationship to community. He suggests that building social relationships can be problematic because identities are never fixed. Individuals, rather than be readily accepted, can become isolated because SL has its own cultural codes, norms and etiquette and reading them is not straightforward. Trust and authenticity, critical factors in promoting successful groups, must be developed over time through scaffolded activity. He concludes that the barriers to the use of SL represent:

> a challenge that requires the careful consideration of a number of design possibilities. Only by constructively approaching each one is it possible to make design decisions that encourage the positive and rewarding use of virtual worlds for learning and teaching. (Warburton, 2009: 425)

Conclusions

New technologies have the potential to support the development of communities of learners which can be just as rich and immersive as those formed through traditional means. In addition, they can enable hard to reach vulnerable groups and those, who for whatever reason are socially isolated to receive and give more fully. They can also transform ideas about how distance learning should be constituted and delivered. They can change the curriculum by forcing traditional subject divisions to become less distinct (Fisher et al., 2006). However, these communities must be founded on a clear understanding of the different ways that they can be constituted. Their internal workings must be governed by appropriate forms of communication, be they synchronous, asynchronous or a combination of both. Virtual communities are subject to the same challenges as their 'real' counterparts. They need to address who does what, engender trust while protecting the vulnerable, deal with unacceptable behaviour, foster appropriate exchange and other concerns such as privacy, all of which have been well rehearsed in the literature (Boulos et al., 2007) For individuals within the community, the leaning experience will be fuller if it encompasses both FtF and virtual components. Teachers must also recognize that these technological tools present conceptual difficulties for both young and older learners, in that initially they are likely to be bounded (time limited and linked to specific outcomes) and formally constituted rather simply spontaneously emerge as a natural consequence of communal activity. It is important to provide training for both teachers and the taught in how best they can be utilized in an educational context. Deed et al. (2010) contend that that effective learning will only emerge from considered pedagogical design, informed by the pupil or student experience and perspective. The young, in particular, inhabit the virtual world with ease and Melville (2009) believes that it has led them to:

> a strong sense of communities of interest linked in their own web spaces, and to a disposition to share and participate. It has also led them to impatience – a preference for quick answers – and to a casual approach to evaluating information and attributing it and also to copyright and legal constraints. (Melville, 2009: 9)

Big question

If teachers fail to make proper use of the technologically mediated communities that are so attractive to the young, are schools in danger of becoming less relevant as agencies of education?

Further reading

Brabazon, T. (2002) *Digital Hemlock: Internet Education and the Poisoning of Teaching,* Sydney: UNSW Press.

Deed, C. and Edwards, A. (2010) Using social networks in learning and teaching in higher education: An Australian case study, *International Journal of Knowledge Society Research*, Vol. 1, No 2, 1–12.

Faux, F., McFarlane, M., Roche, N. and Face, K. (2006) *Learning With Handheld Technologies*, Bristol: Futurelab.

Melville, D. (2009) *Higher Education in a Web 2.0 World, Committee of Inquiry into the Changing Learner Experience*, available from www.jisc.ac.uk/media/documents/publications/heweb20rptv1.pdf – Last accessed 11/02/2011.

Warburton, S. (2009) Second Life in higher education: Assessing the potential for and the barriers to deploying virtual worlds in learning and teaching, *British Journal of Educational Technology*, Vol. 40, No 3, 414–26.

Useful websites

Avatars

www.virtualworldsinfo.com/second-life-avatars.html – Last accessed 11/02/2011.

Blended Learning

www.wlv.ac.uk/default.aspx?page=18446 – Last accessed 11/02/2011.

Communities of Learners

www.league.org/gettingresults/web/module1/introduction/creating_community_video.html – Last accessed 11/02/2011.

Communities of Practice and Inquiry

www.insites.org/CLIP_v1_site/index.html – Last accessed 11/02/2011.

History of the Internet

www.nethistory.info/History%20of%20the%20Internet/global.html y.org.uk/page.aspx?o=135556 – Last accessed 11/02/2011.

Second Life

http://secondlife.com/ – Last accessed 11/02/2011.

Mobile Learning

www.excellencegateway.org.uk/page.aspx?o=135556 – Last accessed 11/02/2011.

Synchronous and Asynchronous Communication

http://web.media.mit.edu/~kkarahal/generals/communication/sync_async.html – Last accessed 11/02/2011.

Virtual Worlds Online

www.virtualworldsinfo.com/index.html – Last accessed 11/02/2011.

Virtual Learning

www.virtuallearning.org.uk/ – Last accessed 11/02/2011.

Creativity, Technology and Education 7

Introduction

De Bono (1993: 169) grandly proclaims that 'creativity is the most important human resource of all. Without creativity, there would be no progress, and we would be forever repeating the same pattern'. Runco (2007) also acknowledges that creativity is of fundamental importance, claiming that it is directly connected to human evolution. The educational community has led the way recently in a revival of interest in notions of creativity. Teachers have many practical opportunities to test out notions of creativity in everyday settings on a regular to basis because of the increasing use of technologies in learning and teaching (Loveless, 2007). It is, however, important that educationalists in particular 'have a clear vision, awareness and understanding of what creativity is and entails in order to fully comprehend how it can be enhanced' (Ferrari et al., 2009: iii). Creativity in an educational context can also mean teaching creatively or teaching creativity. It is the latter aspect of creativity on which this chapter will focus.

What this chapter will seek to establish is that there is a fundamental and increasingly important link between new technologies and creativity in an educational context. It will posit that although creativity was once regarded as the preserve of special individuals, it is an evolving concept now encompassing the mundane and commonplace as well as the extraordinary. It will also establish that creative activity is synonymous with some form of output, regardless of the level at which it is undertaken. Many countries are keen to embrace these expanded notions of creativity in their learning and teaching provision. The affordances of ICTs, particularly when they are combined through the use of modelling and simulations, allow for risk-free experimentation, a condition in which creativity can flourish. This chapter will assert that none of the benefits will be accrued unless there is a corresponding understanding in both the teacher and the taught about how best to employ these technologies. This will be brought into sharp relief by reference to the rise of social networking technology in education.

Towards a definition of creativity

Part of the challenge is that an understanding of creativity is still evolving, despite nearly 150 years of academic interest in the subject (Becker, 1995). Closely associated with genius and madness and oddity in the early nineteenth century, it is now subject to a much broader interpretation. McWilliams et al. (2008) believe that many regard creativity as both mysterious and serendipitous. Notions of creativity are also culturally grounded. There is a striking difference between how creativity has been perceived in the West and the East. Western cultures have tended to regard it as a means of challenging traditional ways of doing things, whilst in the East it has been associated with a remodelling rather than a deconstruction of convention. An additional complicating factor, identified by Runco et al. (1999), is that many believe they have an implicit understanding and tacit knowledge of creativity. This leads some to state that they can recognize creativity, but when pressed they are unable define it. There are indeed at least four challenges, of particular relevance to the educator, that make creativity a problematic concept to grasp. The first challenge is finding a definition that can be applied readily and is relatively easy to understand.

Many recent attempts to define creativity focus on transforming ideas into reality. Kaufman et al. (2006) suggest that we need to identify the purpose of using our creative capabilities and how they contribute to our sense of self as individuals in relation to others and the wider world. Kim (2007) states that it is an individual and cultural phenomenon, which allows us to convert possibilities into things that can be readily used. Craft (2005) regards creativity as the ability to recognize the potential in things that others have not noticed before. Nelson (2005) contends that there is a link between creative thought and problem-solving. Aldous (2005), building on this notion, describes creative thinking as a process that results in unique, usable concepts. The British Educational Communications and Technology Agency (BECTA) (2002) suggests that it relates to the ability to take what one already has or knows and use it in new and different ways. Sternberg et al. (1995) believe that any outcome must be both novel and appropriate at the same time for something to be considered creative. Perhaps the Office for Standards in Education, Children's Services and Skills (OFSTED) in England has come the closest to establishing a definition that is both germane and able to stand up to close scrutiny. It contends that creativity:

1. Always involves thinking or behaving imaginatively
2. Is characterized by purposeful activity
3. Generates something original
4. Produces outcomes that have value in relation to the objective (OFSTED, 2003: 4)

This definition, which will be adopted for the remainder of this work, was derived from a report commissioned by the Secretary of State for Education and Employment for England in May 1999 and entitled 'All our futures, Creativity, Culture and Education (National Advisory Committee on Creative and Cultural Education (NACCCE), 1999). The NACCCE produced the report, and the fact that it was commissioned in the first place is indicative of both the political and educational interest in creativity that still persists today. This interest is international. Countries such as Germany, Japan, the Republic of Korea, the Netherlands and the Americas are attempting to integrate some aspect of creativity in their curriculum (Sharp et al., 2000).

The second challenge is related to the nature of what can be considered a legitimate outcome of creative activity. Gibson (2005) suggests that traditionalists consider paintings, music, dance, drama and films as the only true products of the creative mind. In the West, this viewpoint has dominated attitudes towards creativity in an educational context. In contrast, politicians and economists from across the globe now use the term creativity when talking about an essential skill that needs to be developed in the workforce. This is not the same as that found in the arts. The NACCCE (1999) recognized that creativity in employees is highly valued by employers. Loveless (2007) regards this as a necessary response to the continual fluctuations and rapid transformations of the global market economy.

Activity

Do you think the current use of technology in schools lends itself more readily to the creativity associated with artistic outcomes or to those more akin to the commercial and business world?

The third challenge is that creativity has been regarded as the sole preserve of those with exceptional talent. Stein (1956) states that it requires independence of mind and unusualness to be creative. He comments that less creative individuals seem oriented towards quick achievement, while the more creative appear to work slowly by carefully marshalling their resources. Renzulli (2002) believes that only a small percentage of high-achieving individuals show signs of being creative or innovative, and only then in a restricted number of areas, such as music, where it is regarded as the norm. He suggests that within education, creativity is often associated with the achievement and outcomes of the gifted and talented. However, Runco (2007) asserts that creativity is not confined to those in the arts communities. He states that all can be creative, including children, whether at play or engaging with the world directly. Northcott et al. (2007) contend that everybody has the capacity to produce creative thought. Loveless (2007) likewise suggests that pupils of all abilities are capable of expressing creativity, whether it is through sporting activities or more practical subjects like technology or ICT. The NACCCE (1999) report concludes that we all are, or can be, creative to a lesser or greater degree if given the opportunity. More radically, de Bono (2009) states that creativity can be taught to anyone. Her Majesty's Inspectorate of Education in Scotland (HMIe) suggest that it is possible to be creative in all curriculum areas, but it is easier to encourage more in some that lend themselves to open ended activities, personal interpretation, self expression and choice rather than in others (HMIe, 2006). These claims all hinge on an important development in thinking about the nature of creativity. The concept of big-C and little-c creativity, which builds on the work done by Gardner (1993) and Csikszentmihalyi (1996), has transformed the way educationalists regard creativity. Craft (2001) explains that big-C creativity is restricted to the few. It is an elusive quality. Activity at this level is rare and results in original outcomes that can transform the entire human condition. Vincent van Gogh or Isaac Newton might be said to exhibit big-C creativity. On the other hand, everybody has the capacity for developing little-c creativity. It results in small changes to the more mundane aspects of life. Originality in this context relates to what is new to the individual. Craft (2001) prefers to call it 'possibility thinking'. She regards creativity as a crucial life skill which is far more likely to be what educators see on a regular basis. There is a similar notion, first introduced by Margaret Boden in 1990, which uses the terms psychological or 'P-creativity', and historical or 'H-creativity' rather than big- and little-c. P-creativity occurs when an individual comes up with an idea that they have never thought of before. H-creativity occurs when the idea has never been thought of before. Both concepts acknowledge that the creativity is a broad phenomenon but that degrees of impact and originality separate the extremes. This view of creativity is the basis of much educational thinking across the globe (Boden, 2004).

The fourth challenge relates to the characteristics an individual who is creative might display. Identifying these behaviours is important because they help educators to develop a framework for assessing levels of creativity that do not focus solely on outcome. The NACCCE (1999) suggests that adaptability, the capacity to make connections between things and innovation, are important but has identified five specific qualities of creative individuals. They are able to:

1. Use imagination to come up with solutions that are different
2. Properly manage the growth of an idea
3. Pursue a purpose
4. Evaluate and review
5. Be original

The committee, however, did not entirely forget end product. It also suggested that a solid outcome must be produced as a result of all this activity. This list is quite prescriptive and subjective. Csikszentmilhalyi (1996), a leading

American author on positive psychology, was also concerned with creativity and behaviour. Whilst his list includes some of the NACCCE behaviours, such as the ability to properly manage the growth of an idea, pursue a purpose and evaluate and review, he identifies a number of additional characteristics. He contends that the creative individual:

1. Can eliminate superfluous distractions
2. Displays a lack of fear of failure
3. Is not self-conscious
4. Applies different intelligences to problem-solving
5. Loses all sense of time when engaged in creative activity
6. Does things for the sake of doing them (autotelic activity)

Perhaps he has come the closest to providing a more fulsome list, but this reflects both his professional interests and an overriding concern with the psychology of creativity that was prevalent in the later stages of the last century. There is no indication in either list whether all behaviours must be present equally all of the time.

Activity

Applying either the list of attributes of the creative individual identified by NACCCE or that of Csikszentmilhalyi as a guide, reflect on some learning activity that you have been engaged in that makes extensive use of technology. Decide whether you were being creative or not. State why you have come to that conclusion.

The link between creativity and technology

As a mark of the growing interest and awareness of the role and relevance of creativity, the European Union designated 2009 as the year of creativity and innovation. A major survey (Cachia et al., 2009) involving 10,000 teachers from the 27 member states was undertaken as part of this initiative, which examined creativity in schools. The study sought to answer questions about the nature of creativity, the extent of the link between learning and teaching and creativity, and what role technologies play in the development of creativity.

A majority of respondents from most of the contributing countries were convinced that tools such as computer hardware and software and the World Wide Web (web or www) were useful in promoting creativity. Their views are not unfounded. Alsina (2006) suggests that ICTs provide the catalyst for creative activity. Wegerif et al. (2004) believe that there is a direct link between ICT capabilities and creative processes. BECTA (2002) indicates that ICTs have an important role to play in supporting creativity by providing learners with the facilities to experiment safely in virtual environments. Loveless (2007) suggests that the affordances of digital technologies, mentioned in the previous chapter, directly support the development of creativity. Fisher et al. (2006) believe that these affordances can be grouped into clusters of purposeful activity that they identify as knowledge building, distributed cognition, community and communication and engagement. Knowledge building in this context refers to the capacity of the tools being used to allow an individual to adapt and develop ideas and represent them in a variety of ways, for example, video to capture and critically review some form activity or online conference facilities. Distributed cognition (a branch of cognitive science) refers to being able to find things out through a range of mediating artefacts and tool such as the web. The affordances that enable knowledge building and distributed cognition are closely associated with each other. Community and communication refers to the opportunities (both locally and globally) to exchange and share through tools such as email, chat forums and other network technologies. Engagement is characterized by exploration, experimentation, immediacy, interactivity, play and risk taking, which some digital tools can facilitate. The link between these affordances and the traits identified by both NACCCE and Csikszentmilhalyi is exemplified in Figure 7.1.

Kennewell et al. (2007) suggest that educational settings must involve purposeful activity, something original to the individual and outcomes that are of value in relation to the objective in order for creativity to flourish.

Affordances	Qualities of the creative individual
Knowledge-building	• Properly manage the growth of an idea
	• Evaluate and review
Distributed cognition	• Use different intelligences/imagination to problem solve
Community and Communication	• Lack of self consciousness
Engagement	• Pursue a purpose
	• Unafraid of failure

Figure 7.1 Affordances and the creative individual

Activity

Loveless (2007) believes that digital technologies can allow for non-sequential thoughts and actions. This reflects how the human brain works and, thus, more readily facilitates creativity. Provide examples from your own learning of the capacity for nonlinearity that ICTs in particular have.

Simulation and creativity

There are many ways in which specific technologies can support the development of creativity in education. However, one set of tools which brings together all the unique features of digital technology best exemplifies how this can be done. Modelling or simulation has long been acknowledged as an effective device for promoting learning and teaching because it is founded on making connections, communication and evaluation. They have what Wickens (2007) refers to as provisionality. Diulus et al. (1991) suggest that modelling and simulations lend themselves to learning that is perceived rather than received, discovered rather than given more caught than taught. This is not a new idea in education. Widely employed by the military to train soldiers, simulation has increasingly been used in a range of educational contexts (Smith, 2010). There is some confusion about the terms 'modelling' and 'simulation' (Magee, 2006). In the context of this work, they will be regarded as synonymous. There are a number of distinct types of modelling or simulation available to the educationalist including branching stories, interactive spreadsheets, game based models and virtual simulations. Branching stories enable participants to make choices which influence how a narrative evolves. More and more nodes or branching points can be added to increase complexity. An archetypal branching story may involve a group of children being asked to plan a trip to a major city that involves making choices about how to get there and what to see. At each stage of their virtual journey, they are given options which have different outcomes. They can reflect on these options both before and after choices have been made. Teachers often encourage pupils to create the scenarios themselves as an extension activity. Branching stories can be used with any age range but are more suited to low-level or young learners. Webquests, which are essentially inquiry based online learning activities, are a more sophisticated version of this type of simulation.

Interactive spreadsheets are mathematical models in which inputs and outputs can be varied. They can model any quantitative system, from industrial production to the effect of changing pupil numbers on educational funding, and expose learners to simple decision-making. For example, business or economics students could use an interactive spreadsheet based on a freight business to test ideas about profitability and insolvency. Spreadsheets usually do not make use of anything other than a basic graphical interface.

Game-based models are driven by the need to entertain but have some educational content. Learning can be incidental but because game culture is prevalent amongst the young, they are powerful tools that cannot be ignored for their potential to facilitate creativity. Typical of this type of software are games that allow participants to design and build a virtual theme park. Attractions can be customized and rides developed, the mix of what is on offer varied and employees hired and fired. They use quite sophisticated graphics with varying degrees of realism. Of all the forms of modelling, virtual simulations try to approximate the real world the nearest. What was once the preserve of special groups with enough funding and appropriate hardware, virtual simulations are now widely available. They can be set up to mimic the chaotic and ambiguous nature of reality. Participants can engage with objects or other players in many different ways so that their experience is immersive and interactive. It is this authenticity that makes the learning experience potentially so powerful. As the cost of computers has decreased, their processing power expanded, appropriate software has been developed and the Internet has evolved, so that they are used more frequently in all forms of education. Typical software enables medical practitioners to engage in and manage aspects of health care.

Although all of these tools vary in terms of expense and sophistication, they have a number of things in common, including:

1. Users are required to make decisions
2. Promote abstract thinking
3. Instantaneous feedback
4. Learning can be scaffolded
5. Learning is not confined by geographical or physical boundaries
6. The models can run repeatedly until the learner is ready to move on to the next stage

In addition, interactive spreadsheets, game-based models and virtual simulations can be operate in real or accelerated (or slow motion) time, which means that it is more feasible to observe or participate in activities that normally require hours days or even week to complete or are highly complex. Connecting all forms of modelling and simulations to the Internet vastly increases their scope.

Activity

Use the web to find additional examples of modelling or simulation packages and identify how they might be used in an educational context to promote creativity.

Diulus et al. (1991) recognize that modelling or simulation has great potential for fostering creative activity. They provide a fertile ground in which the conditions established by Seltzer et al. (1999) for creativity to flourish are present. These include:

1. Allowing for variation of contexts in which learners can are able to apply their learning and skills in making connections.
2. Encouraging interactivity through which ideas are readily exchanged and feedback can be quickly received.
3. Drawing upon a diverse range of sources.

However, by themselves, they are only as good as any other resource in promoting creativity unless they contain specific features and are used in particular ways. Risk and experimentation are two additional properties, which modelling and simulation can provide that support the development of creativity in learners.

Risk, technology and creativity

Both NACCCE and Csikszentmilhalyi make the connection between risk-taking and creativity. Beck (1999) highlights the association between creativity and uncertainty. Nickerson (2008) states that risk-taking is central to creativity. Risk-taking in this context is related to having the courage to challenge the orthodox and develop new ideas. Challenging orthodoxy can lead to ostracism and great personal and professional difficulties. Barry Marshall, an Australian pathologist, was not afraid to dispute the prevailing dogma that peptic ulcers resulted mainly from stress and an inappropriate lifestyle. He believed that the bacterium *helicobacter pylorus* was responsible, Challenging orthodoxy with great scepticism from his colleagues. The vast majority of the medical profession worldwide considered him 'to be a quack and really were extremely dismissive for a number of years' (Sweet, 1997). He was proved correct and many people have benefited as a result of his perseverance. There are a number of reasons why creativity and risk-taking are linked. It is important for learners, regardless of the context, to explore the 'what if' scenario without fear of failure in order to test the boundaries of understanding. Learners need to:

- Recognize that constructive failure is an essential part of the creative process.
- Have opportunities to make connections where the risks of uniting things together is unknown.

Simulations and modelling allow learners to take risks which under normal circumstances they would choose not to because of impracticality or because the cost of real failure (in situations where wealth and health are at stake) is unacceptable. They can be reversed at will. Thus, the fear of unfortunate consequences can be minimized. Marshall, who with J. Robin Warren, was awarded the Noble Prize for Medicine in 2005, was so incensed by the professional rejection he suffered at the hands of his doubting colleagues, he swallowed a beaker full of *helicobacter pylorus* in order to prove his point. He became very ill but the link was undeniably proved. This example of big-C creativity might not have occurred if Marshall was not so single-minded and prepared to take enormous risks. However, had a virtual simulation been available, perhaps this dramatic action, which resulted in much pain and discomfort and potential danger, could have been avoided. Beck (1999), Magee (2006) and Runco et al. (1999) suggest that simulations provide a risk-free environment but there is a danger that cannot be removed from any situation involving the generation of new ideas, the fear of failure. Nickerson (2008: 414) believes that fear of exposing ones limitations, and fear of ridicule '... are powerful deterrents to creative thinking, or at least to public exposure of the products of creative efforts. Learners must be free to make mistakes without undue loss of face so that they have the confidence to try again. This is as much about teacher attitudes as it is about technology.

Experimentation and creativity

Most models and simulations support experimentation. Some are configured with a flexible internal architecture so that either the learner or the teacher, or both, can adjust how the systems behave. This is what Runco et al. (1999: 242) suggest will produce 'diverse information, knowledge, and capabilities that can support multiple perspectives and creative approaches'. Experimentation presents learners with opportunities to develop a much broader and deeper understanding of the problem they are investigating. Aldrich (2005) contends that it puts them firmly at the centre of the learning process. In addition, Cropley (2001) believes that self-directed experimentation without fear of sanctions promotes initiative, spontaneity, sensibility, flexibility and divergent thinking. The contexts used can also be outside their immediate experience, which helps learners not only to develop subject knowledge but an understanding of how they deal with the unfamiliar situations. Errors, where they do occur, can be swiftly and painlessly corrected through simple and neutral feedback (Kennewell et al., 2000). In some models and simulations, randomness is factored into how they are designed to operate. This leads to a lack of predictability, which means that users are forced to constantly assess and modify how they engage with the model or simulation.

There are those that doubt the value of modelling and simulation. Monke (2004) is keen to establish the limitations of their use in educational contexts. He contends that there is a danger that the values inherent in what he refers to as real experience are being replaced by a set of abstract values that have more to do with technological ideology. He regards the physical world, with its direct connection to the senses, as an essential component of the learning experience. By focussing unduly on virtual environments, he feels certain qualities are promoted at the expense of others. There are no doubt circumstances when modelling and simulation inhibit, rather than promote, creativity.

Activity

Monke (2004) highlights a simulation package designed to expose users to the decision about resources that early American pioneers faced to illustrate what he perceives as a fundamental weakness. He complains that because the deeply human element of the real story of these explorers has been reduced to no more than deciding whether to take one tin of beans or two, 'the resilient souls of the pioneers are absent from the simulation' (Monke: 2004, 11). What significance does this have for developing creativity in learning and teaching context?

Conclusions

Ferrari et al. (2009) established that in Europe, at least, views held by teachers about creativity closely align with those found in recent academic literature. The key points emerging from their survey are that teachers believe that creativity:

1. Can be applied to every domain of knowledge
2. Is not restricted to certain subject areas
3. Is not exclusive – everybody is capable of it
4. Is about finding out about the connection between things that have not been connected before

They also concluded that creativity is a fundamental skill that can be developed through education. They identified a number of what Ferrari et al. (2009) refer to as enablers that make it more likely to occur in schools, such as assessment regimes, school culture and pedagogy. The respondents to the survey indicated that the use of technology was of paramount importance in this process. Heppell (2006) and Tinio (2003) argue that the affordances of digital technologies in particular put the learner at the centre of the learning process and that this fundamental change is occurring across the globe, albeit at different rates in different countries. Ferrari et al. (2009) concur suggesting that technology now plays a central role in learners' lives. However, the technology alone is not sufficient to maximize opportunities to promote creativity. Teachers must be taught how to deploy technology, and learners must acquire technological literacy in order to liberate their creative leanings. In addition, whilst most teachers appreciate how to do these things with what are ironically referred to as traditional technologies (computers), most have a poor knowledge of how to realise the potential of Web 2 technologies to promote creativity (Deed et al., 2009). 'Web 2.0' is a term used to describe the second generation of the web that enables people to collaborate and share information online in many different forms. Social networking sites like Facebook and MySpace, bookmarking facilities like Delicious and Citeulike, multimedia sharing services like Flickr and YouTube and online gaming like Second Life, blogging and mobile technologies also offer new opportunities for people to express their creativity (Cachia et al., 2009). These remain underutilized and misunderstood in school, and there is a risk that any initiative relating to creativity will be less effective if they are not taken into account. New curriculum models with inbuilt time and space for innovation and experimentation must be allowed to emerge. These should help to maintain the balance between prescription and freedom. Technology can help by allowing subject boundaries to be blurred and generating increased motivation. New technology, education and creativity are linked. However, this does not mean that you cannot be creative without new technology, but it helps if they are employed appropriately.

Big Question

Does technology truly offer the facility for learners to be more creative, or is the caution identified by Monke (2004) about experiencing things one-stage removed in virtual environments (whatever form they take) an impediment to real creative activity?

Further reading

Becker, M. (1995) Nineteenth-century foundations of creativity research, *Creativity Research Journal*, Vol. 4, 219F–29.

Cachia, R., Ferrari, A., Kearney, C., Punie, Y., Van Den Berghe, W. and Wastiau, P. (2009) *Creativity in Schools in Europe: A Survey of Teachers*, Available from http://ipts.jrc.ec.europa.eu/publications/pub.cfm?id=3702 – Last Accessed 11/03/2011.

Loveless, A. (2007) *Creativity, Technology and Learning a Review of Recent Literature*, Report 4, Update for Futurelab. Bristol: Futurelab.

Runco, M. A. and Pritzker, S. R. (1999) *Encyclopaedia of Creativity*, Vol. 1, San Diego: Academic Press.

Wickens, C. (2007) Creativity, in Kennewell, S., Connell, A., Edwards, A., Hammond, M. and Wickens, C. (eds) *A Practical Guide to Teaching ICT in the Secondary School*, London: Routledge.

Useful websites

Creativity

www.ted.com/talks/tags/name/creativity – Last accessed 11/03/2011.

Creativity and the Curriculum

www.rm.com/generic.asp?cref=gp1547323 – Last accessed 11/03/2011.

Creativity and Education

www.ltscotland.org.uk/learningteachingandassessment/approaches/creativity/index.asp – Last accessed 11/03/2011.

Creativity in Education

www.creativityineducation.co.uk/ – Last accessed 11/03/2011.

Creativity and Risk-Taking

www.creativity-portal.com/bc/psychology/rebellion.html – Last accessed 11/03/2011.

Creativity and Technology

http://creativity-online.com/section/cat-creativity-and-technology/680 – Last accessed 11/03/2011.

Simulations in Education

www.uwe.ac.uk/elearning/she/accidentInvestigation.shtml – Last accessed 11/03/2011.

Part 3
THE FUTURE

Future Technology and Education 8

Introduction

The final three chapters of the book will examine the nature of the link between technology and education in the future. This chapter will explore the question of the future from a broad perspective, looking at general trends, and then examine what this might mean for education. The remaining two chapters will concentrate on particular issues in depth.

Thinking about the future is as much part of the human condition as is looking backwards. Predicting what is going to happen is an activity that we have been all tempted to indulge in at some time or other. The vast majority of us fail miserably to do it with any degree of accuracy, regardless of whether we are forecasting the next fashion or how society will develop. Ken Olson, the founder and chairman of Digital Equipment Corporation (DEC) speaking in 1967 could not foresee any reason why anyone would want a computer at home (Goldsborough, 2002). There are those, regarded as savants, who have had spectacular success in anticipating events. Arthur

C. Clarke envisaged the use of geostationary orbits for communications satellites in a paper for a magazine called *Wireless World* in 1945. This was the foundation of all the technologies enjoyed today, such as multichannel television and global positioning technology. Sometimes prediction is the accidental outcome of work that has another purpose. George Orwell's novel *Nineteen Eighty-Four*, written in the middle of the last century, was created to warn of the dangers of Soviet communism (Orwell, 1998). It described a totalitarian state regulated by fear and censorship in which technology was used to suppress individuality. Some now regard it as a prophetic work that clearly illustrates the threat that technocratic modernism poses to privacy and freedom (Posner, 2000). Despite the vagaries of prophecy, an academic discipline called 'futurology' or 'futures studies' has emerged. Those who practice it are regarded as 'futurologists'. Futurology is concerned with being able to identify what will remain constant and what will change, and takes into account all areas of life. A futurologist can either be schooled in the discipline of futures thinking directly, or be an individual who has the necessary technical expertise and, more importantly, the multi-disciplinary approach necessary to be able to offer an appropriate insight. Futures thinking is well established in policy sectors, such as the environment and transportation, but is fairly underdeveloped in education. Yet, it is highly pertinent because it clarifies the societal forces that help to determine how provision should evolve. Technology is a significant transformative agent in the milieu of learning and teaching and deserves significant attention of the educational futurist. Toffler (1972), when writing about the interconnection between education and technology, commented that it was important to anticipate change so that when the future arrives it is not a shock. He suggested that only if we attempt to mange change through the control of technology and by introducing an awareness of the future into education:

> can we begin to choose our personal and social futures, instead of being overtaken and overwhelmed by them. Only in these ways can we soften our collision with tomorrow and prevent what I have called future shock. (Toffler, 1972: 150)

Technological determinism appears to pervade much futures writing but the extent to which the future is shaped solely by technology is questionable. Facer et al. (2010: 78) believe that, to a lesser or greater degree, social and educational change is a 'co-production of technical, discursive and social factors'.

What this chapter seeks to establish is the complexity of trying to determine the nature of the link between technology and education in the future, and yet the necessity of doing so. It will also establish key future economic and demographic trends that may have a bearing on the future. It will contend that the technology will get ever smaller, cheaper and faster. It will identify a number different educational scenarios that may result from these developments in technology and provide the reader with enough background material to make a reasoned decision about the likelihood of any of them coming to fruition. Finally, it will pose the question of whether a technologically determined future is inevitable or even desirable. Facer et al. (2010: 77) believe that any futures work involving technology and education must be clear about 'the values underpinning the vision it is presenting'.

Challenges of looking forward

Education should be founded on futures thinking. While learners need to decide what to study in order to fulfil future aspirations, the educational establishment must decide about curriculum content and teaching methods. Above all, leaders and managers must make decisions based on some recognition of what will happen in the future. However, much policy-making is reactive rather than proactive, despite the fact that the choices made affect communities for decades to come. Looking at social and economic and technological trends rather than trying to second guess what will happen makes this process far less speculative. This approach is concerned less with why something will arise and more with what is occurring.

A number of factors affect the reliability of using a trend to forecast what will happen. They vary in terms of their predictability. Population growth and transportation lend themselves much more readily to long-term planning. Cultural issues or even politics are far less predictable and, therefore, are much more capricious. Some trends develop over a long period of time and are easier to plan for. Others are very dynamic (Pratt-Adams et al., 2010; Race, 2011). The rise in global temperatures has occurred over many centuries, whereas variations in consumer attitudes can be very swift. A trend can have a significant outcome or be of little or no concern. The shift from hand to mass production that occurred in the Industrial Revolution had a deep and long-term effect on the nature of employment. Different fashions come and go with little or no impact on the overall quality of life. Trends which are highly predictable and slow to evolve, but have a significant impact on society, are those that educational futurologist seek. The Organisation for Economic and Cooperative Development (OECD, 2002) undertook a futures-thinking exercise which sought to identify trends that would affect schooling. These included changing demographics, comparative affluence between the West and the East, the growth of a global economy and altered working patterns, among others.

The changing demographic and the future

In the developed world, the birth rate has fallen and continues to fall dramatically. The total fertility rate (TFR), that is, the number of children each woman gives birth to, in OECD countries has decreased (OECD, 2005). In 2007, it had fallen to 1.6 TFR. Statisticians suggest that it needs to be at 2.1 TFR in order to replace the population (OECD, 2008). Parenthood is also starting much later. There is a strong upward trend in the age at which women have children (Office of National Statistics, 2010). This has two significant, but almost contradictory, consequences for education. Falling numbers of children empties schools and eventually forces them to close, because they are no longer viable. Choice is, therefore, reduced. Fewer children also means less competition for resources. At the same time, there is an increasingly ageing population. Life expectancy rose from 66 years in 1950 to 76 years in 2007. By 2050, it could be 83 years, with a significant number of individuals surviving beyond their nineties (National Institute on Ageing, 2006). This trend suggests that providers should think about shifting the centre of gravity of the education system from the young to the old (OECD, 2008). Facer et al. (2010) agree, suggesting that there must be a realignment of educational resources over what they call the 'life course'. Policy-makers will also need to take into account the consequences of motherhood occurring later in life.

Comparative affluence in the future

There has been a spectacular and sustained economic growth in Western nations over the past 100 years. As a result, the gap between the average citizen in the affluent and the poorest parts of the world is wide and getting wider. It is true that the economies of Asia and China are quickly catching up with Western economies. By 2020, China's economy will have overtaken all others, with the exception of America. At the same time, the Indian economy will overtake or be the equivalent of the biggest in Europe (US National Intelligence Council, 2004: 32). Nevertheless, the disparity between the rich and poor persists. There is also a growing inequality within most of the OECD countries. The boundaries between those who have and those who do not have appears to be hermetically sealed. However, what takes place in one part of the world or, indeed, within a country increasingly has consequences for everybody. This disparity, for example, is a contributing factor in international issues such as environmental degradation, disease transmission and political instability.

Activity

The US National Intelligence Council suggests that by 2020, countries that remain behind in adopting technologies are likely to be those that have failed to pursue policies that support the application of new technologies – such as good governance, universal education and market reforms – and not solely because they are poor (US National Intelligence Council, 2004: 34.) The question for policy-makers is how should the education system be used to address this growing trend. What would you suggest?

Global economy and the future

National economies do not exist in isolation. The trend is for globalization. This has led to the development of multinational companies that increasingly function across, rather than within, the confines of one country (OECD 2010). It means that traditional alliances between nation-states and companies operating inside them are more complex than perhaps they were 50 years ago. These companies, which vary in size and origin, can have significant fiscal and political influence that may conflict with the national priorities. In some cases, these companies have greater financial resources than do many small nations. They are, in essence, the equivalent of states with their own operating mores and, as such, they require employees with different allegiances. The trend towards the globalization of the economy raises questions for policy-makers about the competencies and skills required by the potential workforce.

> ### Activity
>
> Why should it be necessary that, regardless of location, future curriculum developments will have more of a focus on multiple language acquisition and a greater emphasis on global history and geography?

Working patterns in the future

In America and Europe, there has been a clear and sustained long-term decline in the number of hours that employees work. The work hours have almost halved between the middle of the last and the start of the present century. At the same time, there has also been an increase in those (both men and women) engaged in either voluntary or imposed part-time work, although the total varies between countries. These combined factors have led to a number of benefits, including increased leisure time, but there are also a number of resulting penalties. More intensity and the need to constantly adapt are significant feature of modern working practices. Earlier retirement and aging populations also mean the rise of what Frost (2010) refers to as a dependency on the young to provide the majority of the workforce. Questions need to be asked about how best to help people to fill their non-working hours and prepare them to manage stress and change.

An OECD (2008) study into the future of the family added two further trends that have a bearing on education. They are social cohesion and immigration.

Social cohesion and family networks in the future

The face of the family is changing. The trend for couples to live together rather than marry is so powerful in some OECD countries that cohabitation is soon likely to become the norm rather than the exception among those in the prime childbearing age (25 – 34 years) bracket (OECD, 2008). There is, however, a trend shared between those who chose to cohabit and those who choose to marry. Both kinds of union appear to be increasingly unstable, particularly in America and some European countries, leading to more frequent reshaping of family groups. Households will, therefore, become smaller and be likely to form and reform more frequently than they have done in the past. The OCED (2008) speculates that, as a result, a culture of separateness will arise in which things are less likely to be done collectively. This debate extends beyond the family into society as a whole. There appears to be a general unease in countries like the United Kingdom that levels of social engagement continue to decline as a result of the breakdown of the family (Brown, 2008). The rise of individualism is also purported to exacerbate this trend. This is extremely difficult to prove. However, policy-makers need to grapple with these trends by strengthening educational provision in out of school settings to help with assimilation and socialization.

Migration and the future

While most people still live and die close to where they were born, some are on the move. Martin et al. state that at least:

> 160 million people were living outside their country of birth or citizenship in 2000, up from an estimated 120 million in 1990. If the world's migrants were in one place, they would create the world's sixth most-populous country after America, Brazil, China, India and Indonesia. (2002: 3)

Migrants are relocating (either temporarily or permanently) from developing countries to developed countries. The reasons for resettlement include helping to address the shortfall that has arisen as a result of shrinking workforces in the West, income differentials, adverse climate change, burgeoning environment disasters such as water shortages, worsening security and, possibly, the attraction of a better education. Migrants, regardless of whether they are high- or low-skilled, can be single or accompanied by family. Although globally the proportion of migrants to non-migrants has only increased marginally, it is a controversial issue (Martin et al., 2002). The trend is for it to increase. Policy-makers must consider issues of assimilation and how best to develop the requisite language skills in situations where migrants do not speak the dominant language of the country to which they migrate.

Activity

It is clear that the developed and developing world display some conflicting trends, although there is a general convergence towards what is happening in the developed world. For example, the birth rate in parts of the developing world is increasing rather than decreasing (Index Mundi, 2009). What is the significance of this variation in terms of education for both the developed and developing worlds?

Technology and the future

Many studies indicate that technology will have an increasingly significant impact on the education of the future (OECD, 2002, 2008; Facer et al., 2010; Such, 2010). The overall trend is for smaller, faster and cheaper devices. This hypothesis is founded on an observation by the cofounder of Intel, Gordon Moore (1965), that transistor density on integrated circuits would double every two years. Moore's Law, as it became known, is now an accepted dictum. In practice, it means that devices can increasingly undertake more complex tasks, even though the scale and cost of them is considerably reduced. This will lead to widely distributed processing power available through invisible networks that are always connected and are located not only in buildings but in devices and even the clothes we wear. It has made possible the rise of what the futurist Ray Kurzweil (1992) called the age of the intelligent machine. A manifestation of this apparent intelligence, machine-to-machine communication, has meant that, as a part of their primary function, devices can undertake a monitoring role in ways that they have not been able to do in the past. This is what Facer et al. (2010) refer to as self-managing systems. It is feasible for refrigerators to warn when the sell-by dates of the goods they contain are exceeded and order replacements. It may well be possible for cars to diagnose what is wrong, book an appointment at the garage for repairs and relay what has been done to correct the fault. What are referred to as assistive technologies could intervene at a very basic level in the daily lives of those with very specific needs. The well-being of the elderly or infirmed living independent lives could be monitored and, in the event of unacceptable variation, either advise what to do or the information could be relayed to others with a duty of care. For education, this could mean that the home could become:

> a fairly technically well-equipped centre for education and vocational training. Distance learning will tend to reduce exclusion from the ICT culture, as ICT literacy is taught as a by-product of the essential learning experience. The range of educational courses could also expand as narrowcast teaching in a specialist subject can be spread over a global classroom, literally, which should hold enough students to justify the course specialism. (OECD, 2008: 69)

Much of this will be made possible because of the miniaturization of components. The advent of speckled computing neatly illustrates the possibilities that can result from making things much smaller. Speckled computers are not conventional computers but are formed from an amalgam of autonomous programmable semiconductor devices called Specks that can sense, compute and connect to wireless networks. These semiconductor grains are minute, no more than one millimetre cubed, and are self-powered or at least rechargeable. The technology to manufacture them is not new but the development of sensors nodes at nano scale and novel power sources will vastly increase what can be done with them. The Specks are designed to seek each other out and unite to form networks that collaboratively process sensory data. They can be sprayed (they are sometimes referred to as 'smart dust') or speckled onto articles or in locations that are difficult to reach. When combined, they create what Arvind (2005) refers to as a 'computational aura' that can endow everyday objects with sensing, processing and networking capabilities. They could be attached to an educational toy so that how and when it was used can be monitored. This technology has the potential to become all-pervasive. Although still in its early development, Arvind contends that speckled computing will mean:

> intelligent ambient spaces, where you have sensing and computational technology embedded into the physical infrastructure so that it disappears into the environment – much in the same way that cable and electricity networks in built spaces. (Arvind in Futurelab, 2006, 1)

Facer et al. (2010) raise the possibility of another interesting extension of Kurzweil's original concept, some kind of direct union between humans and machines. They highlight the possible emergence of invasive and non-invasive interfaces between the brain and machines, enabling prosthetic enhancement and the externalization of cognitive functions. Science fiction is full of dire warnings of the advent of the cyborg (a biological and artificial organism). Perhaps we are not quite there yet but the technology will become increasingly available to make symbiosis happen. Haptic technology, which makes use of signals from the skin to the central nervous system to provide the users of devices with feedback, is already here. There are a number of mobile phones currently available that do this. Moore's law does not mean that the application of technology follows a linear trajectory. Such (2010) and Facer et al. (2010) contend that every decade there is a fundamental shift in focus and predict that the next one will see a change from networked to ubiquitous (all around us) computing.

> ### Activity
>
> Moore's Law implies that computing power will continue to increase, for the foreseeable future at least. This is manifest in Specks and a similar development called mote (very small) computing. What do you think this will mean for learning and teaching?

Such (2010) suggests that, in addition to the effects of Moore's Law, there are a number of other notable technological trends that will have a bearing on education. Specific locations where we previously had access to people and information will be a thing of the past. Heppel (2007) believes that traditional notions of the classroom will become increasingly redundant. He contends that education will occur wherever there is access to information, walking along a street with what he calls learning channels or even inside an aeroplane. The resources used will appear, metaphorically, to float free in virtual space. This gives rise to what Such (2010) and Facer et al. (2010) both refer to as the formation of a personal digital cloud shaped to meet the needs of itinerant individual learners so that they can engage in formal and informal learning. Perhaps the term 'environment' is more appropriate than 'cloud' in this context because educative experiences are supposed to liberate rather than cast shadows. Support networks will form and reform where appropriate. This leads Green (2010) to contend that education will be messier, more informal, exploratory, experimental and improvised and learning to trust the learner to let go may be of paramount importance. She believes that education in the future will be less about doing things for or to people, and more about doing things with and by people themselves. In such an open and:

> collective and hands-on world, new skills such as mediation, facilitation and good communication will be at a premium, as will an intrapersonal intelligence of balancing the rational, logic and reason, with the non rational, intuition, feelings and the senses. (Green, 2010)

Such (2010) believes that accessing information beyond the immediate (in a form of globalization mirrored by that seen in fiscal matters) will become the accepted norm, for those in the developed world at least. This will generate new personal and enriching information landscapes. Facer et al. (2010)

observe that these information landscapes will be denser, deeper and more diverse than those that exist today because of the trend towards:

> accountability and security, the decreasing cost and increasing availability of digital storage capacity, the development of new forms of bio and genetic information, the ability to digitally tag almost any physical object, space or person, the ability to represent information in diverse modes – all of these developments increase the capacity to simply 'know more stuff about more stuff'. We will be able to gather, store, examine, archive and circulate more data, in more diverse forms, about more aspects of ourselves and our world, than ever before. (Facer et al., 83)

Such (2010) contends that the boundaries between many aspects of contemporary living will become weaker or more permeable. What constitutes work, leisure, employment and retirement at the moment will become far less well defined. Even how different elements of a typical day are structured will change. This will result in what Facer et al. (2010) refer to as the disaggregation of information from the institution and vastly increase the capacity to interact at a distance. Consequently where and when learning take place 'will be subject to new choices, new negotiations, new organizations and accountability' (Such, 2010: 3). The Knowledge Works Foundation (2009) contends that these changes will necessitate the creation of a lightweight, modular learning infrastructure.

One incidental but significant outcome of the combined advance of technology is that those who have grown up with computers will far outnumber those who have not. This will effectively change the skill set of those referred to as digital natives as well as their approach to work (Glenn, 2008). They will however, like their parents, still need to learn throughout their lives.

Future educational scenarios

All the trends above, including the ones that focus on technology, are interconnected. It is very difficult to determine which is the most powerful and, therefore, will have the greatest impact on the future. A truly global economy may be able to develop because of the increased connectivity that nano technologies make possible. However, the movement of people from one country to another may be as equally significant. Rather than play one trend against other, futurologists create scenarios to test their ideas. Scenarios have the potential to help overcome some of the limitations of depending upon prediction and can be useful in developing strategic thinking. They are not meant to be totally realistic but constructs of different hypothetical futures that are internally consistent with plausible interrelationships between clusters of variables. They should be applicable in any national context. Various agencies and researchers including the OECD (2002, 2008), Such (2010) and Facer et al. (2010) have identified a number of possible educational futures resulting from these trends. These take three distinct forms explained below.

Maintaining the status quo – This scenario can be best characterized as business as usual. It suggests that educational establishments will be largely unaffected by external trends and closed to outside pressures. It acknowledges that the school system as we know it is highly resistant to change and will remain essentially what it is today, centralized with complex administrative systems. An internal bureaucracy operating with unique conventions and regulation sustains it. Traditional notions of the teacher persist and the question of their professional status continues to be problematic. Although there is an increased use of digital technology, these are absorbed rather than serve to remodel the system.

Schools redefine themselves – This scenario is sometimes referred to as reschooling. It depicts a future in which schools are strengthened by a recognition that they are still valuable, regardless of whatever changes are taking place. The system is transformed so that they can have a more dynamic and diverse role. Schools become organizations with either strong knowledge or social agenda. In the former, the focus is on experimentation, diversity and innovation. In the latter, they are recognised as the most effective bulwark against fragmentation in society and the family. An emphasis on shared responsibly and non-formal learning predominates in these schools. They will also have very strong local focus. Teacher motivation and status in both has improved and the use of new technology is highly valued.

The rise of the market model – This scenario sees learning and teaching move from formal institution into more diverse, privatized and informal enterprises. Governments increasingly withdraw from education and allow private organizations to fill the gap, although some state-sponsored schools continue to exist. Educational services are increasingly brought rather than provided. This leads to radical reform of the system and the rise of market forces that help shape both the curriculum and how it is taught. There is a strong focus on cognitive outcomes in these schools. An extension of this scenario, sometimes referred to as deschooling, suggests that the current education system will be abandoned completely. Dissatisfaction with education reaches an unacceptable level. Schools are replaced by learning networks, although other institutions may follow. These networks might be based on business, cultural, community and religious interests or any combination of all of them. They can be local, national or even international. Teachers in the traditional sense disappear and new learning professionals emerge. The demarcation of roles between all participants in this process, the teacher, the taught and whoever else might be in the networked community become blurred. Digital technology is at the heart of this development (Tinio, 2003; Lovelace, 2007; Deed et al., 2010; Facer et al., 2010; Such, 2010).

Activity

It appears that trends in technology might help to bring about future in which we all have the equivalent of our own personal digital cloud, information landscapes become richer and deeper and traditional locations where learning can take place will be abandoned. Considers each one of these in turn and decide how likely it is to occur, the impact it will have if it does become a reality and how quickly the effect will be felt. Taking into account your thinking on the technology issue and the other trends now decide which one of the three scenarios (if any) is most likely to occur and identify why.

Conclusions

There is always the considerable risk in commenting about the future that it says far more about what is happening today rather than tomorrow. Facer et al. (2010: 89) argue that our ideas are too often based upon the taken-for-granted assumptions of 'inevitable futures promoted by globalizing discourses of dominant economic and political groups'. Who is to say what economic or environmental disaster might befall us that wipes away all previously held assumptions? The rise of China and Asia may prompt new political, social and educational paradigms which are rooted in the ancient cultures on which they are founded and the ideologies that characterise their recent history (Jaques, 2009). It is legitimate however to reflect upon all the forces such as changes in birth rates about which much is known to help to shape our view of the future. Regardless of the effect of other trends, the technology mantra of ever-faster, ever-cheaper and ever-smaller will hold true and increasingly shape life, whether you are one of the chronic poor in Rio di Janeiro or the fashionable elite walking along the boulevards in Paris.

Vernor Vinge, a retired mathematics professor and author of science fiction novels such as *A Fire Upon the Deep* and *Rainbows End*, believes that technology could, in the not so distant future, be used to amplify intelligence to the point of creating superhuman beings. Heppell (2010) contends that even if the future is rich in promise, education does not have a very good track record in using innovative technologies. He points out that ballpoint pens were banned in a number of schools when they first emerged because some argued that handwriting might be ruined as a result of them. This might appear to be a quaint notion, but some pupils were also prevented from using early calculators that could be programmed, on the grounds that it was cheating. Technology could rapidly advance beyond the ability of the educational community to absorb it. To some such, as Brown (2008), this might not be a bad thing. He contends that technology will increasingly promote individualism and erode shared experiences unless we resist its charms. He laments that we no longer have to:

> watch the same film in the cinema as our whole community because we all have televisions at home; we no longer have to watch with our family because we all have TVs in our bedrooms; we no longer watch the same programmes as others because of multi-channel TV. We no longer even have to listen to the chatter of those around us on public transport, as we have an iPod plugged into our ears. (Brown, 2008: 11)

Alienation as consequence of the advance of technology is common theme but the OECD (2008, 22) argues that, although there is a trend towards less contact and cohesion in family groups, 'modern technologies, mobile communications and computers, make such a future far less certain'.

Such (2010), on a more cautionary note, advises that technology of the future should not be regarded as a quick fix, a silver bullet, for the complex problems we will encounter.

Big Question

Watkins (1942: 214), when writing about the future of education during the Second World War, was moved to point out that this new order of things that were emerging was 'not the arbitrary creation of a few geniuses nor of a few fanatical mentalities. Rather, it is the by-product of economic and social forces that have found their way irresistibly, cutting deep channels through the soil of traditions and institutions' (Watkins, 1942: 214). Perhaps then the real question we should be asking about the link between technology and education is not what will happen but what do we want to happen?

Further reading

Facer, K. and Sandford, R. (2010) The next 25 years? Future scenarios and future directions for education and technology, *Journal of Computer Assisted Learning*, Vol. 26, No 1, 4–93.

Kurzweil, R. (2005) *The Singularity Is Near: When Humans Transcend Biology*, New York: Viking Penguin.

OECD (2002) *Schooling for Tomorrow – The Starter Pack: Futures Thinking in Action,* available from www.oecd.org/document/33/0,3343,en_2649_35845581_38981601_1_1_1_1,00.html – Last accessed 11/03/ 2011.

OECD (2008) *The Future of the Family to 2030*, Available from www.oecd.org/dataoecd/11/34/42551944.pdf – Last accessed 11/03/2011.

Such, D. (2010) *Education Futures, Teachers and Technology*, Bristol, Futurelab.

Useful websites

De-Schooling

http://deschoolingsociety.digress.it/ – Last accessed 11/03/ 2011.

http://democracyandeducation.wetpaint.com/page/The+Deschooling+Movement – Last accessed 11/03/ 2011.

Education and the Future

www.teachingexpertise.com/articles/tda-futures-project-the-future-of-education-1790 – Last accessed 11/03/ 2011.

Futures Thinking

www.forumforthefuture.org/projects/futures – Last accessed 11/03/ 2011.

George Orwell Novel *1984*

www.online-literature.com/orwell/1984/ – Last accessed 11/03/ 2011.

Intelligent Ambient Spaces

www.jorgelino.com/index.php?id=45 – Last accessed 11/03/ 2011.

Moore's Law

www.mooreslaw.org/ – Last accessed 11/03/ 2011.

Technology and the Future

www.futureforall.org/ – Last accessed 11/03/ 2011.

The Changing Demographic

www.highereducation.org/reports/pa_decline/decline-impact-demographics.shtml/ – Last accessed 11/03/ 2011.

Virtual Worlds and Education

9

Chapter Outline

Introduction

The term 'virtual education' has been applied to learning and teaching in which a curriculum package is delivered online through the medium of digital technology. It is manifest in two specific forms, virtual schools and virtual worlds. Virtual schools have proliferated in countries like the United States and are fast becoming one of the major growth trends in education (Grubbs et al., 2009). They are a variant of distance learning and although Russell (2004) claims they come in many formats, including those in which students undertake online instruction in a traditional classroom. In the context of this book, they are taken to mean those schools in which the delivery is entirely online, with students unlikely to have any physical contact with their teachers. Virtual education has also been applied to packages or systems that make use of virtual worlds. These are typified by the use of avatars and otherworldliness. The emergence of new and more sophisticated versions of virtual worlds has contributed to a revival of interest by educators in their educational potential. They generally have a game-like quality and allow learning and teaching to be undertaken through the extended use of cyberspace, a term first coined by Gibson (1986) to describe a metaphorical location in virtual space, which facilitates communication on a grand scale between many. Although the definition of virtual worlds is still evolving, Castronova (2005) regards them as synthetic worlds made by humans for humans that can be maintained and regulated by computers under certain circumstances. Minocha et al. (2008: 187) refers to them as a location in cyberspace which 'has simulated bodies in simulated places'.

What this chapter will identify is the nature of all the principle formats of virtual education, although it will be primarily concerned with virtual worlds. It will seek to establish that virtual schools and virtual worlds used in an appropriate context have so many valuable learning affordances that they are here to stay (Dalgarno et al., 2010). This chapter will also establish that both formats position the learner at the heart of the learning process in ways that more traditional approaches do not. They require at the very least a modification in pedagogy that some teachers find problematic. It will contend that a sceptical profession should also develop a greater understanding of the educational possibilities of virtual gaming. This chapter will posit that learning in the virtual and physical worlds has equal validity, providing that ethical issues can be addressed. It will also contend that the disconnection between the virtual and physical worlds sometimes experienced as a result of avatar representation and a lack of realism in virtual worlds have positive as well as negative educational benefits.

The nature of virtual schools

The mode of instruction in virtual schools is mainly done online through Virtual Learning Environments (VLEs) such as Moodle or Blackboard. They are regarded as virtual not only because they use digital technology and the Internet but also because they do not have a campus, buildings or classrooms. At present, no single model prevails, either in terms of organization structure or single source of funding. However, they are to a great extent home schools, in which the 'instructional time, student behaviour and learning expectations are managed in the home setting under the locus of control of the learning coach' (Rodney, 2010: 222). Parents or guardians also play a significant role in them because much of the work is done at home. In a typical virtual school, a learner would log into a learning management system and work through modules and assignments. Some schools supplement this online material with offline resources. Communication is either synchronous or asynchronous and virtual attendance is tracked. The Florida Virtual School is currently one of the largest (154,000 enrolments), offering part-time courses to students in Grades 6 – 12 (as a supplement to their normal education) and fulltime courses to those in Grade 12 (Rodney 2010). The school, which is accredited by the Florida Department of Education, boasts that it provides education at any time, any place, any path and any pace. It is funded through local taxes and is free to residents of the state. Non-residents have to pay fees for the courses in which they are registered. Grubbs et al. (2009) claim that the main reason for the development of virtual schools has been economic. Because they are free of physical infrastructure and allow scarce resources, such as expert teachers, to be employed more widely, they require less funding than does a conventional school. However, the economic benefit may be illusory, because the start-up costs, in particular, can be high. Melnick (2002) rather grandly claims that they offer access to a global classroom in which knowledge can be democratized and the curriculum modified rapidly to meet ever-changing needs. This could be said of other forms of distance learning, but virtual schools more closely reflect contemporary lifestyles of the group they seek to attract in that they are open 24 hours a day and can expose learners to a vast array of resources. Tucker (2007) suggests that perhaps their greatest potential lies not solely as pathfinders, employing technology at the cutting edge, but as decentralizing agencies that could promote system reform. Rodney (2010: 224) concurs, believing that they provide 'a unique bridge between the government, its contractual front line agencies of educational services and parents'. A number of commentators, including Grubbs et al. (2009), note that increased ICT capability for both learners and teachers is an incidental advantage of participation in successful virtual schools. These benefits are not available to that part of the community that does not have access to the relevant software and hardware. However although this inclusion issue is significant pupils like the expanded curriculum offerings, technology rich environment and education at any time and in any place available in virtual schools (Reid et al., 2009). This is despite the fact that they appear to operate in a similar way to traditional schools, in that the education they provide is mediated through the written and spoken word.

Activity

Melnick (2002: 87) suggests technology infrastructures 'can be both supportive and preventative. When networks go down, or applications crash, backlogs are created as the learning process stops. Students lose work, and teachers lose their ability to communicate with their students until the problem is fixed'. This potential frustration is one of the reasons proffered by Roblyer (2008) for the high drop-out rate in virtual schools. Can you think of others?

Overview of virtual worlds

Unlike virtual schools, which are essentially two dimensional, virtual worlds try to emulate three dimensions. The capacity to make smooth temporal changes and interactivity, in addition to their ability to capitalize on the nature of human perception to provide an illusion of three dimensions, are the most important features that distinguish them from the VLEs used in virtual schools. Virtual worlds have what Hew et al. (2010) refer to as the capacity to simulate space. This could mean creating a virtual replica of a real university campus so that potential or even new students can take a tour of various buildings, including libraries and residential accommodation, prior to their arrival. Equally, it could mean creating an alternative universe that users can explore with impunity. These simulated spaces can also be occupied through avatars controlled by external peripheral devices, such as a keyboard or a mouse. Virtual worlds have the capacity to be communication spaces. Like virtual schools, they can employ many forms of asynchronous and synchronous communication tools such as text-based messaging, including email. Opportunities for additional forms communication are also available, including avatars that can gesture and adopt different postures. Heightened levels of realism can result which, according to Minocha et al. (2008: 188), invoke '. . . the Earth and a body as metaphors for interaction' in ways that blogs and wikis (software that allows users to easily create and edit Web page content) and their like cannot. Virtual worlds have an additional capacity that can heighten this ersatz corporeal experience. They allow users to act upon the virtual world in what Hew et al. (2010) regard as experiential spaces, mimicking what happens in the real world. Virtual hands can lift and rotate and drop virtual objects as readily as real hands can do with real objects. These are known as 'virtual manipulatives'. While students in the past might have handled a cube or a sphere to learn about shapes and how they relate to each other, virtual manipulatives can do the same for those currently involved in education. However, they bring the added bonus of being able to accomplish this in a wide range of unlikely contexts that extend the notion of learning by doing to include the fantastic. Zeller (2008) contends that virtual manipulatives have great potential to positively affect the quality of learning. Junior surgeons in some countries find it difficult to acquire the necessary experience to undertake neurosurgical operations because of the increased chance of litigation if something goes wrong and because of the limitations on training hours. Visualization software using images from MRI (magnetic resonance imaging) scans can model relevant parts of the brain so that they can worked upon them with sufficient degree of realism to mimic real surgical training. Vloeberghs et al. (2007: 262) believe that simulations containing virtual manipulatives contribute to 'a decrease in the number of adverse events in surgery'.

Activity

De Freitas (2008) suggests that immersive virtual worlds can be grouped into five categories, although her categorization is not definitive. These are *Role Play Worlds* such as World of Warcraft and Guild Wars, which are role-playing games driven by quests with different levels and rewards; *Social Worlds* such as Second Life and Active Worlds, which tend to be immersive without specific quests and focus community-building activities and communication between individuals; *Working Worlds* such as Project Wonderland and Metaverse which focus on corporate communications and facilities to support business activity; *Training Worlds* such as the Online Interactive Virtual Environment (OLIVE) for the American Army, which has a singular focus on developing specific professional skills and knowledge; and *Mirror Worlds* such as Google Earth and Planet Earth that offer a 3D representation of the real world that can embed onto other unrelated applications. Using the Internet, find and explore different examples of as many of the principle types of virtual worlds mentioned above. Decide which might be used in education and state at what level and why.

Formats of virtual worlds

Massively multiplayer online games (MMOs) and multi-user virtual environments (MUVEs) are currently the two dominant virtual world formats. MMOs, which are sometimes referred to as massively multiplayer online role-playing games, or MMORPGs, are over 20 years old (de Freitas, 2008). Ever

Quest is typical of the genre. In this game, players create their own characters from a menu of 16 different classes of creature, whose roles are guided
by an underlying narrative or mythology. These characters are charged with
exploring a fantasy world, seeking treasure and experience points, thus gain-
ing power and prestige and new abilities as they progress from level to level.
The number of active subscribers currently exceeds 4 million and the system
supports 50,000 simultaneous users, mainly in the United Sates and Europe.
Children under the age of 13 are only allowed limited access to some of the
features of the game. MUVEs are the younger cousin of MMOs. They are less
prescriptive and allow for greater flexibility in how they can be employed.
Some have been used to help students undertake science-based activities,
while promoting socially responsive behaviour. River City is a typical educational MUVE. It helps to demonstrate many of the uses that Dieterle et al.
(2008) suggest that MUVEs have put to in education. It is also worthy of
closer examination because it:

- Is a well established and sophisticated package.
- Draws upon various geographical, historical and social themes that allow complex
  ideas to be explored.
- Makes use of the virtual world as a communication space, an experimentation
  space and a simulation of space to some degree or other.

River City was developed by Harvard and Arizona State universities in 2002
and is housed on a platform called Active Worlds. Harvard was also the
alma mater of Facebook founder Mark Zuckerberg. The National Science
Foundation of America funded the project. It was originally created to teach
pupils from three public middle schools (Grades 6 – 9) about scientific experimentation and has gone through many stages of development as technology has improved and knowledge of how to apply virtual worlds to learning
has increased. By 2007–2008, the Active Worlds project had grown to involve
5,000 students and 100 teachers in 12 states, using both the English and
Spanish languages as the medium for learning and teaching.

The virtual environment in which activities take place is an imaginary
town, typical of late nineteenth-century America, eponymously called River
City. The town is divided into numbered sections with different geographical
characteristics, with a river flowing through them. The mountainous area
in which the river originates is home to the wealthy and is the location for a
university. The middle class live on the periphery, where the river enters the

town. It then flows through a shopping district and finally past tenements and the town dump. A nearby bog provides the residents of the tenements with a place to bathe, swim and wash their clothes. It is a complex terrain that has an impact on where water can run off, and insects propagate.

Although the details can vary in terms of how the MUVE is used in different projects, there are some features common to all. The main goal for participants is to discover why the virtual residents of the town are becoming ill. In particular, they are asked to determine why the incidence of disease among the poor is greater than that among other groups. An integral part of the learning experience is to develop a theory about what causes sickness to pervade River City and create experiments to test this hypothesis. Students can explore the environment as avatars and interact with computer-based agents (virtual residents) and digital objects such as video clips and pictures of real items from the period housed in the Smithsonian Institute. Students can also interact with the avatars of other students. Scattered throughout the virtual environment are signs and books that link to relevant web pages. Data stations allow student to takes samples for analysis in appropriate locations and to examine the water under a microscope. There are also big catcher nets to determine insect numbers. Communication is achieved through a text-based interface that accompanies the principle screen showing the virtual environment. This interface also provides additional information through still and moving images. Student participants encounter muddy streets on their travels through River City and their experience is further heightened by the use of auditory stimuli such as the sound of virtual residents coughing. In their avatar form they can run, swim and even fly as well as walk. Real and virtual notebooks are kept to record ideas as they develop. Pupils are enrolled at River City University and learn about scientific method. They run experiments and collect and analyze data and report to River City officials on their discoveries and make recommendations about what to do and ultimately share their findings with other student participants.

Student participants are able to alter a single factor in one of two identical River Cities to see what happens. Although the actual curriculum material is designed to last approximately 17 hours, life in the virtual world operates on accelerated time (the equivalent of a year) so that participants can observe the effect the change more readily. The phenomena that students investigate in River City are too complex for one individual to master in the time available and therefore they have to work as part of a team. Ketelhut et al. (2010) sought to establish how well River City performs as an aide to learning and teaching. In order to ascertain this, they undertook a research project with 500 seventh-grade students and their teachers from a US Mid-Atlantic school district. The participants were asked to carry out scientific enquiry through either a virtual or non-virtual version of River City. Those in the latter category were allowed to undertake physical experimentation, while those in the former could only use the virtual tools. Ketelhut et al. (2010: 165) established that for both the teachers and the taught, virtual experimentation was 'the highlight of the experience'. In some cases, the students with the virtual experience surpassed the performance of a control group when their capacity for scientific enquiry was compared. Intriguingly, Ketelhut et al. (2010) also discovered that the girls using the virtual version of River City outperformed all other students. They suggested that this has more to do with the collaborative nature of the task rather than the use of technology. Teachers, while recognizing the enthusiasm of their students for virtual experience, also expressed concerns about managing technological resources as well as pedagogical issues.

Activity

Dalgarno et al. (2010) suggest that there are five affordances that virtual worlds possess. They can be used to facilitate learning that enhances the spatial knowledge of the domain being explored. They can allow learning to take place that would be impractical or impossible to carry out in the real world. They increase levels of motivation and engagement. They offer opportunities to transfer knowledge and skills to the real situations. Activities can be richer and more collaborative in nature. Using either the River City example provide in the text or one you have found yourself, identify practical examples of each of these affordances.

Key issues in the educational use of virtual worlds

There are many issues that the use of virtual worlds in education raise including whether they inadvertently create a new digital divide, what moral principles govern their operation, if they generate new forms of identity, what is the right balance between real and virtual experience and their relationship to gaming.

Restricted uptake

Most of the work on the use of virtual worlds in education has taken place in a small number of countries such as the United States and the United Kingdom, which have the appropriate expertise, infrastructure and resources. In these locations, both students and teachers are most likely to be accustomed to virtual worlds. Nevertheless, effective participation virtual worlds have to offer depends on their comfort with a multi-modal set of visual resources and practices. Even so, they may be 'familiar to some . . . but not to all' (Savin Baden et al., 2010: 130). While this may indicate that there are genuine technical and training issues to overcome, a number of commentators believe that there are more fundamental issues affecting uptake. Savin Baden et al. (2010) suggest that immersive virtual learning necessitates that the multiplicity of roles and fluidity of relationships that characterize traditional pedagogy have to be redefined because of the unique nature of the experience. This uniqueness results from what Dalgarno et al. (2010) refer to as presence and immersion. Presence is regarded as the sense of being in a place, and immersion is the objective and measurable property of the system or environment that leads to this sense of presence. It is the size of the step change needed to fully accommodate this phenomenon that causes resistance. The research by Ketelhut et al. (2010) seems to confirm that although teachers can see the benefit of virtual worlds, they are suspicious of what it means for them. Ironically, the situation is compounded because more established text-based digital tools still allow the teacher to continue to act in ways that correspond to face-to-face communication. The research literature, currently available, which could help to address teacher concerns, tends to reflect regional rather than more global issues. In some ways, this corresponds to what happened with the introduction of the teaching machine in the 1950s and the computer in the 1980s.

Savin Baden et al. (2010: 125) believe that, despite the pitfalls, it would be helpful to situate or theorize learning in virtual worlds by turning to:

> newer and emergent learning theories, such as the supercomplexity model (Barnett 2000), threshold concepts (Meyer and Land 2005; Land, Meyer, and Smith 2008) or the conversational framework. (Laurillard, 2002)

Ethics

Olliges et al. (2003: 15) suggest that the idea of social responsibility in an online medium has 'led to the creation of courses in cyber-ethics and to the development of organizations devoted to instilling an understanding of such in all participants of the online medium'. There is no doubt that experiences in cyberspace can contribute to the development of what Sheehey et al. (2007) refer to as 'ethical wisdom'. Indeed, it is one of the cornerstones of River City that combines real and virtual exchanges of ideas. However, the use of virtual worlds as an educational tool raises a set of unique ethical questions. While Cheshire (2010) finds much in virtual education to commend, he is concerned about the accuracy involved in simulating real events and what this might mean to participants. After a visit to Auschwitz in which he movingly describes how the vast size of the grim landscape staggers the senses, he concluded that no virtual re-enactment, regardless of how realistic, would have the authenticity of a genuine visit. He also raises the equally important point that it might lack credibility because:

> it would be all too easy to modify or otherwise tamper with the details and how they are presented. Scale as measured by a finger gliding across a computer touchpad is not the same as distance measured by how fatigued one's legs feel after walking the full length of the grounds at Birkenau. The camp's physical proportions echo its moral proportions. Having recently walked there the camp's dust still clings to my shoes and memories to my mind. (Cheshire, 2010: 140)

Activity

Discuss if it possible to create a virtual world dealing honestly and fully with issues such as the genocide that took place in Cambodia from 1975 to 1979 and avoid the macabre and mawkish? What would you do to maximize the educational value of such a resource?

Avatars

Savin Baden et al. (2010: 130) suggest that the use of avatars 'introduces a set of possibilities surrounding identity work, meaning-making and self-representation'. Peña et al. (2009) believe they can improve confidence and generate empathy between those who adopt such a form of online personality. Avatars also appear to provide a level of anonymity that is liberating to those who find normal communication difficult (Dickey, 2005; Martino, 2007). The fact that avatars can be given powers in the virtual world that we don't possess in real life raises a number of interesting possibilities. Zielke (2009, 12) notes that one of the key motivators for people with disabilities who participate in Second Life (SL) is the ability to:

> virtually experience physical activities such as dancing, running, walking, and even flying. Accordingly, some SL residents with real-life disabilities create avatars that do not display these same physical characteristics and thereby explore the fantasy of not being bound to their real-life bodies, which might require wheelchairs, canes or other mobility aids. (Zielke, 2009: 12)

Participants are also given the option of being represented by avatars with obvious physical disabilities. Peña et al. (2009) welcome the opportunity that virtual worlds have to embed more positive stereotypes within them. However, *The Lancet* (1991) warned that there is a danger that those who are challenged in real world in one way or another may prefer what appears to be an angst-free virtual world. Avatars have been successfully used with younger as well as older children as a means of facilitating interaction (Bailey et al., 2003). However, Riedl (2004) found that a number of adults had difficulty interacting with the avatars of those they did not know. This may be because, although avatars can be moved next to each other, they currently lack the facility to clearly signal emotions, often staring into space, inert and appearing to be unengaged (Minocha et al., 2008). In addition, Savin Baden et al. (2010: 125) observed that among some groups 'online modes of identity formation were viewed negatively, primarily as the true self being deceitfully threatened by the online being'.

Activity

It appears that younger rather than older users of virtual worlds have fewer problems with adopting an avatar identity. What implications dose this have for teachers and teacher training?

Real or not

The degree of presence and immersion an individual feels in a virtual world is contingent to a certain extent on what Dalgarno et al. (2010) regard as the level of representational fidelity and the range of facilities available to promote learner interaction. Representational fidelity depends upon a number of factors, including the realism of the display, the smoothness and speed with which changes and motion occur and the consistency of object behaviours. Learner interaction results from features such as the ability to manipulate objects and the capacity to engage in verbal and non-verbal forms of communication. It is, therefore, tempting to suggest that, depending on the context, the transfer of learning from the virtual to the actual world is somehow dependent upon the levels of realism. However, even in packages with relatively low levels of realism such as River City, participants engaged in virtual experimentation have little problem with applying this learning in the real world (Ketelhut et al., 2010). Indeed, they suggest that the virtual experience is more beneficial than real experimentation. Yet there is a commonly held assumption that experiences in some virtual worlds are not real. Ketelhut et al. (2010) suggests that that the expression 'real world' be replaced with the phrase 'physical world'. Twining (2009) contends that they are different realities with equal legitimacy. Even if it is impossible to reconcile the virtual and physical world in this way, White et al. (2010) regards the disjuncture between them as an education opportunity and not as a threat. The fantastical nature of some virtual worlds is so far beyond anything real that they cause participants discomfort, which can be the foundation of experiential learning (White et al., 2010).

To play or not to play

It is clear that the education community on the whole has more readily adopted MUVEs rather than MMOs, in pursuit of new and innovative approaches to learning and teaching. MUVEs are easier to employ because their inherent openness allows users to modify them to fit an extensive range of contexts. They have been employed to:

- Create online communities for pre and in service teacher training
- Help students understand and experience history
- Promote social development through cultures of enrichment
- Provide an environment in which programming can take place
- Explore new mathematical concepts
- Undertake scientific enquiry (Dieterle et al., 2008)

MMOs have been less widely adopted in educational circles because they are strongly connected with entertainment. White et al. (2010) suggest that educators find it impossible to see beyond the fantastic creatures, elves, goblins and their like that populate them. In addition, MMOs like EverQuest, a fantasy game involving dwarves and wizards, appear to have an unashamed association with conflict and commerce, whereas MUVEs like Quest Atlantis, in which participants gain points for social responsibility and compassionate behaviour rather than slaying dragons and acquiring wealth, are more obviously value driven. However, Sandford et al. (2005) notes that teachers appear to underestimate the depth of knowledge required to participate fully in games and some older pupils need to be convinced that playing can equate to learning. They suggest that formal educational environments are:

> very different to the informal contexts in which games are usually played, and bring with them many constraints that make introducing games as learning tools more of a challenge than might be thought. (Sandford et al., 2005: 11)

Despite the association of some MMOs with violence, it would be a mistake to ignore their educational potential. Gee (2003) argues that good teaching, after all, allows the learner in any context to play the game of a geographer or historian or a scientist. Additionally, the great depth of expertise that resides in both the amateur and professional gaming communities for developing interesting and exciting virtual activities should not be marginalized or ignored by those involved in education. However, while there are some who are quick to question the educational worth of virtual gaming, research investigating their learning potential in classrooms is still in its infancy (Merchant, 2010).

Conclusions

Learners and teachers and those who manage education systems all concede that virtual schools and virtual worlds have worth. Students and pupils value being able to figuratively move around freely and act in, and on, a three dimensional virtual space and the opportunity to form virtual relationships in virtual worlds (Hew et al., 2010). Teachers recognize the value of learning in this context, although some struggle with the overly student-centred nature of the experience (Ketelhut et al., 2010). Managers and policy-makers seem to be attracted to the notion of using virtual schools in particular because of the apparent efficiency gains that can be accrued from not having capital and transportation costs (Anderson et al., 2006). The creation of virtual teachers, another potential use of avatars, also appears to offer the potential to make financial savings in much the same way as the expert teacher was purported to do so when both radio and television were first employed in an educational context. Education in both virtual schools and virtual worlds is dependent upon the availability, cost and reliability of the necessary technology. Levels of understanding on how best to engage with them on the part of both the teacher and the taught determine their effectiveness as educational tools. A whole set of virtual behaviours and protocols and perhaps a new pedagogy must be established. Virtual worlds could distort or even create an alternative and possibly addictive reality for participants. This latent capacity must be considered in any debate about their educational value. There is almost a need for some form of acculturation as we transcend from the physical to the virtual world. Although this can be challenging, distinct opportunities for learning can result and they should not be lost. Despite these challenges, White et al. (2010) contend that in virtual worlds learning would appear to:

> carve a different path, in which participants' experience is actually secondary, mediated through vision, yet such is its power to draw in and engage that, together with the human ability to project and imagine, participants have the impression of learning through primary experience. (White et al., 2010: 192)

Educators need to understand how best to make use of this capacity and resolve the tension between virtual gaming and learning. They should recognize that as well as being a motivational tool, virtual games can also help the teacher to meet curricular objectives and develop skills and competencies (Sandford et al., 2005).

Big question

The technology to make virtual worlds more immersive will be available shortly. The clamour from the young in particular will be to embrace them fully in all aspects of life. Is it necessary or desirable to resist their use, particularly in education?

Further reading

Cheshire, W. (2010) Doing no harm to Hippocrates: Reality and virtual reality in ethics education, *Ethics and Medicine*, Vol. 23, No 3, 137–42.

Ketelhut, D. and Nelson, B. (2010) Designing for real-world scientific inquiry in virtual environments, *Educational Research*, Vol. 52, No 2, 151–67.

Savin Baden, M., Gourlay, L., Tombs, C., Steils, N., Tombs, G. and Mawer, M. (2010) Situated pedagogies, positions and practices in immersive virtual worlds, *Educational Research*, Vol. 52, No 2, 123–33.

Tucker, B. (2007) *Laboratories of Reform: Virtual High Schools and Innovation in Public Education, Education Sector Reports*, Available from www.educationsector.org/publications/laboratories-reform-virtual-high-schools-and-innovation-public-education – Last accessed 11/03/2011.

White, D. and Le Cornu, A. (2010) Eventedness and disjuncture in virtual worlds, *Educational Research*, Vol. 52, No. 2, 183–96.

Useful websites

AppEdTech

www.lesn.appstate.edu/aet/aet.htm – Last accessed 11/03/11.

Education and Virtual Worlds

www.vwbpe.org/ – Last accessed 11/03/11.

Latin American Virtual School

www.world-virtual-school.com/latinamerica/ – Last accessed 11/03/11.

Mirror Worlds

www.youtube.com/watch?v=ArgE5nDjmgE – Last accessed 11/03/11.

Quest Atlantis

http://atlantis.crlt.indiana.edu/ – Last accessed 11/03/11.

River City

http://128.103.176.29/rivercityproject/ – Last accessed 11/03/11.

Schome

www.schome.ac.uk/wiki/The_Schome_Park_Programme – Last accessed 11/03/11.

Tapped IN

http://tappedin.org/tappedin/ – Last accessed 11/03/11.

Training Worlds

www.defense-aerospace.com/articles-view/release/3/125263/-pentagon-plans-avatar_based-virtual-training-world.html – Last accessed 11/03/11.

Virtual Schools

http://devvirtualschool.ncsl.org.uk/ – Last accessed 11/03/11.

www.shambles.net/pages/school/vschools/ – Last accessed 11/03/11.

Whyville

www.whyville.net/smmk/nice – Last accessed 11/03/11.

10 Enhancement Technologies, Transhumanism and Education

Introduction

Education has long been regarded by writers from Dewey (1966) to Freire (1974) as a means of improving the human condition (Bostrom, 2003). Technology has been viewed similarly, particularly in relationship to helping those who for one reason or another have additional needs. New technologies are emerging which can enhance not only the physical but cognitive abilities of the majority as well as those with disabilities. The resulting devices, many of which are connected to the user in some form of symbiosis between human and machine, are either here now or well on the way to becoming a reality. At the same time, experimentation with chemical rather than electro–mechanical enhancement of intellectual performance is being undertaken. Advances in neuroscience are also increasing the range of what can be done to improve cognition. The impact of these developments on educational provision required in the future will be significant. These enhancement technologies and the ideas that surround them are also being enthusiastically seized upon by a group of thinkers such as Bakhurst (2008), Bostrom (2003) and

Doede (2009), who believe they offer a golden opportunity to address many of the ills that currently blight us, such as ageing. They contend that a confluence of all these technologies will result in the division between man and machine becoming indistinguishable. Education in this context will not only be different but beyond anything already imagined.

This chapter accordingly will examine challenging issues. It seeks to bring together some of the principle themes evident in previous parts of the book by exploring the transformative and fantastical future that is possible through technology and education. The evolutionary journey into a post human future (humanity in a form unrecognizable today) that it signals will help to bring into sharp relief the following questions:

- To what extent is it desirable for education to embrace these new technologies?
- What role should education have in informing the wider societal debate about these technologies?

Enhancement technology and education

Prosthetic devices of one sort or another have been around for a long time. They are generally used to allow those with damaged limbs or some form of impairment to function more readily. However, a new generation of prosthetic devices controlled by the brain are emerging, which make it possible to enhance the human condition rather than simply address a deficit. Cochlear implants which improve the hearing of those who suffer from deafness and replacement limbs regulated by direct connection to the body are typical of this new genus. Both are controlled by an interface that links the brain and machine together. In the past the connection between user and the device has been far less intimate. It will not be long before it is possible to enhance cognitive abilities in a similar way. The technology used to develop cognitive prosthetics, which are currently designed to address the needs of those with brain injuries, could be applied to augment the intellectual abilities of the majority (Geake, 2008). So-called smart pills or cognitive enhancers are a similar development. They evolved from drugs which were designed to help Alzheimer suffers with memory loss. One of these drugs, Donepezil, which operates by inhibiting the chemical cholinesterase in the brain, thus allowing it to work at higher levels of efficiency, has been found to significantly improve the memory of healthy young adults (Gron et al., 2005). Addereral, which is normally used to treat attention deficit hyperactivity disorder (ADHD), has been found to boost concentration. Much current educational practice would be directly challenged by the idea that any technology could be routinely employed to bypass natural aptitude. It would give rise to a debate that has resonated for many years in sport about the legitimacy of enhancing performance by what are regarded as artificial means (Rigney, 2004). This is becoming such a pressing issue that Turner et al. (2008) urge that as our scientific understanding advances, there is a need for 'educators, the government, academics and the public to start an open debate about these issues' (Turner et al., 2008: 110–11).

Activity

A school has decided to boost the performance of its pupils by offering a freely available smart pill, proven to have no detrimental physical side effects, to all who want it. While a number of parents welcomed this action, a vociferous few object in the strongest possible terms that human intelligence is a sacred gift and to tamper with it in this way is contrary to divine will. The school has called a meeting to discuss this issue. With which group would you side and why?

Neuroscience and education

Teachers with a clear appreciation of how the brain acquires a particular canon of knowledge would be able to provide suitable learning experiences founded on this understanding. Cognitive neuroscience and the technology it employs can now offer such insight.

Educational neuroscience, although not as directly invasive as the new generation of prosthetic devices or smart pills, can also be regarded as an enhancement technology. In the past educators have had a poor record of making use of neuroscience. Samuels (2009) has suggested that it was once possible for educators to ignore the relationship between the science of how the brain functions and learning, because the technological means to study it *in vivo* (within the living) was not available. Many recent advancements in neuroimaging technology have now given neuroscientists unprecedented opportunities to view the live brain at work. The tools used most frequently to do this are magnetic resonance imaging (MRI) and functional MRI (fMRI) scanners, which convert the measurement of blood flow in the brain into images that can be displayed readily on a computer screen. Blood flow, in this context, can be equated with levels of brain activity. This allows researchers to observe what happens when an individual is engaged in actions such as computation, recalling previously learned information or even reasoning about social situations and the like. It also allows them to determine how an impaired brain functions in comparison to an undamaged brain. The neural basis of reading in particular is one area that has become better understood because of the use of MRI and fMRI scanners. Research into the neurological basis of reading has revealed that phonological and orthographic processing, essential to the act of reading in both children and adults, occur in different regions of the brain (Ansari, 2008). This is very helpful in addressing dyslexia and other similar difficulties. By examining the brain activity profiles of those with this condition before and after the use of different structured reading remediation programmes, the most effective treatment can be determined. There is also another benefit that can directly enhance a human being in a similar way to a prosthetic device. Neurofeedback, made possible by MRI scanners and other technologies, not only allows the scientist to view brain activity but for the individual to positively alter his or her brain state. These scanners can generate visual, audio or hepatic (or a combination of all three) stimuli that represent levels of specific activity in different regions of the brain. An individual would, as result of this information, be able to adjust the appropriate region in order to cope best with a stressful situation or an activity of some sort such as art or music. Singer (2006) describes being cocooned in an MRI machine trying to manage the chronic back pain that plagued him for years by controlling an image of a series of fires on a screen using only thought. The image represented activity in the cingulated cortex and right and left insula regions of his brain, which are associated with pain control. His task was to manage the size of the fires. Such is the power of neurofeedback that by repeatedly exercising targeted parts of the brain, permanent changes in the circuitry responsible for hearing or vision can be achieved (Singer, 2006). When employed with cognitive behavioural therapy, this technique can also alter negative thought patterns that are associated with depression. In education, neurofeedback could be put to a number of uses when the technology required becomes less cumbersome and expensive and less dependent on expert input. A computer-based teaching tool with such a capacity could monitor the state of the user, be they bored, excited or confused, and adjust the features of a learning activity to reflect such a brain state. Research into gaming technology has already made it possible to take account of the affective state of players (Ulicsak, 2009).

Play Attention, a rather expensive system that is purported to help pupils with ADHD to focus, is one such tool. The system, available since 1996, is composed of a series of computer-based games in which the player moves objects on screen by the use of brainpower alone. Each game has been designed to improve the ability of the player to maintain focus by developing a requisite series of skills, such as the ability to discriminate between important and unimportant stimuli. Lack of concentration, determined by the sensors in a helmet that a player wears, is penalized. Thus, it is hoped the behaviour can be changed. This is akin to operant conditioning so favoured by Skinner (1954), in which desirable behaviour is rewarded and undesirable behaviour is discouraged. There are a number of other uses for neurofeedback information. An individual could be made aware of their own brain state and, in time, learn to modify it accordingly to facilitate understanding or prepare them for a musical or sporting performance. Thus, intrinsic motivation rather than the external rewards and penalties found in Play Attention apply. Teachers or guardians could determine the propensity of their pupils or those in their care for certain subjects by examining the neurofeedback data. This could pertain to very young children, in particular, because the information-gathering process does not rely on the collection of verbal indicators, which they may not be capable of providing. Another technology which makes use of neural networks, brain computer interfaces (BCI), could make it possible for a computer to 'sense' what an individual wants rather than help them modify their brain state. Although more invasive than conventional neurofeedback systems, implants may be required in the brain, BCI offers the tantalizing prospect of a computer being able to detect the choices we wish to make without the need for protracted training. Pages in a virtual book could be literally turned at will or an individual could dictate a missive without any apparent physical effort or obvious contact with any machine (Ulicsak, 2009). Perhaps a more immediate benefit of neuroscience when it is applied to education is the debunking of what Geake (2008) calls 'neuromyths' or folk psychology derived from brain science folklore. There has been a tendency in the education community to adopt an oversimplified view of the way the brain functions. As a result, a number of doctrinal beliefs have arisen, often without scientific foundation, which are now buried deep within the educational psyche. First among these is the notion that learning styles are tied to the sensory modalities of the brain and, therefore, individuals can be classified as visual, auditory or kinaesthetic (VAK) learners. There is a considerable scarcity of neurological evidence to support this claim. In fact, the opposite is probably true. We do not learn through one sense alone.

Howard-Jones's (2007) comments that recent psychological investigations concluded that attempts to focus on learning styles by teachers were wasted because there was no apparent benefit from doing so. Ansari (2008) suggests that VAK, although appealing, is fundamentally inaccurate. It may be useful for teachers to present learning materials in different ways, simply to add variety, but 'existing research does not support labelling children in terms of a particular learning style' (Howard-Jones, 2007: 16). Sharp et al. (2008: 89) conclude that VAK is an over-rated phenomenon, 'one offering no diagnostic or pedagogical power whatsoever, and one with no independently verifiable claim to validity and reliability'. Another fallacy is the notion that we can categorize learners into right- or left-brain dominant groups (Howard-Jones, 2007). Advocates suggest that those with a predisposition for right brain activity are intuitive and governed by feelings while those with left-brain leanings are analytical and logical. It may be true that certain activities can be associated with either the left or the right hemisphere (language is left orientated) there is no reliable neuroscientific evidence suggesting that learners can be divided into either group (Howard-Jones, 2007). Neuroimaging research indicates that to undertake most tasks, including learning, both sides of the brain are required to work in unison in a sophisticated parallel fashion (Ansari, 2008; Geake, 2008). There is constant communication between them via a thick bundle of white matter called the *corpus callosum*. Neuroimaging research also provides evidence that the brains of young and gifted children appear to be enhanced by strengthening these connections (Geake, 2008). Gardener's theory of multiple intelligences (MI) does not escape the scrutiny of the neuro sceptics. In his theoretical model traditional notions of intelligence are replaced by up to eight or nine cognitive competences separated into linguistic, logical-mathematical, musical, bodily kinaesthetic spatial, interpersonal and intrapersonal intelligences designed to encompass a broad set of abilities, talents or mental skills. MI theory has been adopted unquestionably but it is not supported by neuroscience. Geake (2008) is categorical in his opposition to it, stating that there are no multiple intelligences, only one general multifaceted intelligence that can be applied to many different situations. White (2006) complains that the trouble with MI is that it corrals all the:

> heterogeneous forms of human intelligence into a few categories of dubious provenance. Some may find it impressive because it is backed by the authority of

a famous Harvard professor. But teachers should be wary of appeals to authority. Evidence is what counts; and MI is evidentially weak. (White, 2006: 83)

Perks (2004) is equally vociferous in his condemnation of this theory, yet there is a whole educational industry based on it. MI has had a huge influence on educational reform, especially in school improvement, around the world. It has shaped policy on curriculum content, methods of learning and teaching and pupil aptitudes. It is clear that the educational community has invested a great deal of energy and money in untested brain based ideas that have no scientific foundation at all. However, neuroscience is not without criticism. It is essentially a laboratory based activity that, when applied to education, is not without its limitations. Even with the best intentions it is difficult to transfer what has been learned under controlled conditions to the ever changing landscape of the classroom. Care should be taken when doing so. Geake (2008) boldly states that:

due to the nonlinearities of morphogenesis, and the uniqueness of subjective experiences, every human brain that ever was, and ever will be, is unique. This includes the brains of identical twins . . . and human clones should any ever be developed'. (Geake, 2008: 57)

To him, it is, therefore, impossible to predict educational performance from what current neuroimaging technology tells us about brain structure. Thus, Purdy et al. (2009: 105) suggest that rather than representing a panacea, 'the cognitive neuroscientific enterprise in relation to education is therefore necessarily limited'. Even if we manage to resist the wholesale use of enhancement technologies to those that we regard as commensurate with existing notions of humanity, there are those such as Agar (2007) who contend our values will inevitably change. Rigney (2004) argues that we need a kindness pill foremost rather than enhancement technology or advances in neuroscience, because the resulting augmented intellect alone would not necessarily be compassionate.

Activity

Can you suggest reasons why the educational community has been slow to adopt legitimate neuroscience and what would you do to address this deficiency?

Transhumanism and education

As a result of a convergence of developments in artificial intelligence, genetic engineering, information technology and molecular nanotechnologies, human intellectual and physical and emotional capacities could be enhanced way beyond that which is currently possible. A group of thinkers belonging to a loosely defined movement called transhumanism have started to identify what this future might be as a result of these technologies. They judge that human beings will be transformed into what they refer to as a post-human state with vastly increased capacities. These post-humans may be resistant to disease and impervious to ageing, have unlimited vigour, and reach intellectual heights as far above any current human genius:

> as humans are above other primates. They may have increased capacity for pleasure, love, artistic appreciation, and serenity and experienced novel states of consciousness that current human brains cannot access. (Agar, 2010: 14)

Bostrom (2008: 70) suggests that a post-human from the future, would point out to his or her human forebears that, among other things, in order to attain this elevated state it is important that human cognition is upgraded. The brain must grow beyond any current genius of humankind in its 'special faculties as well as its general intelligence, so that you may better learn, remember, and understand' (Bostrom, 2008: 70). Subcutaneous data ports and their like could make this possible. As a result, a post-human could engage directly with a computer, providing instant access to a vast library of information held in whatever form the Internet may take in the future. Some sort of symbiosis with an artificial intelligence could also be formed, making it possible to be uploaded into a virtual reality. It is probable that our enhanced post-human descendants will not require schools in which they are inducted into one canon of knowledge or another. Instead, they will be engineered towards a state that Nietzsche (1969) referred to as overhuman (Sorgner, 2009). Transhumanists are able to envisage this future because they believe human nature is 'a work-in-progress, a half-baked beginning that we can learn to remold in desirable ways' (Bostrom, 2003: 1). They claim that technology is simply the continuation of evolution by other more efficient means and:

> the painfully slow biological phase of evolution involved in a few billion years of chance and necessity to produce homo sapiens, the technology creating species

> that through recent technological development, is now poised to launch itself into
> the self designing phase of evolution. (Doede, 2009: 47)

Transhumanists share Koepsell's (2007) instrumentalist viewpoint that technology is neutral, it is neither good nor bad and even:

> the atomic bomb and its deadlier cousin the thermonuclear bomb are neutral.
> Their uses and the intentions that humans have in producing and stockpiling
> weapons can be criticized as immoral, but the tools themselves are neither moral
> nor immoral. (Koepsell, 2007: 465)

They believe that humans and their successors will remain masters and not slaves of technology and it is up to them to control what happens. Cave et al. (2005) describe transhumanists as utopians who want to use technology as a tool to engineer the individual so that a better collective future can be created. This means a life without disease or decline in which the energy and food supply, concerns that blight us today, are solved by superior intelligences working for the collective good. However, this requires morally motivated post-humans who are without the homicidal tendencies of their unimproved forebears (Agar, 2007). Transhumanism has found a receptive audience in Western cultures, which have been conditioned to a certain extent to accept that technology and the development of human beings are intimately entwined (Doede, 2009). There is some evidence for this. Koepsell (2007) contends that human evolution has altered because technology, in the form of the clothing and shelter that made it possible to exist in harsh environments, allowed humans to migrate and subsequently every stage of our culture and development since then:

> has been enabled and guided in part by technologies. Agriculture, tools for hunt-
> ing, languages, mathematics, and every innovation that has lifted us beyond reac-
> tionary instinct has been technological. (Koepsel, 2007: 446)

No less a thinker on philosophical issues than John Dewey would have found things to welcome in the transhumanist rhetoric. He contended that 'when the machine age has thus perfected its machinery, it will be a means of life and not its despotic master. Democracy will come into its own, for democracy is a name for life of free and enriching communion . . . It will have its consummation when free social enquiry is indissolubly wedded to the art of full and moving communication' (Dewey, 1927: 350). Postman (1993) argues that at the same time as technology increases our capacity to access information, it also creates new knowledge monopolies that could undermine what is regarded as traditional wisdoms. Doede (2009) contends that technology is not inert. It implants certain individual and social biases, certain telic (leading towards a definite end) tendencies in those who employ it in subtle yet non-trivial ways. Thus, technology must never be accepted as part of the natural order of things and that all devices are 'a product of a particular economic and political context and carries with it a program, an agenda, and a philosophy that may or may not be life enhancing and that therefore requires scrutiny, criticism and control' (Postman, 1993: 185). Goodman (1970) believes that technology should be regarded as a branch of moral philosophy rather than as a science because it not only *does things for us but to us*, taking away as much as it gives. Marcus (2009: 41) warns that the industrial society which makes technology and science its own 'is organized for ever more effective domination of man and nature . . . It becomes irrational when the success of these efforts opens new dimensions of human realization'. Education is at the very heart of the debate generated by the future predicted by the enhancement technologists, and more poignantly the transhumanists such as Koepsell (2007) and Bostrom (2003), in three very distinct ways. By its very nature, it is the one area of human activity which is solely concerned directly with human potential. It is also a laboratory in which many technological experiments are undertaken, that sometimes have negative as well as positive implications. Postman (1993: 63) characterizes schools as secular bureaucracies governing the ecology of information with systems that legitimize some parts of the flow and discredit others. Education embodies values (Ozolins, 2010). Thinkers from Confucius to Bertrand Russell all believed that there was some transcendental, political, spiritual or social idea that can be advanced through education (Postman, 1993). Sylwester (2006) suggests that some technological developments applied to learning and teaching are bound to have an impact on values. Any increased knowledge of the conscious mind that accrues from technology, so useful to the educationalist, has much wider ramifications since consciousness is also integral to religious belief and cultural behaviour. Sylwester (2006) argues that this cannot be ignored in the formulation of educational theory.

Activity

The enhancement technologists and transhumanists sometimes disparagingly refer to those who contest their viewpoint as bio conservatives or bio Luddites. They argue that opponents fail to see the opportunities that technology is presenting to shape the human future in ways unimagined before. What would you do through education to prepare for or resist it' with 'What would you do through education to prepare for or resist this view of the human future

---

Conclusions

At various times in various cultures, no doubt there have been similar questions about the direction our lives have taken as a result of technology, but the situation we now face is radically different (Koepsell, 2007). Enhancement technology and neuroscience and the combination of all other existing and emerging technologies, brought together spectacularly in transhumanism, all signal that some form of post-human future is possible. By degrees, they appear to be part of the same technological continuum in which the division between man and machine is becoming ever less clear. For the educationalist, they raise questions about not only how best to employ them but whether they should be employed at all. While enhancement technologies bring to the majority a number of tantalizing cognitive gifts previously only bestowed on the few, they also generate their own educational issues. Would they solve or amplify existing problems? Turner et al. (2008) believes that they could create a new form of intellectual poverty that would blight those who do not have the means to purchase the necessary enhancement technology. Education in the way that is constituted at present could never be an antidote to those who suffer from this form of deprivation. Social division could also be further magnified because enhancement might be applied selectively using criteria other than wealth, leaving many behind or even worse, making them redundant beings. These technologies could also have further and somewhat unexpected ramifications, as individuals are deprived of a sense of satisfaction at their own achievements. Rigney (2004) asks what would happen to intrinsic motivation if human beings could buy harder rather than try harder to overcome their limitations. Might they become lazy and lack the challenge that appears to be an integral part of the human condition? The transhumanists desire to shape human evolution through the use of technology raises the spectre of creating some kind of future Frankenstein, albeit one with a vastly more increased intellectual capacity than the original. Mary Shelly (1984) titled her work *Frankenstein, the Modern Prometheus*. Prometheus, a figure from Greek mythology, stole fire from the sun and gave it to mankind to fashions technologies such as tools and weapons. Zeus, the father of the gods, punished Prometheus for his transgression because his intervention led to conflict between mankind and the deity. Although this apocryphal story of the dangers of tampering with the very fabric of the human condition could be regarded as an exaggeration it highlights the importance of engaging in the debate about a future that is shaped largely by technology. Postman (1993) suggests that help is at hand if the right kind of education is applied. Bakhurst (2008) contends that the right kind of education will only result if the right kinds of questions are asked such as; if we stop students from taking computers into examinations because it undermines the nature of the challenge, why should we look any more favourably on the prospect of them downloading material directly into their brains? He believes that such questions, no matter however fanciful, raise ethical questions which 'force us to confront the issue of what education is and ought to be . . . we must not let excitement about scientific innovation and technological possibility distort our conception of education and of the values it ought to embody' (Bakhurst, 2008: 428). Despite Cuban (1985) suggesting that educators have an errant passion for technology, they do not have a good track record of asking the right kind of questions about it. The rise of neuromyths that have influenced contemporary learning and teaching, referred to earlier in this chapter, is evidence of this lack of incisiveness. Yet, educators require a sound understanding of both the possibilities and limitations of neuroscience and the psychological and philosophical implications of current and future research in this field. Howard-Jones (2007: 16) contends that in the future an improved dialogue between educators and scientists 'will be critical in supporting the development, application and evaluation of educational programmes based on a sound scientific understanding of the brain'. The need for dialogue is a pressing issue even today. Educationalists might very well employ the results of current work on the conscious brain, but they also need to be aware that it raises fundamental questions about the nature of self. Purdy et al. (2009: 105) suggest that while cognitive neuroscience at its best offers insights into the neural concomitants of thinking, it does not offer privileged access into the 'hidden world of the inner, that inner world being already manifest in external behaviour'. Ilyenkov (1977) contends that the brain does not think but the human being thinks with the help of her brain. Cuban (1985) believes that although the brain's cortex is important, it only represents a fragment of the whole human being. Bakhurst agrees, suggesting that what he calls our 'mindedness' does not consist 'in the occurrence of a special class of events inside us; rather, it lays in our mode of engagement with the world, a mode of engagement possible only because we are social beings' (2008: 426). This has long been the territory of philosophers and theologians who associate 'mindedness' with concepts of the spirit and the soul but it also needs to become the province of educationalists. Kass warns that through technology human nature itself lies on the operating table ready for alteration:

> for eugenic and psychic enhancement, for wholesale redesign. In leading laboratories, academic and industrial, new creators are confidently amassing their powers and quietly honing their skills, while on the street their evangelists are zealously prophesying a post human future. For anyone who cares about preserving our humanity, the time has come to pay attention. (Kass, 2010: 311)

Big Questions

Can we (or should we) resist the benefits that enhancement technologies clearly offer both generally and specifically in education?

What do educators need to do to help us *pay attention*?

Further reading

Geake, J. (2008) Education: education and human potential, In Zonneveld, L., Dijstelbloem, H. and Ringoir, D. (eds). *Reshaping the Human Condition: Exploring Human Enhancement*, the Hague, Netherlands: Rathenau Institute, 53–65.

Howard-Jones, P. (2007) *Neuroscience and Education: Issues and Opportunities*, TLRP Commentary (London, Teaching and Learning Research Programme), London: Institute of Education.

Koepsell, D. (2007) Robots bowling alone: Evolving post-technological humans, *Scripted*, Vol. 4, No. 4, 462.

Postman, N. (1993) *Technopoly*, New York: Vintage Books.

Sharp, J., Byrne, J. and Bowker, R. (2007) VAK or VAK-uous? *Educational Futures*, Vol. 1, 76–93.

Useful websites

Enhancement Technologies

www.ucl.ac.uk/~ucbtdag/bioethics/ – Last accessed 11/03/2011.

Mary Shelley

www.kirjasto.sci.fi/mshelley.htm – Last accessed 11/03/2011.

Neuromyths

www.oecd.org/document/53/0,3746,en_21571361_44559030_33829685_1_1_1_1,00.html – Last accessed 11/03/2011.

Neuroimaging and Children

www.parentingscience.com/neuroimaging.html – Last accessed 11/03/2011.

Neuroscience and Education

http://royalsociety.org/policy/reports/brainwaves2/ – Last accessed 11/03/2011.

The Cyborg Revolution

www.youtube.com/watch?v=urVXWUD8Q3Y&feature=related – Last accessed 11/03/2011.

The Singularity

http://singinst.org/overview/whatisthesingularity/ – Last accessed 11/03/2011.

Technopoly

http://techliberation.com/2010/01/31/are-you-an-internet-optimist-or-pessimist-the-great-debate-over-technology%E2%80%99s-impact-on-society/ – Last accessed 11/03/2011.

Transhumanism

www.nickbostrom.com/ethics/genetic.html – Last accessed 11/03/2011.

Bibliography

Agar, N. (2007) Where to transhumanism? The literature reaches a critical mass, *Hasting Centre Report*, Vol. 37, No. 3, 12–17.

Aldous, C. (2005) Creativity in problem solving: uncovering the origin of new ideas, *International Education Journal*, Vol. 5, 43–56.

Aldrich, C. (2005) *Learning by Doing: a Comprehensive Guide to Simulations, Computer Games, and Pedagogy in E Learning and Other Educational Experiences*, San Francisco: Pfeiffer.

Alexander, R. (1992) *Policy and Practice in Primary Education*, London: Routledge.

Alsina, P. (2006) *ICT and Creativity – Creative Contents and Community Building*. Available from www. ict-tutors.co.uk/index.php?sec=4&tp=14&ts=9&skip=1 – Last accessed 11/03/2011.

Ambrose, S. (2001) Palaeolithic technology and human evolution, *Science*, Vol. 291, No. 5509, 1748–1753.

Anderson, A., Augenblick, J., DeCesore, D. and Conra, J. (2006) *Costs and Funding of Virtual Schools*, BellSouth Foundation, Available from www.inacol.org/research/docs/Costs&Funding.pdf – Last accessed 11/03/2011.

Anderson, J. (2010) *A Regional Guide ICT Transforming Education*, Paris: UNESCO.

Anderson, T., Rourke, L., Garrison, D. R. and Archer, W. (2001) Assessing teaching presence in a computer conferencing environment, *Journal of Asynchronous Learning Networks*, Vol. 5, No. 2, 1–17.

Ansari, D. (2008) The brain goes to school: Strengthening the education neuroscience connection, *Education Canada*, Vol. 48, 6–10.

Apple, M. W. (1998) Selling our children channel one and the politics of education. In: R. W. McChesney, E. Meiksins Wood and J. B. Foster (eds), *Capitalism and the Information Age: The Political Economy of Global Communications*, New York: Monthly Review Press.

Arvind, D. K. (2005) *Speckled computing, Proceedings Nanotech 2005*, Vol. 3, Anaheim CA. Available from www.specknet.org/publications/4th_Workshop/ – Last accessed 11/03/ 2011.

Attewell, P. (2001) The first and second digital divides, *Sociology of Education*, Vol. 74, 252–9.

Bailey, F. and Moar, M. (2003) The VERTEX Project: Designing and populating shared 3D virtual worlds in the primary (elementary) classroom, *Computers and Graphics*, Vol. 27, No. 3, 353–9.

Bakhurst, D. (2008) Minds, brains and education, *Journal of Philosophy of Education*, Vol. 42, Nos 3–4, 415–32.

Balakrishnan, M., Rossafri, M. and Soon, F. (2007) Synergizing pedagogy, learning theory and technology in instruction: How can it be done? *US China Education Review*, Vol. 4, No. 9, 46–52.

Baldauf, R. B. (1981) Educational television, enculturation and acculturation: a study of change in American Samoa, *International Review of Education*, Vol. 27, No. 3, 227–45.

Barab, S.A., Dodge, T., Ingram-Goble, A., Volk, C., Peppler, K., Pettyjohn, P. and Solomou, M. (2010) Pedagogical dramas and transformational play: Narratively rich games for learning. *Mind, Culture, and Activity*, Vol. 17, No. 3, 235–64.

Barnett, R. (2000) *Realizing the University in an Age of Supercomplexity*, Buckingham: SRHE and Open University Press.

Barrantes, B. (2007) Analysis of ICT Demand: What is digital poverty and how to measure it? In Galperin, H. and Mariscal, J. (eds), *Digital Poverty: Latin American and Caribbean Perspective*, Rugby: Intermediate Technology Publications.

Baxter, A. (2008) *Second Life for Classrooms,* London, Financial Times, February 29th. Available from www.ft.com/cms/s/2/a89ec97c-e6f3-11dc=b5c3-0000779fd2ac.html#axzz1VToW6esF – Last accessed 11/02/2011.

BBC, (2009) *Mali Villagers Fight Back Against the Sahara*, Available from http://news.bbc.co.uk/l/hi/world/africa/8408568.stm – Last accessed 15/02/2011.

Beck, U. (1999) *World Risk Society*, Cambridge: Polity Press.

Becker, M. (1995) Nineteenth-century foundations of creativity research, *Creativity Research Journal*, Vol. 4, 219–29.

Beckett, F. (2010) *Help Is at Hand to Beat the Digital Poverty Trap; Looks at How Technology Enriches Us*, London: Times Newspapers.

BECTA, (2001) *The 'Digital Divide': A Discussion Paper,* London: DFES.

—. (2002) *How to Encourage Pupils' Creativity Using ICT*, Available from http://schools.becta.org.uk/index.php?section=tl&catcode=ss_tl_use_02&rid=594 – Last accessed 11/03/2011.

—. (2008) *How Do Boys and Girls Differ in Their Use of ICT?* Research Report. www.bee-it.co.uk/Guidance%20Docs/Becta%20Files/Reports%20and%20publications/46%20Gender%20and%20technology%20How%20do%20boys%20and%20girls%20differ%20in%20use%20of%20ICT.pdf – Last accessed 07/03/2011.

Belgrove, M., Griffin, J. and Makepeace, B. (2008) Using e-learning tools to build a community of distance learners: a progress review and call for collaboration. In *Proceedings of the 7th European Conference on e-Learning* (ECEL 2008), Reading: Academic Publishing Limited, 90–6.

Benjamin, L. (1988) A history of teaching machines, *American Psychologist*, Vol. 43, No. 9, 703–12.

Bennett, S., Maton, K. and Kervin, L. (2008) The 'digital natives' debate: A critical review of the evidence, *British Journal of Educational Technology*, Vol. 39, No. 5, 775–86.

Berger, P. and Luckmann T. (1966) *The Social Construction of Reality*, London: Penguin University Books.

Bianchi, W. (2002) The Wisconsin School of the Air: Success story with implications, *Educational Technology and Society*, Vol. 5, No. 1, 141–8.

—. (2008) Education by Radio: America's Schools of the Air, *TechTrends: Linking Research and Practice to Improve Learning*, Vol. 52, No. 2, 36–44.

Bijker, W. (1997) *Of Bicycles, Bakelites, and Bulbs: Toward a Theory of Sociotechnical Change*, Cambridge, MA: MIT Press.

Bimber B. (1990) Karl Marx and the three faces of technological determinism, *Social Studies of Science*, Vol. 20, No. 2, 333–51.

Bingham, C.W (2005), Who are the philosophers of education? *Studies in Philosophy and Education*, Vol. 24, 1–18.

Blanchard, A. (2004) Virtual behavior settings: An application of behavior setting theories to virtual communities. *Journal of Computer-Mediated Communication*, Vol. 9, No. 2. Available from http://jcmc.indiana.edu/vol9/issue2/blanchard.html – Last accessed 23/09/11.

Block, W. (2004) The digital divide is not a problem in need of rectifying, *Journal of Business Ethics*, Vol. 53, 393–406.

Boden, M (2004) *The Creative Mind: Myths and Mechanisms*, 2nd edn, London: Routledge.

Bonner, S. (1977) *Education in Ancient Rome: From the Elder Cato to the Younger Pliny*, Berkeley: University of California Press.

Bostrom, N. (2003) Human genetic enhancements: a transhumanist perspective, *Journal of Value Inquiry*, Vol. 37, No. 4, 493–506.

—. (2008) Letter from Utopia, *Journal of Evolution and Technology*, Vol. 19, No. 1, September, 67–72.

Boulos, M., Hetherington, L. and Wheeler, S. (2007) Second Life: An overview of the potential of 3-D virtual worlds in medical and health education, *Health Information and Libraries Journal*, Vol. 24, No. 4, 233–45.

Boyle, T. and Cook, J. (2004) Understanding and using technological affordances: A commentary on Conole and Dyke, ALT-J, *Research in Learning Technology*, Vol. 12, No. 3, 295–99.

Brabazon, T. (2002) *Digital Hemlock: Internet Education and the Poisoning of Teaching*, Sydney: UNSW Press.

Brooks, J. and Brooks, M. (1993) *In Search of Understanding: The Case for Constructivist Classrooms*, Alexandria, VA: ASCD.

Broue, P., Birchall, I. H. and Pearce, B. (2004) *The German Revolution 1917–1923*, Leiden: Brill Academic Publishers.

Brown, A. (2008) Has there been a decline in values in British society, *The Social Evil Series*, Joseph Rowntree Foundation. Available from www.jrf.org.uk/publications/has-there-been-decline-values-british-society – Last accessed 11/03/ 2011.

Brown, D. E. (1991) *Human Universals*, New York: McGraw Hill.

Burling, R. (2007) *The Talking Ape: How Language Evolved*, USA: Oxford University Press.

Butany, C. (2008) Scrambled for it *Literacy at First Digital Village*. Available from www.nation.co.ke/News/regional/-/1070/498064/-/view/printVersion/-/13lx0hgz/-/index.html – Last accessed 07/03/2011.

Cachia, R., Ferrari, A., Kearney, C., Punie, Y., Van Den Berghe, W. and Wastiau, P. (2009) *Creativity in Schools in Europe: A Survey of Teachers*. Available from http://ipts.jrc.ec.europa.eu/publications/pub.cfm?id=3702 – Last accessed 11/03/2011.

Campbell, J. (1989) The invisible rhetorician: Charles Darwin's third party strategy, *Rhetorica*, Vol. 7, No. 1, 55–85.

Castronova, E. (2005) *Synthetic Worlds*, London: The University of Chicago Press.

Catania, A. (1999) Thorndike's legacy: Learning, selection and the law of effect. *Journal of the Experimental Analysis of Behaviour*, Vol. 72, No. 3, 425–8.

Cave, S. and Cave, F. T. (2005) The most dangerous idea on earth? The bioethics of transhumanism – applying science to enable us to live forever – have shot up the political agenda. For the theory may become stark reality in our lifetime. *Financial Times*, May 27, 21.

Chambers Journal (1871) The international exhibition of 1871, *Chambers Journal of Popular Literature, Science and Arts*, August 26, 538.

Cheshire, W. (October 2010) Doing no harm to Hippocrates: Reality and virtual reality in ethics education, *Ethics and Medicine*, Vol. 23, No. 3, 137–42.

Chomsky, N. (1996) *Powers and Prospects: Reflections on Human Nature and the Social Order*, Boston: South End Press.

Church, A. (2011) *Bloom's and ICT tools*, Available from http://edorigami.wikispaces.com/ Bloom%27s+and+ICT+tools – Last accessed 07/03/2011.

Clark, D. (2006) *BlendedLearning*, London: Epic.

Clegg, S., Hudson, A. and Steel, J. (2003) The Emperor's new clothes: Globalization and e-learning in higher education, *British Journal of Sociology of Education*, Vol. 24, No. 1, 39–53.

Clough, G., Jones, A., McAndrews, P. and Scanlon, E. (2007) Informal learning with PDAs and smartphones, *Journal of Computer Assisted Learning*, Vol. 24, 359–71.

Cohen, L., Manion, L. and Morrison, K. (2007) *Research Methods in Education,* 6th edn, London: RoutledgeFalmer.

Collis, B. (1996) *Tele-Learning in a Digital World: The Future of Distance Learning*, London: International Thomson Publications.

Compaine, B. M. (2001) *The Digital Divide: Facing a Crisis or Creating a Myth?* Cambridge: MIT Press.

Conole, G. and Dyke, M. (2004) What are the affordances of information and communication technologies? ALT-J, *Research in Learning Technology*, Vol. 12, No. 2, 113–24.

Cook, D. (1962) The automization of Socrates, *Theory into Practice*, Vol. 1, No. 1, 9–19.

Corbeil, J. (2006) *The (r)evolution of synchronous communication in distance education, Issues in Information Systems*, Vol. VII, No. 1, 388–92.

Coulson, J. E. (1966) Automation, electronic computers, and education, *The Phi Delta Kappan*, Vol. 47, No. 7, 340–4.

Cox, M., Webb, M., Abbott, C., Blakeley, B., Beauchamp, T. and Rhodes, V. (2003) *Ict and Pedagogy: a Review of the Research Literature*, Annesley: DfES Publications.

Craft, A. (2001) *An Analysis of Research and Literature on Creativity Education*: A report prepared for the Qualifications and Curriculum Authority (QCA). Available from www.euvonal.hu/images/ creativity_report.pdf – Last accessed 11/03/2011.

—. (2005) *Creativity in Schools: Tensions and Dilemmas*, London: Routledge.

—. (2006) Fostering Creativity with Wisdom, *Cambridge Journal of Education*, Vol. 36, No. 3, 337–50.

—, Jeffrey, B. and Leibling, M. (2001) *Creativity in Education*, New York, Continuum International Publishing Group.

Craig, J. (1980) *Brittain's Open University: Text, Telly and Tutor, Change*, Washington D.C.: Heldref Publications, Vol. 12, No. 7 (October), 43–8.

Cranmer, S. (2006) *How Families Use the Internet in the Home.* Unpublished PhD thesis, University of London Institute of Education.

Crook, D (2007) School broadcasting in the United Kingdom: An exploratory history, *Journal of Educational Administration and History*, Vol. 39, No. 3, 217–26.

Cropley, A. (2001) *Creativity in Education and Learning. A Guide for Teachers and Educators*, London: Routledge.

Csikszentmilhalyi, M. (1996) *Creativity: Flow and the Psychology of Discovery and Invention*, New York: Harper Collins.

Cuban, L. (1985), *Teachers and Machine: The Classroom Use of Technology*, New York, Teachers College Press.

—. (1986) *Teachers and Machines: The Classroom Use of Technology Since 1920*, New York: Teachers College Press.

—. (2001) *Oversold and Underused: Computers in the Classroom,* Cambridge: Harvard University Press.

Cubberley, E. (2007) *The History of Education*, Vol. 1, Charleston: BiblioBazaar.

Curoe, P. R. V. (2008) *Outline of the History of Education*, India: Bibliolife.

Daele, A., Deschryver, N., Gorga, D. and Künzel, M. (2007) *Managing Knowledge within Communities of Practice*: *Analysing Needs and Developing Services*, e-Learning Papers, No. 5, Available from www.elearningpapers.eu/index.php?page=doc&doc_id=10222&doclng=6 – Last accessed 11/02/2001.

Dale, E. (1967) Historical setting of programed instruction. In P. C. Lange (ed.), *Programed Instruction: The Sixty-Sixth Yearbook of the National Society for the Study of Education*, Part II, Chicago: The University of Chicago Press, 28–54.

Dalgarno, B. and Lee, J. (2010) What are the learning affordances of 3-D virtual environments? *British Journal of Educational Technology*, Vol. 41, No. 1, 10–32.

de Bono, E. (1993) *Sur Petition: Going beyond Competition*, London: Harper Collins.

—. (2009) *Lateral Thinking*, London: Penguin Books.

De Freitas, S. (2008) *Serous Virtual Worlds: A Scoping Study*, JISC, Available from www.jisc.ac.uk/publications/reports/2008/seriousvirtualworldsreport.aspx – Last accessed 11/03/2011.

de la Bédoyère, G. (2010) *Roman Britain: A New History*, London: Thames and Hudson.

Deed, C. and Edwards, A. (2010) Using social networks in learning and teaching in higher education: An Australian case study, *International Journal of Knowledge Society Research*, Vol. 1, No. 2, 1–12.

Dewey, J. (1927) *The Public and Its Problems*, New York: Holt.

—. (1966, first published in 1916) *Democracy and Education: An Introduction to the Philosophy of Education*, New York: Macmillan.

DFEE, (2000) *Bridging the Digital Divide*, by Michael Wills MP. Available from www.dfee.gov.uk/kew/wills.shtml. Last accessed 07/03/2011.

Dickey, M. (2005) Three-dimensional virtual worlds and distance learning: Two case studies of Active Worlds as a medium for distance learning, *British Journal of Educational Technology*, Vol. 36, No. 3, 439–51.

Dieterle, E. and Clarke, J. (2008) Multi-user virtual environments for teaching and learning. In Pagani, M. (ed.), *Encyclopaedia of Multimedia Technology and Networking*, 2nd edn, Hershey, PA: Idea Group.

Dijstelbloem, H., and Ringoir, D. (eds) *Reshaping the Human Condition: Exploring Human Enhancement*, The Hague Netherlands, Rathenau Institute.

Diulus, F. and Baum, R. (1991) Simulation, creativity and learning, *Contemporary Education*, Vol. 34, No. 1, 1–17.

Doede, B. (2009) Transhumanism, technology, and the future; Posthumanity emerging or subhumanity descending? *Appraisal*, Vol. 7, No. 3, 39–54.

Donaldson, J. A. and Conrad, R.. (2003) *Moving F2F Activities Online,* Proceedings of the 18 th Annual Conference on Distance Teaching and Learning. Available from http://uwex.edu/disted/conference/ Resource_library/proceedings/02_22.pdf – Last accessed 11/03/2011.

Dreher, C., Reiners, T., Dreher, N. and Dreher, H. (2009) Virtual worlds as a context suited for information systems education: Discussion of pedagogical experience and curriculum design with reference to second life, *Journal of Information Systems Education*, Vol. 20, No. 2, 211–14.

Dudeney, G. (2009) View from the plateau, *English Teaching Profession*, Vol 61, 66–9.

Duffy, T. M. and Cunningham, D. J. (1996) *Constructivism: Implications for the Design and Delivery of Instruction.* New York: Simon and Schuster Macmillan.

Earthmovers (2010) *Giant Copper Trio*, Vol. 76, 7–13.

Eisenstein, E. (1980) *The Printing Press as an Agent of Change*, Vol. 1, Cambridge: Cambridge University Press.

—. (1990) *The Printing Revolution in Early Modern Europe*, Cambridge: Cambridge University Press.

European Schoolnet (2010) *Greece, Country Report on ict in Education*. Available from www.xplora.org/ ww/en/pub/insight/policy/policies/2009_country_reports.htm – Last accessed 11/03/2011.

Evans, D (1998) *A Critical Examination of Claims Concerning the Impact of Print*. Available from www. aber.ac.uk/media/Students/dle9701.html – Last accessed 23/02/2011.

Facer, K. and Sandford, R. (2010) The next 25 years? Future scenarios and future directions for education and technology, *Journal of Computer Assisted Learning*, Vol. 26, No. 1, 4–93.

Faux, F., McFarlane, M., Roche, N. and Face, K. (2006) *Learning with Handheld Technologies*, Bristol: Futurelab.

Feenberg, A. (1992) Subversive rationalization: Technology, power and democracy with technology, *Inquiry*, Vol. 35, Nos 3 and 4, 301–22.

Ferrari, A., Cachia, R. and Punie, Y. (2009) *Innovation and Creativity in Education and Training in the EU Member States: Fostering Creative Learning and Supporting Innovative Teaching Literature* review on Innovation and Creativity in E and T in the EU Member States, Luxemberg, JRC. Avaiable from http://ipts.jrc.ec.europa.eu/publications/pub.cfm?id=2700 – Last accessed 11/03/2011.

Feurzeig, W. (2006) Educational Technology at BBN, *IEE Annals of the History of Computing*, Vol. 28, No. 1, 18–31.

Field, J. (2007) Behaviourism and training: The programmed instruction movement in Britain, 1950–1975, *Journal of Vocational Education and Training*, Vol. 59, No. 3, September, 313–29.

Field, M. (1958) TV in schools, *British Journal of Educational Studies*, Vol. 6, No. 2, 169–70.

Field, T. (1897) The Academy, *Educational Supplement*, 105.

Finn, J. (1960) Automation and education: A new theory for instructional technology, *AV Communication Review*, Vol. 8, No. 1, 5–26.

Fisher, R. and Williams, M. (2004) *Unlocking Creativity – Teaching Across the Curriculum*, London: David Fulton Publishers.

Fisher, T., Higgins, C. and Loveless, A. (2006) *Teachers Learning with Digital Technologies: A Review of Research and Projects*, Bristol: Futurelab.

Flynn, J. (1965) A rationale for using teaching machines, *The Clearing House*, Vol. 39, No. 6, 365–7.

Fonseca, J. R. (1965) *Will programmed learning destroy us? Improving College and University Teaching*, Vol. 13, No. 2, 100–1.

Fox, R. (2001) Constructivism examined, *Oxford Review of Education*, Vol. 27, No. 1, 23–35.

Freeman, S. L. (1967) Teachers and television: The master-slave relationship, *The Clearing House*, Vol. 42, No. 4, 198–203.

Freire, P. (1974) *Education: The Practice of Freedom*, London: Writers and Readers Publishing Cooperative.

Frost, A. (2010) Youth Dependency. In Bremner, J., Frost, A., Haub, C., Mather, M., Rimgheim, K. and Zuehlke, *Population Bulletin, Population Reference Bureau*, Vol. 65, No. 2, 4–5, Available from www.prb.org/pdf10/65.2highlights.pdf – Last accessed 11/03/ 2011.

Fry, E. (1959) Teaching machines: The coming automation, *The Phi Delta Kappan*, Vol. 41, No. 1, 28–31.

Füssel. S. (2005) (Trans. Martin D.) *Gutenberg and the Impact of Printing*, Aldershot: Ashgate.

Futurelab (2006) Here there and everywhere, *Vision, Issue* 3, Bristol, Futurelab. Available from www2.futurelab.org.uk/resources/documents/vision/VISION_03.pdf – Last accessed 11/03/2011.

Futuresource Consulting (2010) *1 Million Interactive Whiteboards Will Be Sold in 2010 According to New Futuresource Report*. Available from www.futuresource-consulting.com/pdfs/2010-02_IWB_release.pdf – Last accessed 11/03/2011.

Gagné, R. M. (1965) The analysis of instructional objectives for the design of instruction. In R. Glaser (ed.), *Teaching Machines and Programmed Learning II: Data and Directions*, Washington, D.C.: National Educational Association, 21–65.

Galperin, H. and Mariscal, J. (eds) (2007) *Digital Poverty: Latin American and Caribbean Perspective*, Rugby: Intermediate Technology Publications.

Gardner, H. (1993) Seven creators of the modern era. In Brokman, J. (ed.). *Creativity*, New York: Simon and Shuster.

Garner, W. L. (1966) *Programmed Instruction*, New York, The Center for Applied Research in Education.

Garrison, D. R. and Anderson, T. (2003) *E-Learning in the 21st Century: A Framework for Research and Practice*, London: Routledge Falmer.

— and Archer, W. (2000) Critical inquiry in a text-based environment: Computer conferencing in higher education, *The Internet and Higher Education*, Vol. 2, Nos 2 and 3, 87–105.

Gartner (2010) *Gartner Says More Than 1 Billion PCs in Use Worldwide and Headed to 2 Billion Units* by 2014. Available from www.gartner.com/it/page.jsp?id=703807 – Last accessed 07/03/2011.

Gathanju, D. (2010) Kenya Builds Digital Villages. Available from www.econtentmag.com – Last accessed 07/03/2011.

Geake, J. (2008) Education: Education and human potential. In Zonneveld, L., Dijstelbloem, H. and Ringoir, D. (eds) *Reshaping the Human Condition, Exploring Human Enhancement*, The Hague: Rathenau Institute, 53–64.

Gee, J. (2003) *What Video Games Have to Teach Us about Learning and Literacy*, London: Palgrave Macmillan.

Gerard, R. W. (1965) Computers and education, Proceedings of the Fall Joint Computer Conference,

Gibson, H. (2005) What creativity isn't: The presumptions of instrumental and individual justifications for creativity in education. *British Journal of Educational Studies,* Vol. 53, No. 2, 148–67.

Gibson, W. (1986) *Burning Chrome* , New York: Arbour House.

Glenn, M. (2008) *The Future of Higher Education: How Technology Will Shape Learning, New Media Consortium.* Available from www.nmc.org/pdf/Future-of-Higher-Ed-(NMC).pdf – Last accessed 11/03/ 2011.

Goethe, J. W. and Karabab, G. (2006) Culturally appropriate pedagogy: The case of group learning in a Confucian Heritage Culture (CHC), *Intercultural Education,* Vol. 17, No. 1, March 2006, 1–9.

Goldsborough, R. (2002) The perils of prophesying the future of digital technology, *Community College Week,* Available from http://www.amazon.com/perils-prophesying-digital-technology-technology/ dp/B0008EFOIQ – Last accessed 11/03/2011.

Goldstein, A., Pinaud, N. H. and Chen, X. (2006) *China and India: What's in it for Africa?* Paris: OECD.

Goodman, P. (1970) *New Reformation: Notes of a Neolithic Conservative*, New York: Vintage Books.

Gorski, P. and Clark, C. (2002) Multicultural education and the digital divide: focus on language, perspectives on technology, *Multicultural Perspectives*, Vol. 4, No. 2, 30–4.

Graham, C. (2006) Blended learning systems: Definitions, current trends and future directions. In C. Bonk and C. Graham (eds), *The Handbook of Blended Learning: Global Perspectives, Local Designs.* San Francisco: John Wiley & Sons.

Grant, L. (2010) *Developing Home School Relationships using Digital Technologies*, Bristol: Futurelab.

Green, J. (2010) Innovation in Education, *Education Guardian.* Available from www.guardian.co.uk/ innovation-education/speaker-interview-josephine-green – Last accessed 11/03/ 2011.

Gron, G., Kirstein, M., Thielscher, A., Riepe, M.W. and Spitzer, M. (2005) Cholinergic enhancement of episodic memory in healthy young adults, *Psychopharmacology*, Vol. 182, No. 1, 170–9.

Grubbs, S., Pate, L. and Leech, D. (2009) Distance learning and virtual schools: A journey towards the future, *Journal of Technology Integration in the Classroom*, Vol. 1, No. 1, 29–41.

Guillén, M. F. and Suárez, S. L. (2005) Explaining the global digital divide: Economic, political and sociological drivers of cross-national Internet use, *Social Forces*, Vol. 84, No. 2, 681–708.

Hackbarth, S. (1996) *The Educational Technology Handbook: a Comprehensive Guide: Processes and Products for Learning*, Englewood Cliffs: Educational Technology Publications.

Hagner, P. and Schneebeck, C. (2001) Engaging the faculty. In Barone, C. and Hagner, P. (eds), *Technology-Enhanced Teaching and Learning: Leading and Supporting the Transformation on Your Campus*, San Francisco: Jossey Bass Publishers.

Hague, C. and Williamson, B. (2009) Digital Participation, *Digital Literacy, and School Subjects*, Bristol: Futurelab.

Hansen, B. P. (1970) The computer in education, *The Clearing House*, Vol. 45, No. 4, 195–200.

Heppell, S. (2006) *Learning 2016* – What it might be like. Available from www.multiverse.ac.uk/ viewarticle2.aspx?contentId=14157 – Last accessed 11/03/2011.

—. (2007) What will colleges of the future look like, *The Independent*. Available from www. independent.co.uk/news/education/further/what-will-colleges-of-the-future-look-like-400366. html – Last accessed 11/03/2011.

—. (2010) In Fraser, F. *The Innovators* – No. 12 Stephen Heppell. Available from www.agent4change. net/innovators/536.html – Last accessed 11/03/ 2011.

Hew, K. and Cheung, W. (2010) Use of three-dimensional (3-D) immersive virtual worlds in K-12 and higher education settings: A review of the research, *British Journal of Educational Technology*, Vol. 41, No. 1, 33–55.

HIF-net (2011) *Working Together to Improve Access to Reliable Information for Healthcare Workers in Developing Countries*, Available from http://dgroups.org/Community.aspx?c=a4287629-aff1-40b6-a560-4e91e6f568bb – Last accessed 11/02/2011.

Hilberry, C. B. (1957) The computer's challenge to education, *Mathematics Magazine*, Vol. 30, No. 3, 149–53.

HMG (2008) *Delivering Digital Inclusion: An Action Plan for Consultation*, HMG. Available from http://www.communities.gov.uk/publications/communities/digitalinclusionresponses. Last accesed 07/03/2011.

HMIe (2006) *Emerging Good Practice in Promoting Creativity*, A report by HMIe. Available from www. hmie.gov.uk/documents/publication/hmieegpipc.html – Last accessed 11/03/2011.

Holden, H. (1895) *M Tulli Ciceronis Pro Publio Sestio, Oratio ad Iudiced*, London: Macmillan and Co.

Hoth, W. (1961) From Skinner to Crowder to chance: a primer on teaching machines, *The English Journal*, Vol. 50, No. 6, 398–401.

Hough, J. (1962) Research vindication for teaching machines, *The Phi Delta Kappan*, Vol. 43, No. 6, 240–2.

Howard-Jones, P. (2007) *Neuroscience and Education: Issues and Opportunities, TLRP Commentary* (London, Teaching and Learning Research Programme), London: Institute of Education.

Howell, D. (2010) The riddle of the smart machine, *Tech Trends*, Vol. 54, No. 1, 33–7.

Huxley, A. (1932) *Brave New World*, London: Chatto and Windus.

IEA (2011) *The Computers in Education Study*, www.iea.nl/computers_edu_study.html?&type=98&no_cache=1&sword_list[0]=computers – Last accessed 14/02/2011.

Ilyenkov, E. V. (1977) *Dialectical Logic: Essays in its History and Theory*, Moscow, Progress Publishers.

Index Mundi (2009) *Birth Rate: Colour Coded World Map*. Available from www.indexmundi.com/map/?v=25&l=en – Last accessed 11/03/2011.

Insight (2011) 2009/2010 *Insight Country Reports* www.xplora.org/ww/en/pub/insight/policy/policies/2009_country_reports.htm – Last accessed 07/03/2011.

Internet World Stats (2011a) Internet usage statistics. *The Internet Big Picture*. Available from www. internetworldstats.com/htm – Last accessed 07/03/2011.

—. (2011b) *Usage and Population Statistics*. Available from www.internetworldstats.com/stats7.htm – Last accessed 07/03/2011.

Isaacson, P. (1978) Personal computing – A little past and a lot of future, *Proceedings of the National Computer Conference*, 359–62.

Jackson, R. (2010) *The Warwick REDCo Community of Practice*. Available from www2.warwick.ac.uk/fac/soc/wie/research/wreru/research/completed/redco_warwick/ – Last accessed 11/02/2011.

Jaques, M. (2009) *When China Rules the World: The End of the Western World and the Birth of a New Global Order*, New York: Penguin Press.

Jasanoff, S. (2004) Ordering knowledge, ordering society. In Jasanoff, S. (ed.), *States of Knowledge: The Co-production of Science and Social Order*, London: Routledge, 13–45.

Jefferies, P., Carsten-Stahl, B. and McRobb, S. (2007) Exploring the relationships between pedagogy, ethics and technology: Building a framework for strategy development, *Technology, Pedagogy and Education*, Vol. 16, No. 1, 111–26.

John, P. D. and Sutherland, R. (2004) Teaching and learning with ICT, new technology, new pedagogy? *Education, Communication and Information*, Vol. 4, No. 1, 101–7.

Jones, P. (2010) *Equality and Human Rights Commission Triennial Review: Education* (Lifelong Learning). Internet Access and Use. Available from www.equalityhumanrights.com/uploaded_files/triennial_review/triennial_review_internet_access.pdf – Last accessed 11/03/2011.

Kanuka, H. (2008) Understanding eLearning technologies-in-practice through philosophies-in-practice. In Anderson, T. (ed.), *The Theory and Practice of Online Learning*, 2nd edn, Edmonton: AU Press, 91–118.

Kass, L. (2010) Preventing a brave new world. In Hanks, C. (ed.), *Technology and Values: Essential Readings*. Malden, MA: Wiley-Blackwell.

Kaufman, James C. and Sternberg, Robert J. (eds) (2006) *International Handbook of Creativity*, Cambridge: Cambridge University Press.

Kennewell, S. (2003) *Developing Research Models for ICT-Based Pedagogy* – paper was presented at the IFIP Working Groups 3.1 and 3.3 Working Conference: ICT and the Teacher of the Future, held at St. Hilda's College, The University of Melbourne, Australia 27 – 31 January, 2003. Available from www.acs.org.au/documents/public/crpit/crpitv23kennewell.pdf – Last accessed 11/03/2011.

— (2006) *Reflections on the Interactive Whiteboard Phenomenon: A Synthesis of Research from the UK.* Paper presented at the AARE Conference, 2006 Adelaide, Available from www.aare.edu.au/06pap/ken06138.pdf – Last accessed 11/03/2011.

—, Connell, A., Edwards, A., Hammond, M. and Wickens, C. (2007) *A Practical Guide to Teaching ICT in the Secondary School*. Oxon: Routledge.

—, Parkinson, J. and Tanner, H. (2000) *Developing the ICT Capable School*. London: Routledge Falmer.

Ketelhut, D. and Nelson, B. (2010) Designing for real-world scientific inquiry in virtual environments, *Educational Research*, Vol. 52, No. 2, 151–67.

Kim, U. (2007) *Creating a World of Possibilities Indigenous and Cultural Perspectives in Tan A (2007) 9Ed Creativity, A handbook for teachers*, Singapore, World Scientific Publishing, Available from www.scribd.com/doc/38502037/Creativity-A-Handbook-for-Teachers – Last accessed 11/03/2011.

Kirscher, P. and Davis N. (2010) Pedagogical benchmarks for information and communications technology in teacher education, *Technology, Pedagogy and Education*, Vol. 12, No. 1, 125–47.

Kitchener, R. (1972) B. F. Skinner: The Butcher, the Baker, the Behaviour-Shaper, *The Philosophy of Science Association*, Vol. 1972, 87–98.

Klausmeier, H. J. and Lambert, P. (1961) Teaching machines and the learning process, *Educational Leadership*, Vol. 18, No. 5, 278–324.

Kline S. J. (1985) What is technology? *Bulletin of Science Technology and Society*, Vol. 5, 215.

Kneszevich S. and Eye, G. (eds) (1970) *Instructional Technology and the School Administrator*, Washington: American Association of School Administrators.

Knowledge Works Foundation (2009) *2020 Forecast: Creating the Future of Learning*. Available from www.futureofed.org/ – Last accessed 11/03/2011.

Knowles, E. (1999) *The Oxford Dictionary of Quotations*, Oxford: Oxford University Press.

Koepsell, D. (2007) Robots bowling alone: Evolving post-technological humans, *Scripted*, Vol. 4, No. 4, 462.

Krause, S. D. (2000) Among the greatest benefactors of mankind: What the success of chalkboards tells us about the future of computers in the classroom, *The Journal of the Midwest Modern Language Association*, Vol. 33, No. 2, 6–16.

Kruger, K. (2000) Using information technology to create communities of learners, *New Directions for Higher Education*, Vol. 109, 59–70.

Kulik, C. C., Schwalb, B. J. and Kulik, J. A. (1982), Programmed instruction in secondary education: A meta analysis of evaluation findings, *Journal of Educational Research*, Vol. 75, No. 3, 133–8.

Kurzweil, R. (1992) *The Age of Intelligent Machines*, Cambridge, MA: MIT Press.

—. (2005) *The Singularity Is Near: When Humans Transcend Biology*, New York: Viking Penguin.

Lally, E. (2003) *At Home With Computers*, Oxford: Berg.

Lancet, The (1991) Being and believing: Ethics of virtual reality, *The Lancet*, Vol. 338, No. 8762, 283–4.

Land, R., Meyer, J. H. F. and Smith, J. (eds) (2008) *Threshold Concepts within the Disciplines*, Rotterdam: Sense Publishers.

Langeveld, M. J. (1967) Programmed learning: Some preliminary considerations from a pedagogical point of view, *International Review of Education*, Vol. 13, No. 1, 14–25.

Laurillard, D. (2002) *Rethinking University Teaching: a Conversational Framework for the Effective Use of Learning Technologies*, London: RoutledgeFalmer.

—. (2007) Technology, pedagogy and education: Concluding comments, *Technology, Pedagogy and Education*, Vol. 16, No. 3, 357–60.

Lave, J. and Wenger, E. (1991) *Situated Learning: Legitimate Peripheral Participation*, Cambridge: Cambridge University Press,

Law, N., Pelgrum, W. J. and Plomp, T. (eds) (2008) Pedagogical practices and ICT use around the world: Findings from an international comparative study, *CERC Studies in Comparative Education*, Hong Kong: CERC and Springer, 1–296.

Lawler, L, J. (1965) Educational television and its role in developing countries, *International Review of Education*, Vol. 11, No. 3, 326–36.

Lawson, D. (1973) Who thought of it first. In Perry, G. and Lipsitz, L. (eds), *Using Programmed Instruction, Educational Technology*, Vol. 10, 93–5.

Layton, E. (1974) Technology as knowledge, *Technology and Culture*, Vol. 15, 31–41.

Leeds Mercury, The, Practical Teaching, *Leeds*, Saturday, September 25; No. 13249, Vol. (1880)291, No. 5509, 1748–53.

Lenhart, A., Horrigan, J., Rainie, L., Allen, K., Boyce, A., Madden, M. and O'Grady, E. (2003) *The Ever-Shifting Internet Population: A New Look at Internet Access and the Digital Divide*, Washington: Pew Internet and American Life Project.

Levin, R. and Hines, L. (2003) Educational television, Fred Rogers, and the history of education, *History of Education Quarterly*, Vol. 43, No. 2, 262–75.

Li, J. (2009) *Hong Kong Primary School Bolsters Interactive Learning*, Asia Pacific futuregov. Available from www.futuregov.asia/articles/2009/may/29/hong-kong-primary-school-bolsters-interactive-lear/ – Last accessed 11/03/2011.

Light, A. and Luckin, R. (2008) *Designing for Social Justice: People, Technology and Learning*, Bristol: FutureLab.

Lim, H. L., (2007) Community of inquiry in an online undergraduate information technology course, *Journal of Information Technology Education*, Vol. 6, 153–68.

Lipponen, L. (2002) Exploring foundations for computer-supported collaborative learning. In G. Stahl (ed.) *Computer Support for Collaborative Learning: Foundations for CSCL Community*, Proceedings of the Computer-supported Collaborative Learning 2002 Conference, Hillsdale, NJ: Erlbaum, 72–81.

Livingston, S. and Helesper, E. (2007) Gradations in digital inclusion: Children, young people and the digital divide, *New Media and Society*, Vol. 9, No. 4, 671–96.

Loop, Liza (2006), Why look back? Arguments for a history of computing in education, In *ICALT 2006 – Proceedings of the 6th IEEE* International Conference on Advanced Learning Technologies, 5–7 July 2006, Kerkrade. The Netherlands, 1087–8.

Loveless, A (2002) *A Literature Review in Creativity, New Technologies and Learning*. A Report for Futurelab. Bristol: Futurelab.

—. (2007) *Creativity, Technology and Learning: A Review of Recent Literature*, Report 4, Update for Futurelab. Bristol: Futurelab.

—. (2008), Creative learning and new technology? A provocation paper. In Sefton-Green, J. (ed.), *Creative Learning*, London: Arts Council, 61–72.

—, and Wegerif, R. (2004) Creativity and ICT. In R. Fisher and M. Williams (eds). *Unlocking Creativity*. London: David Fulton, 92–102.

Luppicini, R. (2005) A systems definition of educational technology in society, *Educational Technology and Society*, Vol. 8, No. 3, 103–9.

Magee, M. (2006) State of the field review: Simulation in education, *Final Report*, Alberta Online Learning Consortium.

Marcus, H. (2009) The new forms of control. In Kaplan, D. (ed.), *Readings in the Philosophy of Technology*, Second Edition, Latham, Rowman and Littlefield, 34–43.

Markle, J., Petersen, C. and Pinch, T. (eds), *Handbook of Science and Technology Studies*, Thousand Oaks, CA: Sage.

Marshall, I. V. (1924) The Art of Teaching, *The High School Journal*, Vol. 7, No. 2, UNC Press, 49.

Martin, P. and Widgren, J. (2002) *International Migration: Facing the Challenge*, Population Bulletin, Vol. 57, No. 1, 1–40. Available from www.prb.org/Source/57.1IntlMigration_Eng.pdf/ – Last accessed 11/03/ 2011.

Martino, J. (2007) *The Avatar Project: Connected But Not Engaged – The Paradox of Cyberspace*. Available from http://art.tafe.vu.edu.au/avatar/wp-content/uploads/. AvatarLitReview-revision%202.doc – Last accessed 11/3/2011.

Mason, R. and Rennie, F. (2006), *e-Learning: The Key Concepts*, London: Routledge.

McCluskey, L. (1994) Gresham's Law, technology, and education, *The Phi Delta Kappan*, Vol. 75, No. 7, 550–2.

McDonald, J. K.,Yanchar, S. C. and Osguthorpe, R. T. (2005) Learning from programmed instruction: Examining implications for modern instructional technology, *Educational Technology Research and Development*, Vol. 53, No. 2, 84–98.

McKeachie, W. J. (1974) Instructional psychology, *Annual Review of Psychology*, Vol. 26, 161–93.

McLuhan, M. (1962) *The Gutenberg Galaxy*, London: Routledge.

—. (1995) *Understanding Media*, London: Routledge.

McRobb, S., Jefferies, P. and Stahl B. C. (2007) Exploring the relationships between pedagogy, ethics and technology: Building a framework for strategy development, *Technology, Pedagogy and Education*, Vol. 16, No. 1, 111–26.

McWilliam, E. and Hanukkah, S. (2008) Educating the creative workforce: New directions for twenty-first century schooling, *British Educational Research Journal*, Vol. 34, No. 5, 651–66.

Mead, G. (1934) *Mind, Self and Society*, Chicago: University of Chicago Press.

Means, B., Toyama, Y., Murphy, R., Bakia, M. and Jones, K. (2010 revised edn), *Evaluation of Evidence-Based Practices in Online Learning*, A Meta-Analysis and Review of Online Learning Studies, U.S. Department of Education. Available from http://ctl.sri.com/publications/displayPublication. jsp?ID=770 – Last accessed 11/02/2001.

Melnick, B. (2002) Virtual schools: The changing face of education? *The English Journal*, Vol. 91, No. 5, 85–8.

Melville, D. (2009) *Higher Education in a Web 2.0 World*, Committee of Inquiry into the Changing Learner Experience. Available from www.jisc.ac.uk/media/documents/publications/heweb20rptv1. pdf – Last accessed 11/02/2011.

Merchant, G. (2010) 3D virtual worlds as environments for literacy learning, *Educational Research*, Vol. 50, No. 2, 135–50.

Meyer, J. and Land, R. (2005) Threshold concepts and troublesome knowledge (2): Epistemological considerations and a conceptual framework for teaching and learning, *Higher Education*, Vol. 49, No. 3, 373–388.

Minocha, S. and Roberts, D. (2008) Laying the groundwork for socialization and knowledge construction within 3D virtual worlds, *Research in Learning Technology*, Vol. 16, No. 3, 181–96.

Molnar, A. (1997) Computers in education: a brief history. *T.H.E. Journal*, Vol. 24, No. 11, 63–8.

Molphy, M., Pocknee, C. and Young, T. (2007) *Online Communities of Practice: Are They Principled and How Do They Work?* Available from www.ascilite.org.au/conferences/singapore07/procs/molphy. pdf – Last accessed 11/02/2001.

Monke, L. (2004) *The Human Touch*, Education Next. Available from http://educationnext.org/ thehumantouch/ – Last accessed 11/03/2011.

Monro, K. (1918) Blackboard work and the card system, *The English Journal*, Vol. 7, No. 7, 460–4.

Moore, G. (1965), Cramming more components onto integrated circuits, *Electronics*, Vol 38, No. 8, April 19, 114–17.

Morrill, C. S. (1961) Teaching machines: a review, *Psychological Bulletin*, Vol. 58, No. 5, 363–75.

Morton C. (1996) The modern land of Laputa: Where computers are used in education, *The Phi Delta Kappan*, Vol. 77, No. 6, 416–19.

Moss, G., Jewitt, C., Levacic, R., Armstrong, V., Cardini, A. and Castle, F. (2007) The interactive whiteboards, pedagogy and pupil performance evaluation. *An evaluation of the Schools Whiteboard Expansion (SWE) Project*, London Challenge, London: DfES.

Mullis, E. (2009) The Device Paradigm: a consideration for a Deweyan philosophy of technology, *The Journal of Speculative Philosophy*, Vol. 23, No. 2, 110–17.

Nachmias, R., Ram, J. and Mioduser, D. (2006) Virtual TAU: The study of a campus-wide implementation of blended learning. In C. Bonk and C. Graham (eds), *The Handbook of Blended Learning Environments*, San Francisco, CA: Pfeiffer.

Nagel, D. (2009) *Most College Students to Take Classes Online by 2014* Available from http://campustechnology.com/articles/2009/10/28/most-college-students-to-take-classes-online-by-2014.aspx?sc_lang=en – Last accessed 11/02/2011.

National Advisory Committee on Creative and Cultural Education (NACCCE) (1999) *All Our Futures, Creativity, Culture and Education*, London: DEEE.

National Institute on Aging (2006) The future of human life expectancy: Have we reached the ceiling or is the sky the limit? *Population Reference Bureau*, No. 8. Available from www.prb.org/pdf06/nia_futureoflifeexpectancy.pdf – Last accessed 11/03/ 2011.

Neill, M. (1995) Computers, thinking and schools in the new world order. In J. Brook and I. A. Boal (eds), *Resisting the Virtual Life: the Culture and Politics of Information*, San Francisco: City Lights, 181–94.

Nelson, B. (2005) *The Creative Process: A Phenomological and Psychometric Investigation of Artistic Creativity*, Melbourne: The University of Melbourne.

Nichol, R. (2010) *Growing Up Indigenous: Developing Effective Pedagogy for Education and Development*, Rotterdam: Sense Publishers.

Nickerson, R. S. (2008) Enhancing creativity. In R. J. Sternberg (ed.), *Handbook of Creativity*, New York: Cambridge University Press.

Nietzsche, F. (1969) *Thus Spoke Zarathustra: A Book for Everyone and No One*, Harmondsworth, Penguin.

Northcott, B., Miliszewska, I. and Dakich, E. (2007) *ICT for Inspiring Creative Thinking*. Available from www.ascilite.org.au/conferences/singapore07/procs/northcott.pdf – Last accessed 11/03/2011.

Nulden, U. and Hardless, C. (1999) *Activity Visualization and Formative Assessment in Virtual Learning Environments*. Available from www.viktoria.se/nulden/Publ/Publicationwindow.html – Last accessed 11/02/2011.

Nye, E. and David, T. (2006) Technology and the production of difference, *American Quarterly*, Vol. 58, No. 3, 597–618.

Ochoa Morales, H. (2004) The effect of information and communication Technology (ICT) on the globalization paradigm, *Issues in Information Systems*, Vol. V, No. 2, 647–53.

OECD (2002) *Schooling for Tomorrow – The Starter Pack: Futures Thinking in Action*, Available from www.oecd.org/document/33/0,3343,en_2649_35845581_38981601_1_1_1_1,00.html – Last accessed 11/03/2011.

—. (2005) *Health at a Glance*. Available from www.oecd.org/dataoecd/58/47/35624825.pdf – Last accessed 11/03/2011.

—. (2008) *The Future of the Family to 2030*. Available from OECD (2010) Measuring Globalization: OECD Economic Globalization Indicators 2010. Available from www.oecd-ilibrary.org/industry-and-services/measuring-globalisation-oecd-economic-globalisation-indicators-2010_9789264084360-en – Last accessed 11/03/2011.

Office for National Statistics (ONS) (2007) *Internet Access Module. Statistical First Release*, August. Available from www.statistics.gov.uk/pdf – Last accessed 11/03/2011.

Office of National Statistics (2010) *Live Births*. Available from www.statistics.gov.uk/CCI/nugget.asp?ID=369&Pos=2&ColRank=2&Rank=240 – Last accessed 11/03/2011.

OFSTED (2003) *Expect the Unexpected: Developing Creativity in Primary and Secondary Schools*. Available from www.ofsted.gov.uk/Ofsted-home/Publications-and-research/Browse-all-by/Documents-by-type/Thematic-reports/Expecting-the-unexpected2 – Last accessed 11/05/2011.

Okojie, M., Olinzock, A. and Okijie-Boulder, T., The pedagogy of technology integration, *The Journal of Technology Studies*, Vol. 32, No. 2, 66–70.

Olaniran, B. A. (2006) Applying synchronous computer-mediated communication into course design: Some considerations and practical guides, Campus-Wide Information Systems, *The International Journal of Information and Learning Technology*, Vol. 23, No. 3, 210–20.

Oliver, M. (2005) The problem with affordance, *E-Learning and Digital Media*, Vol. 2, No. 4, 402–13.

Oliver, M and Trigwell, K. (2005) Can 'blended learning' be redeemed? *E Learning*, Vol. 2, No. 1, 17–262.

Olliges, R. and Mahfood, S. (2003) Teaching and learning in the new millennium: Transformative technologies in a transformable world, *Communication Research Trends*, Vol. 22, No. 2, 3–28.

Olsen, M. (2004) Foucault and Marxism: Rewriting the theory of historical materialism, *Policy Futures in Education*, Vol. 2, No. 3 and 4, 454–82.

Olson J. K. and Clough M. P. (2001) Technology's tendency to undermine Serious Study: a Cautionary Note, *The Clearing House*, Vol. 75, No. 1. Heldref Publications, pp. 8–13.

Orwell, G. (1998) *Nineteen Eighty-Four*, London: Penguin.

Ozolins, J. (2010) Creating public values: Schools as moral habitats, *Educational Philosophy and Theory*, Vol. 42, No. 4, 410–23.

Paine, T. (1819) *The Age of Reason*, London: Robert Carlile.

Papert, S. (1987) Computer criticism versus technocentric thinking, *Educational Researcher*, Vol. 16, No. 1, 22–30.

Park, Y. (2011) a pedagogical framework for mobile learning: Categorizing educational applications of mobile technologies into four types, *International Review of Research in Open and Distance Learning*, Vol. 12, No. 2, 78–102.

Parker, L. (1939) British school broadcasting, *The English Journal*, Vol. 28, No. 4, 296–302.

Peña, J., Hancock, J. and Merola, N. (2009) The priming effects of avatars in virtual settings, *Communication Research*, Vol. 36, 838–56.

Perks, D. (2004) The shattered mirror: A critique of multiple intelligences. In D. Hayes (ed.), *The Routledge Falmer Guide to Key Debates in Education*. London: Routledge Falmer.

Person, I. (2008) Our virtual future, *Engineering Technology*, Vol. 3, No. 3, 18–21.

Pesce, M. (2008) *Inflection Points*. Available from http://blog.futurestreetconsulting.com/2008/12/11/inflection-points/ – Last accessed 11/02/2011.

Petrina, S. (2004) Sidney Pressey and the automation of education, 1924–1934, *Technology and Culture*, Vol. 45, No. 2. 305–30.

Phipps, R. and Merisotis, J. (1999) What's the difference? A review of *Contemporary Research on the Effectiveness of Distance Learning in Higher Education*. Washington, DC: The Institute for Higher Education Policy.

Picciano, A. G. and Seaman, J. (2007) *K–12 Online Learning: A Survey of U.S. School District Administrators*. Boston, MA: Sloan Consortium.

Pickering, S. J. and Howard-Jones, P. (2007) Educators' views on the role of neuroscience in education: Findings from a study of uk and international perspectives, *Mind, Brain and Education*, Vol. 1, No. 3, 109–13.

Pinch T. and Bijker, W. (1984) The social construction of facts and artefacts: Or how the sociology of science and technology might benefit each other, *Social Studies of Science*, Vol. 14, 399–441.

Plomp, T., Anderson R. E. and Kontogiannopoulou-Polydorides, G. (eds) (1996) *Cross-National Policies and Practices on Computers in Education*, Dordecht: Kluwer Academic Publishers.

Pool, R. (1999) *Beyond Engineering: How Society Shapes Technology*, New York: Oxford University Press.

Posner, R. (2000) Orwell Versus Huxley: Economics, technology, privacy, and satire, *Philosophy and Literature*, Vol. 24, No. 1, 1–33.

Postman, N. (1986) *Amusing Ourselves to Death*, London: Methuen.

—. (1992) *Technopoly: The Surrender of Culture to Technology*, New York: Vintage.

—. (1993) *Technopoly*, New York: Vintage Books.

Power, E. (1964) Plato's academy: a halting step toward higher learning, *History of Education Quarterly*, Vol. 4, No. 3, 155–66.

Pratt-Adams, S., Maguire, M. and Burn, E. (2010) *Changing Urban Education*, London: Continuum.

Prensky, M. (2001) *Digital Game Based Learning*, New York: McGraw-Hill.

Press, G. (1982) *The Development of the Idea of History in Antiquity*, Toronto: McGill Queens.

Pressey, S. (1933) *Psychology and the New Education*, New York: Harper.

—. (1962) Basic unresolved teaching machine problems, *Theory into Practice*, Vol. 1, 30–7.

Pringle, R.M. (2002). Developing a community of learners: Potentials and possibilities in web mediated discourse. *Contemporary Issues in Technology and Teacher Education*, Vol. 2, No. 2, 218–33.

Prior (2005) *How the Interactive Whiteboard Has Changed the Way I Teach*. Available from www.evaluation.icttestbed.org.uk/research/show/P28 – Last accessed 11/03/2011.

Purdy, N. and Morrison, H. (2009) Cognitive neuroscience and education: Unravelling the confusion, *Oxford Review of Education*, Vol. 35, No. 1, 99–109.

Quiles, C. (2007) A Grammar of modern Indo-European: Language and culture, *Writing System and Phonology, Morphology and Syntax*, UK: Dnghu Associates.

Race, R. (2011) *Multiculturalism and Education*, London: Continuum.

Reid, K., Aqui, Y. and Putney, L. (2009) Evaluation of an evolving virtual high school, *Educational Media International*, Vol. 46, No. 4, 281–94.

Renzulli, J. S. (2002) Emerging conceptions of giftedness: Building a bridge to the new century. *Exceptionality*, Vol. 10, No. 2, 65–6.

Resta, P. (ed.) (2002) *Information and Communication Technologies in Teacher Education: A Planning Guide*, Paris: UNESCO.

Reus Smit, C. (2008) Reading history through constructivist eyes, Millennium – *Journal of International Studies*, Vol. 37, No. 2, 395–41.

Riedl, R. (2004). Building a program in a virtual world. In L. Cantoni and C. McLoughlin (eds), Proceedings of World Conference on Educational Multimedia, *Hypermedia and Telecommunications*, 424–31.

Rigney, D. (2004), What if you could be instantly smarter? A thought experiment: The pros and cons of 'smart pills' – mind-enhancing pharmaceuticals – are weighed by students as an exercise in critical thinking, *The Futurist*, Vol. 38, No. 2, 34–6.

Roblyer, M. (2008) Predicting success for virtual school students: Putting research-based models into practice, *Online Journal of Distance Learning Administration*, Vol. XI, No. IV, Available from www.westga.edu/~distance/ojdla/winter114/roblyer114.html – Last accessed 11/03/2011.

Rodney, B. (2010) Virtual schools: The nexus between parental autonomy and centralized management of k-12 education, *Journal of Philosophy and History of Education*, Vol. 60, 221–5.

Rogers, E. (1995) *Diffusion of Innovations*, 4th edn, New York: Free Press.

—. (2003) *Diffusion of Innovations,* 5th edn, New York: Free Press.

Roth (2009) Following Plato's advice: Pedagogy and technology for the Facebook generation, *Journal of Philosophy and History of Education*, Vol. 59, 125–8.

Rudd, T. (2007) *Interactive Whiteboards in the Classroom*, Bristol: Futurelab.

Runco, M. A (2007) *Creativity: Theories and Themes: Research*, Development and Practice, San Diego, CA: Elsevier Academic Press.

Runco, M. A. and Pritzker, S. R. (1999) *Encyclopaedia of Creativity*, Vol. 1, San Diego, Academic Press.

Russell, G. (2004) Virtual schools: A critical view. In Cavenaugh, C. (ed.), *Development and Management of Virtual Schools: Issues and Trends*, Hershey, PA: Information Science Publishing, 1–25.

Russell, S. (1986) The social construction of artefacts: A response to Pinch and Bijker, *Social Studies of Science*, Vol. 16, No. 2, 331–46.

Sackville, A. and Sherratt, C. (2010) *Creating a Community of Learners* (and Teachers) – At One Remove! Paper presented at Improving University Teaching (IUT) Conference 2010, Washington D.C. Available from www.iutconference.org/papers.html – Last accessed 11/02/2011.

Salmon, G. (ed.) (1993) *Distributed Cognition*, Cambridge: Cambridge University Press.

Samuels, B. (2009) Can the differences between education and neuroscience be overcome by mind, brain, and education, *Mind, Brain and Education*, Vol. 3, 44–54.

Sandford, R. and Williamson, B. (2005) *Games and Learning*, Bristol: FutureLab.

Santander-Gana, M. T. and Trejo-Fuentes, L. (2006) As 'a human practice with social meaning'–a new scenery for engineering education, *European Journal of Engineering Education*, Vol. 31, No. 4, 437–47.

Santayana, G. (1905) *The Life of Reason: Reason in Common Sense*, New York: Charles Scribner and Sons.

Savin Baden, M., Gourlay, L., Tombs, C., Steils, N., Tombs, G. and Mawer, M. (2010) Situated pedagogies, positions and practices in immersive virtual worlds, *Educational Research*, Vol. 52, No. 2, 123–33.

Sayre, K. M. (1970) Teaching ourselves by learning machines, *The Journal of Philosophy*, Vol. 67, No. 21, 908–18.

Scharfe, H. (2002) *Education in Ancient India*, Leiden: Brill.

Sciadas, G. (ed.) (2003) *Monitoring the Digital Divide and Beyond*, Montreal: Orbicom.

Seltzer, K. and Bentley. T. (1999) *The Creative Age: Knowledge and Skills for New Economy*, Demos: London.

Selwyn, N. and Facer, K. (2007) *Beyond the Digital Divide: Rethinking Digital Inclusion for the 21st Century*, Bristol: Futurelab.

Selwyn, N., Gorard, S. and Williams, S. (2001) Digital divide or digital opportunity? The role of technology in overcoming social exclusion in us education, *Educational Policy*, Vol. 15, 258–77.

Sharp, C. and Le Métais, J. (2000) *The Arts, Creativity and Cultural Education: an International Perspective* (International review of curriculum and assessment frameworks). London: QCA.

Sharp J. G., Byrne, J. and Bowker, R. (2008) The trouble with VAK, *e-journal of the British Education Studies Association*, Vol. 1, No. 1, August, 89–97. Available from www.educationstudies.org.uk/materials/sharp_et_al_2.pdf – Last accessed 11/03/11.

—. (2007) VAK or VAK-uous? *Educational Futures*, Vol. 1, 76–93.

Sharpes, D. K. (1968) Computers in education, *The Clearing House*, Vol. 43, No. 3, 135–6.

Shea, P., Vickers, J. and Hayes, S. (2010) Online instructional effort measured through the lens of teaching presence in the community of inquiry framework: a re-examination of measures and approach, *The International Review of Research in Open and Distance Learning*, 11(3).

Sheehy, K., Ferguson R. and Clough, G. (2007) Learning and teaching in the panopticon: Ethical and social issues in creating a virtual educational environment, *International Journal of Social Sciences*, Vol. 2, No. 2, 89–96.

Shelley, M. (1984) *Frankenstein, the Modern Prometheus*, Berkeley, University of California Press.

Simon, H. (1969), *The Science of the Artificial*, Cambridge, MA: MIT press.

Singer, E. (2006) Seeing your pain, *Technology Review*, Vol. 109, No. 3, 70.

Skinner, B. (1954) The science of learning and the art of teaching, *Harvard Educational Review*, Vol. XXIV, No. 2, 86–97.

—. (1960) Teaching Machines, *The Review of Economics and Statistics*, Vol. 42, No. 3, Part 2, 189–91.

—. (1983) *A Matter of Consequences*, New York: Knopf.

Skinner, B. F. (1953) *Science and Human Behaviour*, New York, MacMillan.

Skinner, B. F. (1968) *The Technology of Teaching*, New York: Meredith Corporation.

Smith, F., Hardman, F. and Higgins, S. (2006) The impact of interactive whiteboards on teacher–pupil interaction in the National Literacy and Numeracy Strategies, *British Educational Research Journal*, Vol. 32, No. 3, 443–57.

Smith, M. and Kollock, P. (eds) (2002) *Communities in Cyberspace*, London: Routledge.

Smith, R. (2010) The long history of gaming in military training, *Simulations and Gaming*, Vol. 41, No. 6, 898–920.

Soffer, T., Nachmias, R. and Ram, J. (2010) Diffusion of web-supported instruction in higher education – The Case of Tel-Aviv University, *Educational Technology and Society*, Vol. 13, No. 3, 212–23.

Somekh, B. (1994) Inhabiting each other's castles: Towards knowledge and mutual growth through collaboration, *Educational Action Research*, Vol. 2, No. 3, 357–81.

Sorgner, S. (2009) Nietzsche, the overhuman, and transhumanism, *Journal of Evolution and Technology*, Vol. 20, No. 1, 29–42.

Stacey, E. and Gerbic, P. (2008) *Success Factors for Blended Learning*. Available from www.ascilite.org.au/conferences/melbourne08/procs/stacey.pdf – Last accessed 11/02/2011.

Stanistreet, P. (2009), A university of the air, *Adults Learning*, Vol. 20, No. 7, 8–11.

Stein, M. I. (1956) A transactional approach to creativity. In C. W. Taylor (ed.), *University of Utah Research Conference on the Identification of Creative Scientific Talent*, Salt Lake City: University of Utah Press.

Sternberg, R. J. and Lubart, T. (1995) *Defying the Crowd: Cultivating Creativity in a Culture of Conformity*. New York: Free Press.

Stewart, W. I. (1963) Programmed Learning and Mass Education, *Africa Today*, Vol. 10, No. 3, 4–6.

Such, D. (2010) *Education Futures, Teachers and Technology*, Bristol: Futurelab.

Suter, W. N. (2005) *Introduction to Educational Research: A Critical Thinking Approach*. London: Sage.

Sweet, M. (1997) *Smug as a Bug*, Sydney Morning Herald. Available from www.vianet.net.au/~bjmrshll/features2.html – Last accessed 11/03/2011.

Sylwester, R. (2006) Cognitive neuroscience discoveries and educational practices: seven areas of brain research that will shift the current behavioural orientation of teaching and learning, *School Administrator*, Vol. 63, No. 11, 32.

Taylor, D. (2009) *Widening Access with the Virtual World of Second Life*. Available from www.egos-cip.eu/riga2009/abstracts/TAYLOR_abstract.pdf – Last accessed 11/02/2011.

Taylor, P. H. (1975) Education and a new technology: Problems and promise, *Paedagogica Europaea*, Vol. 10, No. 2, 159–70.

Thinh, D. and Dung, V. (2009) *Interactive Teaching and Learning with Low-cost Interactive Smart Boards*, Paper presented at 13th UNESCO-APEID International Conference and World Bank-KERIS High Level Seminar on ICT in Education 24–26 March 2009, Bangkok, Thailand.

Thoman, E. and Jolls, T. (2005) *Literacy for the 21st Century: An Overview and Orientation Guide to Media Literacy Education*, Los Angeles: Centre for Media Literacy.

Thomas, E. (1952) BBC lessons on TV, *The Children's Newspaper*, London: Amalgamated Press, September 21, 4.

Thorndike, E. L. (1912) *Education: A First Book*, New York: The MacMillan Company.

Timucin M. (2009) Diffusion of technological innovation in a foreign languages unit in Turkey: A focus on risk-aversive teachers, Technology, *Pedagogy and Education*, Vol. 18, No. 1, 75–86.

Tinio, V. (2003) *ICT in Education*, E-Primers. Available from www.apdip.net/publications/iespprimers/eprimer-edu.pdf – Last accessed 04/09/2010.

Toffler, A. (1972) English education and future shock, *English Education*, Vol. 3, No. 3, 145–50.

Torrance, E. (1979) Can we teach children to think creatively? *Journal of Creative Behaviour*, Sage, Vol. 6, 114–43.

Tucker, B. (2007) *Laboratories of Reform: Virtual High Schools and Innovation in Public Education*, Education sector reports. Available from www.educationsector.org/publications/laboratories-reform-virtual-high-schools-and-innovation-public-education – Last accessed 11/03/2011.

Turner, D. and Sahakian, B. (2008) The cognition-enhanced classroom. In Zonneveld, I., Dijstelbloem, H. and Ringoir, D. (eds), *Reshaping the Human Condition: Exploring Human Enhancement*. The Hague Netherlands: Rathenau Institute, 107–113.

Twining, P. (2009) Exploring the educational potential of virtual worlds: Some reflections from the SPP. *British Journal of Educational Technology*, Vol. 40, No. 3, 496–514.

Tyack, D. and Hansot, E. (1982) *Managers of Virtue: Public School Leadership in America, 1820–1980*, New York: Basic Books.

Ulicsak, M. (2009) *Neurofeedback: Is There a Potential for Use in Education?* Bristol: Futurelab.

Underwood, J., Baguley, T., Banyard, P., Dillon, G., Farrington-Flint, L., Hayes, M., Le Geyt, G., Murphy, J. and Selwood, I. (2010) *Understanding the Impact of Technology: Learner and School Level Factors*, London: BECTA.

UNESCO (1985) *Technology Education within the Context of General Education*, Paris: UNESCO.

—. (2004) *ICT in Education*. Available from www.unescobkk.org/education/ict/online-resources/features/ict-pedagogy/ – Last accessed 11/03/2011.

—. (2005) *The Role of UNESCO in the Construction of Knowledge Societies through the UNITWIN/UNESCO Chairs Programme*, France: UNESCO.

—. (2007) *Education for All: Global Monitoring Report 2007*, France: UNESCO.

U.S. National Intelligence Council (2004) Mapping the Global Future: Report of the National Intelligence Council's 2020 Project, Based on *Consultations With Nongovernmental Experts Around the World*. Washington, DC: National Intelligence Council, Available from www.foia.cia.gov/2020/2020.pdf – Last accessed 11/03/2011.

Veblen, T. (1921) *The Engineers and the Price System*, New York: Huebsch.

Vernon, P. (1984) Encouraging creative learning. *Journal of Creative Behaviour*, Vol. 6, 186–97.

Vloeberghs, M., Glover, A., Benford, S., Jones, A., Wang, P. and Becker, A. (2007) Virtual neurosurgery, training for the future, *British Journal of Neurosurgery*, Vol. 21, No. 3, 262–7.

Vredeveld, G. (1982) Economics and programmed instruction, *The Journal of Economic Education*, Vol. 13, No. 2, 14–25.

Vygotsky, L. (1962 – Originally printed in 1934) *Thought and Language*, Cambridge: M.I.T. Press.

Wajcman, J. (1995) Feminist theories of technology. In Sheila Jasanoff, Gerald E. Markle, James C. Petersen, and Trevor Pinch (eds), *Handbook of Science and Technology Studies*. London: Sage Publications, 189–204.

Walker, L. and Logan, A. (2009) *Using Digital Technologies to Promote Inclusive Practices in Education*, Bristol: Futurelab.

Warburton, S. (2009) Second Life in higher education: Assessing the potential for and the barriers to deploying virtual worlds in learning and teaching, *British Journal of Educational Technology*, Vol. 40, No. 3, 414–26.

Watkins, C. and Mortimore, P. (1999) Pedagogy: What do we know? In Mortimore, P. (ed.), *Understanding Pedagogy and its Impact on Learning*. London: Chapman, 1–19.

Watkins, G. (1942) The future of education, *The Phi Delta Kappan*, Vol. 24, No. 5, 212–18.

Way, J., Lilley, E., Ruster, C., Johnco, S. and Mauric, M. (2009) *Symposium: Interactive Whiteboards and Pedagogy in Primary Classrooms*, Australian Association for Research in Education – Annual Conference, Canberra.

Webb, M. and Cox, M. (2004) A review of pedagogy related to information and communications technology, *Technology, Pedagogy and Education*, Vol. 13, No. 3, 235–86.

Wegerif, R. and Dawes, L. (2004) Thinking and Learning with ICT – *Raising Achievement in Primay Classrooms*. London: RoutledgeFalmer.

Wenger, E. (2007) *Communities of practice: A brief introduction*, Communities of Practice. Available from www.ewenger.com/theory/ – Last accessed 11/02/2011.

Wertsch, J. (1988) *Vygotsky and the Social Formation of Mind*, Cambridge, MA: Harvard University Press.

Westbrook, V. (2006) The virtual learning future, *Teaching in Higher Education* Vol. 11, No. 4, 471–82.

Wheeler, S., Waite, S. J. and Bromfield, C. (2002) Promoting creative thinking through the use of ICT. *Journal of Computer Assisted Learning*, Vol. 18, No. 3, 367–78.

WHES (2011) 2011 *World Hunger and Poverty Facts and Statistics*. Available from www.worldhunger. org/articles/Learn/worldhungerfacts 2002.htm. Last accessed 11/03/2011.

White, D. and Le Cornu, A. (2010) Eventedness and disjuncture in virtual worlds, *Educational Research*, Vol. 52, No. 2, 183–96.

White, J. (2006) The trouble with multiple intelligences, *Teaching Geography*, Vol. 31, No. 2, 82–3.

Wickens, C. (2007) Creativity. In, Kennewell, S., Connell, A., Edwards, A., Hammond, M. and Wickens, C (eds.) *A Practical Guide to Teaching ICT in the Secondary School*, London: Routledge.

Willett, R. (2007) Technology, pedagogy and digital production: a case study of children learning new media skills, *Learning Media and Technology*, Vol. 32, No. 2, 167–81.

Williams, B., Copestake, P., Eversley J. and Stafford B. (2008) *Experiences and Expectations of Disabled People*, London: HMG.

Willmann, O. (2009) (Trans. Kirsch, F. M.), *The Science of Education in its Sociological and Historical Aspect*, Vol. 1, Michigan: University of Michigan Library.

Winner, L. (1993) Upon opening the black box and finding it empty: Social constructivism and the philosophy of technology, *Science, Technology, and Human Values*, Vol. 18, No. 3, 362–78.

Xiaoping, W. (2010) *Rethinking historical materialism: The new edition of the German ideology, Science and Society*, Vol. 74, No. 4, 489–508.

Zandberg, I. and Lewis, L. (2008) Technology-based distance education courses for public elementary and secondary school students: 2002–2003 and 2004–2005, *National Centre for Education Statistics*,

Institute of Education Sciences, Washington, D.C., U.S. Department of Education. Available from nces.ed.gov/pubs2008/2008008.pdf – Last accessed 11/02/2001.

Zeller, D. (2008) The future of Internet-based education through virtual worlds, *The International Journal of Learning*, Vol. 15, No. 10, 45–56.

Zielke, M., Roome, C. and Krueger, B. (2009) A composite adult learning model for virtual world residents with disabilities: A case study of the virtual ability Second Life island, pedagogy, *Education and Innovation in 3-D Virtual Worlds*, Vol. 2, No. 1, 4–21.

Index